CHARLES DE FOUCAULD

BOOKS BY MARGARET TROUNCER

Courtesan of Paradise
The Pompadour
Go, Lovely Rose
Why so Pale?
The Smiling Madonna
Oriflamme
She Walks in Beauty
Madame Récamier
The Bride's Tale
The Nun
Madame Elisabeth
The Reluctant Abbess
A Grain of Wheat
Miser of Souls
A Duchess of Versailles
The Gentleman Saint
The Passion of Peter Abélard
Eleanor
The Dividing Sword

Charles de Foucauld

BY

MARGARET TROUNCER

GEORGE G. HARRAP & CO. LTD
London · Toronto · Wellington · Sydney

For James Laver and to the memory of Veronica Laver

First published in Great Britain 1972
by GEORGE G. HARRAP & Co. LTD
182–184 High Holborn, London WC1V 7AX

© *Margaret Trouncer* 1972

ISBN 0 245 50840 6

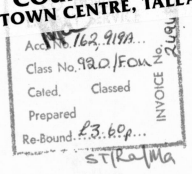
*Composed in Intertype Baskerville type and printed
by Western Printing Services Ltd, Bristol
Made in Great Britain*

Acknowledgments

I want to thank most warmly Dom Philippe Jobert, O.S.B., librarian of Solesmes, for his loan of about a hundred and twenty books, and Reverend Father Abbot for permission to work in the Abbey. Also, Mr Browne of the Farm Street Jesuit library, Mother Bede, librarian of the Assumption convent, and Madame Castro of the Institut Français, for the loan of books. Finally, I am grateful to the Royal Geographical Society for permission to work in their library on the text of *Reconnaissance au Maroc*.

My great appreciation goes to Mademoiselle Raymond of Solesmes, who was the perfect secretary, and, last but not least, to a friend, who wishes to remain unknown, who so kindly and ably revised this manuscript.

Margaret Trouncer December 8th, 1970

CONTENTS

INTRODUCTION

The Paris of his Day

THIS dynamic man, who became a blend of soldier, mystical contemplative, explorer and hermit, was in his early days a dissolute Parisian *roué*, a *bon viveur*. His life-span was fifty-eight years, from his birth at Strasbourg in 1858, to his assassination by the Touaregs in 1916.

So this extraordinary adventure story opens in the days of the crinoline and ends with the divided skirt and the hobble. Those years saw the birth of a new social era, particularly for women. They witnessed the vanishing of the costly courtesan, the *grande cocotte* of Paris, the farewell to elegant château life, with an aristocracy served by bevies of highly trained and often devoted servants.

I like to think that I lived in Paris very near Charles de Foucauld and his relations. After his conversion, he had a flat at 50 Rue de Miromesnil. His uncle and aunt, Monsieur and Madame Moitessier and their family, lived together in a large mansion surrounded by its garden and stables, just at the corner of the Rue d'Anjou and the Boulevard Malesherbes, which I passed often when our British nannies took us beyond the Parc Monceau. Like me, he must have enjoyed the candles of the chestnut-tree flowering in May. Like me, he must have sniffed delightedly the Spanish chestnuts roasting in the fiery cauldron at the street corner, under the aegis of the benign giant from Auvergne. Sarah Bernhardt passed him in her barouche, driven by greys whose blinkers were decorated with fresh Parma violets. Later, we might easily have seen Charles himself, an unkempt hermit, for he came to Paris on three separate occasions towards the end of his life. Or we might have glimpsed his confessor, the Abbé Huvelin, on an errand of mercy, twisted by his infirmities, clinging to the wall, bent under the wind. As for St Augustin, that monstrosity of a church where Charles was converted, we often went to it, and I also knew all the Paris churches where Charles prayed for faith during long, weary months.

He described his face as pig-like: his eyes were imbedded in layers of fat. At Saint-Cyr Military Academy, he ate *foie gras* neat in bed in the middle of the night. His friends in the dormitory could hear the spoon clicking against the tin. He had numberless mistresses, for brief spells. He was dismissed from his regiment for lack of discipline. But by then a miracle was dawning. He had known Africa, and Africa had cast her powerful spell on him. Eventually, he left his last mistress, Mimi, and became the first European to explore Morocco. On his return he was converted by the Abbé Huvelin, who told him to make his confession in St Augustin. (There is a commemoration plaque on the wall.) He became a Trappist monk, joining quite the severest Order in the Church. By now, his whole appearance had changed, he was slender, and his eyes were large and brilliant: a lay brother said of him that 'he was as beautiful as St Francis of Assisi'.

After a while, he felt called to leave the Trappists. He became, for a time, the ragged servant of the Poor Clare nuns in Nazareth and Jerusalem. Finally, after being ordained, he became the hermit saint of North and Central Africa, living for months alone, without attracting a single disciple to the Order he wanted to found, ill from a bad diet, converting no one, and eventually being assassinated.

But after his death, the world slowly filled with his Little Sisters and Brothers of Jesus, with their ideal of universal brotherhood. In great poverty, they form contemplative fraternities, earning their living among the most forgotten peoples of mankind, and each adoring the Blessed Sacrament for one hour every day.

To return to Paris: like Charles, we saw the last horse-drawn omnibuses, we drove in carriages with my mother when she left visiting cards with her friends. We could easily cross the streets reading a book, without looking to left or right, and arrive unscathed on the other side. Marcel Proust lived near, and there was Maxim at the end of the Boulevard Malesherbes, which was haunted by my Russian Chevalier Garde uncle on his yearly visit from St Petersburg: he used to hire the dray horse outside St Augustin at three in the morning, and ride back to our place in his top hat and monocle. He was let in by a member of that now dying race—the *concierge*. Ours had trained her parrot to squawk out *"sale petite Anglaise"* to one of our British nannies.

But enough of this frivolity and nonsense. Although Lenin and

Marx were emerging, Charles's era was one of famous pontiffs—
Pope Pius IX, Leo XIII with his fine Encyclicals on social justice,
St Pius X and Benedict XV. For France, this was a time of
spiritual renewal, after the revolutionary troubles of several reigns.
Dom Guéranger founded his two Benedictine abbeys of monks
and nuns at Solesmes, and restored the ancient Gregorian plain-
chant in all its ethereal beauty. But it was also an era which saw
the separation of Church and State. Religious congregations
were turned out of their convents by the police and driven into
exile. Charles himself was born shortly after the death of the Curé
d'Ars; he must have heard a great deal about him and St Bernadette of Lourdes. Also, St Thérèse of Lisieux and Father Damien
lived in his day.

There was a passionate movement against slavery, about which
Charles too felt most strongly. He knew a North Africa radiant
with the memory of Cardinal Lavigerie and his White Fathers.
There was an upsurge of devotion to the Sacred Heart, and after
the defeat of 1870 national pilgrimages began streaming into
Paray-le-Monial, where, in the seventeenth century, St Margaret
Mary has had her visions of Christ's Heart.

In France alone, there were writers like Renan, Huysmans,
Anatole France, Gide, Péguy, Psichari, Bloy, Claudel, Proust, the
Maritains. And the composers—Ravel and Debussy, to name but
two. Charles was still alive when Nijinsky was dancing in Paris,
thereby creating a furore for everything Eastern. I remember the
smarter women walking about the streets in turbans with aigrettes,
in gowns of exotic colours. In fact, the East was penetrating more
and more to the West, in other ways than by the tales of missionaries and explorers.

Finally, it was the age of holy French priests: the Abbé
Huvelin, who directed people like Pasteur and Baron von Hügel,
and converted Littré; Père Lamy, priest of the rag-pickers, who
used to have visions of Our Lady surrounded by angels whilst he
was scrubbing the floors of his poor churches in the shabbier out-
skirts of Paris. There was the Abbé Mugnier, who converted
Huysmans, and who was noted for a flair for understanding high
society, and whose enchanting letters to Princesse Bibesco will
remain a classic.

Charles lived in the smart Faubourg Saint-Honoré where the
last great eccentrics blossomed. For example, there was the Duc

d'Albufera who had trained his many parrots to chant Vespers. Raymond Roussel had taught his poodle to smoke a pipe. Some enchanting lunatic had scribbled on a plaque on the very walls of the Church of St Philippe du Roule, *Ici repose Chatte Blanche*. In the neighbourhood of the Place Vendôme, very late at night, there could be seen wandering a hideous frump, the Italian Comtesse de Castiglione. She, who had been the most beautiful woman in Europe and Napoleon III's mistress for a short time, was now a dried-up pea-pod, dressed in an old woman's cape. She detested the vanishing of her beauty so much that she veiled all the looking-glasses in her house, and lived in filthy sheets littered with dirty poodles. In spite of her immense wealth, she was known to be a miser.

Above all, there were the singers like Mistinguette, actresses like the Duse, Réjane, and Sarah Bernhardt of the golden voice, whose many eccentricities were the talk of Paris and who was idolized by Parisians. For a time she kept three shabby lion cubs, very malodorous and almost bald, in the Parc Monceau. Her house near our part of the city was like a sanctuary, full of the scent of incense, the melodies of far-away music and the roaring of captive animals. Charles went to see her act, and remembered her, with pity, at the end of his life.

The Place de l'Étoile—now the Place Charles de Gaulle—was deserted. It was a very lonely district in those days, quite dangerous to walk in at night, and I possess an engraving of an old woman collecting a bundle of faggots on the unpaved, countrified road leading to the Arc de Triomphe.

The motor-car was a dangerous novelty. I remember, in the Place St Augustin, the beautiful delivery vans of Félix Potin, the Fortnum and Mason of the day, with their resplendent horses, so perfectly groomed, their harnesses so highly polished. What a pleasant world it was, before the advent of the automobile, and how different the air smelt—that special odour of Paris, unlike any other in the world. We would sometimes go and sit in the Champs-Elysées and watch the coupés returning from the races at Longchamp. Oh, those high-stepping horses, so highly bred, with their gleaming hooves and plaited manes and that delightful click-click sound of their foam-covered curb-chains being shaken. It all created such an atmosphere of luxury and power. And how much one enjoyed seeing the coachmen in their fur capes. And the footmen—quite alarming. You could hear their voices booming at night, when their masters returned from the theatre or a ball, as they called out to the sleeping *concierge* to open the door. The horse was the king of the Paris streets. Charles had his own footman and his own carriage, with a low footboard as he was too idle, in his early youth, to lift his foot into some higher vehicle. His aunt's Paris house had its stables, and the courtyard was full of the pleasant associated sounds, with horses neighing, French swear words, water being sluiced over the horses as they were rubbed down.

And what carriages! So beautifully upholstered inside, decorated with crystal vases filled with orchids and other rare flowers. Real little drawing-rooms. If ever Charles condescended to take a hansom cab, he would never ask the cabby for change from his gold piece, such were his *grand seigneur* ways. When eventually a friend of his saw him on the top of a Paris bus before he left the world for good, he thought it most extraordinary. That in itself pointed to a conversion.

The lesser vehicles were the horse buses, painted yellow, green, maroon, and the coachman was dressed in a triple cape and a round feathered hat with soaring wings and a silver ribbon. His legs were wrapped in a rug. Then there were the cabs which supplied one with a hot-water bottle in cold weather. The horses were painfully thin; their cabbies' swear words and bad language were famous. One amusing detail: women's corsets, which were supposed to defend their virtue, were often found in the lost-property office, having been picked up on the seats of cabs.

As dusk fell, there were the men who lit the street oil lamps, for even in smart quarters like the Étoile, gas and electric lighting in the streets was an innovation as late as the end of the century. Many of the shops had their traditional ensigns swinging outside, depicting the emblems of their trade. For example, barbers always displayed a shaving bowl. The unpaved streets were either covered in dust or thick in mud. If they walked at all, smart women always picked up their skirts, but avoided showing their ankles, for that was considered fast. I remember the little street merchants who sold rat poison and carried rows of withered mice on the end of a long stick. There was the woman who made Parisian potato chips like little golden crisps, well salted.

And then the street cries. Among the sounds of Paris, I

remember the cries of the man who trafficked in rabbit skins, and the man who mended china or chairs on the edge of the pavement. Then there was the shepherd, sounding his horn, who sold curds; another man who blew a trumpet to announce the arrival of his goat; and the she-asses, heralded by a bell, which trotted from door to door with their health-giving milk. Not to mention the mechanical pianos, and the organ-grinder with his brightly dressed monkey. Very early in the morning, before daylight, we used to hear the strange, sad cries of the rag-and-bone men down our street, and of course there were innumerable flower sellers, carrying baskets on their hips.

Everywhere there were the Paris police, nicknamed '*sergots*'. Massive, with huge moustaches, their terrible weapon was not the truncheon of the British policeman, but their capes, rolled into a stiff sausage. And we children always gaped at the gold-helmeted fireman, driving his huge greys at a terrific speed. There were many chimney sweeps. These were people of great importance, and quite terrifying, not only because of their blackened faces, but because of their strange bellowings down the chimney from the roof. In an age when so many people were illiterate, the public scrivener could still be seen at street corners, with his enormous quill pens.

Around the year 1880, when Charles was twenty-two, he would admire the first women bicyclists dressed as Zouaves in little straw hats, heavily veiled, as if they were rather ashamed of being seen. And indeed, it was rather a daring thing in the days when a young girl was so protected. Her maid or a man-servant always accompanied her to shops, to her classes or her friends. The servant walked behind her at a respectful distance.

The *Manual of good manners*, written in 1893, tells us that a well-bred man would never dare to sit on the same sofa as a young girl. And if a woman were caught smoking, she was looked upon as a painted Jezebel and would probably be cut off from good society for ever.

There was a reverse side of the medal to this luxurious quarter of Paris. One barely knew of the wretched misery of the poorer districts, like the Passage Longcheval that was an enormous tenement building of seven hundred rooms, which housed both beggars and honest working folk. It was damp, dark and stinking, full of people who worked very long hours but did not earn a living wage, and had no form of insurance against accidents or illness. The filthily clad beggars were numberless on all the pavements, pathetically silent or noisily persistent, very often barefooted. There is an engraving of a family evicted by the bailiff for non-payment of rent, sitting in resigned despair in the street, surrounded by their few shabby belongings; and another of a poor woman miserably dressed, with an expression of passive misery on her face, staring at a smart lady emerging from a cab. One of the things which Charles de Foucauld regretted after his conversion was that he had not given enough to these Paris beggars, and he wrote to his sister, Mimi de Blic, beseeching her to remember them. In the days when benevolence took the place of social justice, even the Impératrice Eugénie would visit the poor in the slums. She had a special plain, small hat for these expeditions, and a particular kind of reticule.

Among the stranger aspects of the Paris streets in those days were the numerous funerals—first, second and third class. (The poor were shuffled into a common grave.) For the rich, the coffins in churches were covered with sumptuous mortuary cloths, embroidered in silver, and the church doors were draped in black, embroidered with silver tears and cross-bones. You could measure the importance of the dead person by the number of these majestic draperies. The law of mourning was inexorable, though we always thought the widows with their long, black veils sweeping the ground very fascinating.

The Left Bank, with its marvellous old street names, was the refuge of the monarchist aristocracy. The quarter was still almost intact, and had survived the so-called improvements of the Baron Haussmann. After the revolutionary troubles which followed the Franco-Prussian war, the Tuileries were burnt down only the ruins remained, and these were finally demolished in March 1883, when Charles was twenty-four. The Bois de Boulogne had no trees after the war.

Charles was born in the era of the crinoline. His mother wore it when photographed. It did not really go out until 1867, and lingered on with some very old ladies until the end of the century. Of course the king of fashion was Mr Worth of Lincoln, some time of Swan and Edgar in London. It was his dresses which filled the trunks destined for the Compiègne Imperial week-ends which piled up in the special train leaving the Gare du Nord.

One had to change about four or five times a day, and what charming fashion-plates emerged! Winterhalter's famous picture of the Impératrice Eugénie and her maids-of-honour is one of the most romantic pictures in the world, and these are the kind of women whom Charles saw as a small boy. In case of mischance to the crinoline in a high wind, it was customary to wear long linen pantaloons edged with lace and sometimes reaching to the ankle. Although the crinoline was a symbol of the supposed unapproachability of women, it was in itself an instrument of seduction. Then, towards the end of the 1860s, the bustle emerged, bonnets vanished, and very small hats were perched over the forehead, on top of a high coiffure like Queen Alexandra's. Only later was a bun worn at the nape of the neck.

The French aristocrats of the Left Bank, on the other hand, made a point of being very simply dressed. They would have raised their eyebrows at the portrait by Ingres of Madame Moitessier, Charles de Foucauld's aunt, now in the National Gallery, with its elaborate white evening dress painted with clusters of rosebuds, its bracelets and rings and fan and complicated hairstyle. But then Madame Moitessier had married a very rich bourgeois, and though she received men like the Duc de Broglie in her Paris salon, one gets the vague impression that she was not 'quite right', and she made up for her feeling of insecurity by emphasizing social exclusiveness, particularly when it came to the day when her nephew Charles became engaged to a young lady without the *de* of nobility to her name. The later de Foucauld family photographs show all the hideous sartorial simplicity of aspiring aristocrats. By the time Charles was of an age to notice these things, the rustling of countless silk petticoats became a kind of erotic symbol and hat-makers scattered cherries on their creations.

As for men, if they were wealthy, they were very particular about their appearance. One woman said: "I want my husband to smell of Eau-de-Cologne, Russian leather and the English pipe." When Charles came of age, he spent plenty of money on elegant and expensive clothes. Surrounded as they were by women who loved ribbons, frills and feathers, and the very romantic fashions which we can see in Tissot's pictures, Charles and his friends were not to be outdone. It was the thing for every man of fashion to have a 'library' of shoes and boots for all occasions, and he supervised the polishing of this collection by his man-servant. We are told Charles went in full evening garb almost every night to dine with his aunt on the Boulevard Malesherbes. White trousers were worn at dinner-time, even in the country. Our English dinner-jacket never became popular with the French. If they went skating, men wore fur coats. Anyway, Charles spent a fortune at the bootmakers and hatters when he was a cavalry officer at Saumur. He did everything to attract the fair sex, even to having the hairdresser call on him every day. And the members of the fair sex itself, in their exotic clothes, were a constant source of temptation which he rarely resisted. His mistresses, of course, were socially from rather doubtful circles, but that did not prevent them from being very *chic*, and imitating, almost for the first time in history, the clothes of the aristocrats. Complaints were beginning to be heard that underlings could no longer be distinguished from their employers by their clothes.

All these things filled the young days of Charles, and it is a proof of the originality and nobility of his character that he soon outgrew them, and became the saint of modern times, for Paul VI has said that his charity earned him the title of 'Universal Brother'.

CHAPTER 1

Early Childhood

CHARLES DE FOUCAULD was six, and his only sister Marie, nicknamed Mimi, four, when they lost both their parents in the same year. But in the brief time before their deaths, these parents had left their mark: the father by inspiring Charles with a love of nature, taking him for long woodland walks—walking, that occupation of the wise and good—the mother by her simple piety.

Is it a sign of predestination to be born on a Feast of Our Lady? Charles came into the world on the Feast of Our Lady of Sorrows, September 15th, 1858, at Strasbourg. The family did not originate in Alsace, but came from a much more exciting and violent part of France, the Périgord in the South-west, full of woods, mountains and castles, a land haunted by legends and feuds. The family, which was known from the tenth century, had given to Christendom and to France men of varied vocations. There was Hughes de Foucauld, who became a hermit, another Hughes who went on a crusade with St Louis and was killed at the battle of Mansourah defending his king against the Moslems. Another, Gabriel, was chosen by François II to marry our Queen Mary Stuart by proxy. Another, Jean, assisted at the coronation of the Dauphin at Rheims, next to St Joan of Arc. A very great number of them became soldiers. In fact, there was a strong military tradition in the family.

But the ancestor of whom they were most proud was Charles's own great-uncle, the Archbishop Prince of Arles, who died a martyr in the garden of the Abbaye des Carmes during the French Revolution. Perhaps it was stories about him overheard in his early youth which filled Charles's mind throughout his life with a longing for martyrdom. In a written meditation, he made Christ say: "You desire to give me the mark of the greatest love. Live as though you should die today a martyr." After all, it was not impossible for children in the early 1860s to listen to the tales of the children of eye-witnesses of events which happened about seventy years before that. And we today can still see that sombre convent, intact in the Rue de Vaugirard. We can picture the priests as they were led into the garden, that early September day, between the guards armed with pikes and wearing red Phrygian caps. We can hear the insults screamed at them from the windows by other national guards. A group of priests had made a refuge near a little oratory in a corner of the garden; and they were there, quietly reciting Vespers, when suddenly the garden door swung open and heavily armed men rushed at them, calling out, "The Archbishop of Arles! The Archbishop of Arles!" This great-uncle of Charles turned to the other priests and said, "*Messieurs*, let us thank God that He calls us to seal with our blood the Faith which we profess." His priests tried to surround him and protect him, but he would not allow it. He walked calmly towards his assassins, his hands crossed on his breast. He was instantly struck on the forehead by a sword, then somebody lashed at him from behind and split his skull. A pike was thrust into his breast with such violence that it could not be drawn out again. Finally, the body of this holy prelate was trodden underfoot.

After this example, the others met their deaths with serenity, looking, it was said, like angels, with an expression of gentle charity towards their murderers. The police superintendent was so struck by them that he commented, as our own saint Sir Thomas More said in the Tower of London when he saw the Carthusians being led to their martyrdom, "I cannot understand it . . . your priests face death with the joy of a man going to his wedding." A priest dressed as a layman, crossing the street at that moment, heard the groans of the victims and the shrieks of the fiends who murdered them.

In May 1867, when Charles was only nine years old, many bodies and skulls were found in a well, still with marks of wounds, but none had an offensive odour. A wine merchant has told how during the days of the massacres his shop was streaming in blood and the guards came in with their hands and their clothes, their pikes and their *sabots* crimsoned with the blood of the martyrs. One of the maniacs carried a picture representing a flaming heart which he had taken from a corpse. He said it was their rallying sign. Another of these men, who really seemed to have gone crazy, stopped a peaceful young man in the street and said, "You've

never yet seen the blood of an aristocrat, well I shall show you."
Instantly he killed his prisoner, opened him up, tore out his heart
and made the trembling young man kiss it. Indeed, they had
become cannibals, and when one of them, a clothes-merchant,
boasted that he had eaten a part of the heart of Madame de
Lamballe, this horrified his wife so much that she nearly died of
fear.

Besides the hermits, soldiers and martyrs who were Charles's
ancestors, there were also brigands. And as Pope Leo XIII has
told us that, when we make historical researches, we must not
suppress the truth, I think it only fair to say that when I visited
the Périgord this year and clambered about the ruins of the
Château de Lerm, whose owners were noted for rapacity, lust and
murder, I bought a book which gave the genealogy of the
seigneurs of Lerm. In it I found, to my horror, that a certain
Foucauld d'Aubusson was the father of François d'Aubusson who
had his wife strangled in 1605 in order to get the Château de
Lerm and all her inheritance and later to marry the beautiful
seventeen-year-old Marie d'Hautefort. François d'Aubusson did
not do the strangling himself, but hired four men to do it when
she was alone in her room in the castle, and amongst the four
murderers was a bastard son of this Foucauld d'Aubusson.
François afterwards seized her necklace and rings, and when the
officials came to examine the body, he would only allow them to
search below the neck. He had her head covered. Then he hid in
the woods with his companions and killed about twenty men who
went in search of him. No doubt the child Charles de Foucauld
was not told any of this by either of his parents.

Does some law of expiation for shady ancestors prevail? Anyway, a photograph of Charles taken with his mother and his
sister shows a ferocious little boy with scowling dark eyebrows
drawn together and a sulky, angry mouth. An earlier sketch
which his mother made of him is much more endearing. That
was when he was quite a baby, with long eyelashes. She caught
him in his high chair, intent upon the little wooden horse which
he was holding. Before his birth, the mother of St Dominic
had dreamed that she saw a hound bounding into the world, with
a lighted torch in its jaws. Apparently one day Elizabeth de
Foucauld, too, thought she heard a voice telling her that her son,
if she guided him aright, would become a great saint. And much

help towards sanctity was placed in his way, in those happy years before tragedy struck the family. When he was a year old, his father was appointed Chief Inspector of Waters and Forests, so the family moved from Strasbourg to Wissembourg at the foot of the Geisberg mountains. Mountains are often associated with great saints. Francis Thompson said that Nature is God's daughter. St Bernard's early teachers, he tells us, were oaks and elms. In his walks in the mountains with his father, even at so early an age, Charles learned to love the silence and the solitude which were eventually to prepare him for Africa.

As a young man, he used to say that he found his greatest happiness in being surrounded by books and his loved ones, *dans la belle nature*, in beautiful natural surroundings. In fact, in his childhood he was so quiet and retiring that he gave the impression to a tutor that he was more like a girl than a boy. Someone else has said that he was golden-hearted—*un coeur d'or*—and remarkably intelligent.

Elizabeth de Foucauld was a woman of tender devotion, with a great love for the Blessed Sacrament. She loved to go into country churches, and there silently adore the Host hidden in the tabernacle.* It is said that Christianity is caught rather than taught. It was no doubt as a result of her silent influence that Charles was to write in later life to a devoted woman of Lyons, Suzanne Perret, who had offered her life for him, and whom he was never to meet: "To adore the Host should be the core of every human life." When he wrote the rule for his Fraternity, he was an ardent believer in the sanctifying power of the Host, that silent Presence in Africa which would eventually influence the Infidel without a word being spoken. And later, as a contemplative, true son of his mother, Charles spent long nights of vigil adoring the Host in the silence of those African nights. His mother had made a little altar for him which she put on the chest of his bedchamber. And he kept that altar even during his thirteen years of unbelief.

Elizabeth de Foucauld also loved the month of May, a month

* Cardinal Herbert Vaughan and his nine brothers and sisters—most of whom became priests and nuns—used to peep through the window at their mother adoring the Blessed Sacrament in their private chapel, and the secret of her great love for God could be read in her rapt gaze towards the Host.

dedicated to the Virgin Mary. She would pick flowers in the woods and mountains, make them up into little nosegays, take Charles with her into those shabby old country churches, which smell of incense and Madonna lilies, and place them before Mary's shrines. When he explored Morocco as a young man, he went into raptures over the flowers, and indeed he had been trained to observe them in all their beauty, not only in Alsace during walks with his father, but at the Lady altars where he knelt with his mother.

But the devotion he recalled with most joy was that of praying before the little Christmas crib which his mother always prepared for the children. It was there, as he gazed at the little waxen image of a poor baby lying in a manger surrounded by ox and ass, that he learned his truly Franciscan love of Dame Poverty, the bride of St Francis of Assisi.

The Christmas of 1863 was the last which the de Foucaulds spent together. His father had become tubercular, and rather than pass on the infection to his family, he made the sacrifice, left them in Strasbourg with his wife's father, and went to Paris to live with his sister, Inez Moitessier, in her large house at the corner of the Rue d'Anjou and the Boulevard Malesherbes, where he waited for death. The disease was a killer at the end of the nineteenth century; the fear of draughts, in fact the fear of any fresh air at all, paralysed most Frenchmen. They thought that the best way of nursing the victims of tuberculosis was to shut them up in airless rooms. The disease was so pitiless that they even feared to give it its true name. It was evasively called '*maladie de langueur*' or 'a decline'.

The parting from her adored husband was too much for Elizabeth. In her father's house, in March 1864, she suffered a severe miscarriage and died soon afterwards. On her death-bed Charles heard her say, "Thy will, not mine, be done." Five months later, in August, his father died in Paris. And thus peace, security and love vanished from Charles's life. Later, this led to despair, heedlessness and rebellion.

Charles's maternal grandfather, Colonel de Morlet, was kindness itself. Among other things, he fostered a deep love of family which in the end was to be Charles's salvation. One may well be amused by the almost rapturous affection which he showed to cousins, even cousins once or twice removed, ending his letters, "I love you with all my heart." He was a great letter writer, even at an early age, and the letters he wrote when he was eight to his cousin Adolph Hallez, then a young naval officer, are enchanting and very revealing.

"I wish you a happy new year, and I rejoice at the thought of seeing you this year. There was a big ball at the Latouches', and if you had been there, you would have been able to dance nicely and throw your partner to the ground. I kiss you, your little cousin, Charles de Foucauld."

February 5th, 1866
"Your letter pleased me very much. You ought to have sent me a piece of bacon, I like it very much. I would have exchanged it for a piece of *crême-au-chocolat* cake. I go composing once a week in college, and then on Thursdays and Sundays, I go to Catechism and to Mass and to the first composition where I have been fourteenth and to other compositions where I have been the thirteenth out of twenty pupils.

"I had a sore thumb but now it's cured and it's peeling. I kiss you with all my heart and Mimi also.

Charles."

"My dear Mouc,
"I wish you a happy new year. On the Sunday after Christmas I went to the Town Hall, and in that reunion there were 150 children of all heights, at five o'clock they put up a Christmas tree which almost reached the ceiling; I send you my photograph. I am dressed as a soldier and Mimi as a canteen girl. I kiss you with all my heart.

Charles."

1867
"My dear little Mouc,
"Your letter amused me very much. I also would have loved to see the blacks dancing and uttering cries of joy, that must have been very funny, I hope you are well. It must be very funny to be carried in a palanquin. Today I have won my medal of honour. We are amusing ourselves by travelling, the chairs are boats. We go much further than you, and however we do

not leave the room. We go to Spitzberg, I am the father, I am fifty years of age. Mimi is the son who is twenty-three and Rosine is the grandfather, aged a hundred and twenty-two.

"I hope big Charles is cured.

"I kiss you with all my heart and Mimi does so also.

Charles de Foucauld."

"The Madagascar monkeys all dressed up made me laugh very much. Also the people with rings in their noses must have been very funny. The Arabs must have been frightening with their great swords.

"I will be very much amused when you play the part of the father giving spankings, only they should also stuff a pipe into your mouth when you're asleep."

1870

"We must build my fortress up again, which I had pulled down and buy some Prussian soldiers."

October 11th, 1870

"Now we have arrived at Berne. But I should very much like to come and help you kill Prussians; that task would suit me better at the moment than my Latin and Greek. I go to a drawing class where I am almost always alone with the master, which means he can really explain things to me. I go there every day for two hours."

The child is indeed father of the man. So many things, except the bad punctuation, give one a foretaste of what Charles was to become. The voracious appetite is there, indeed his cousin Général Gamelin, who remembers Charles being held up at Saumur as an example not to follow, wrote, "I was about ten years old at the time and I have a very clear recollection of my cousin; whenever we found ourselves together at any family reunion, I was terrified if I saw Charles moving towards the children's table, for in a few seconds, he invariably gobbled up all the cakes which had been set aside for us."

And so the two little orphans were put in the charge of seventy-year-old Colonel de Morlet. The children lived in his house in Strasbourg until the exodus in 1870, when they went to Switzerland for a short time and then finally settled at Nancy. The colonel was the best kind of retired French soldier, with a deep love for France and his family. Perhaps he was too kind, for when Charles wept in order to get his own way, he usually gave in, saying with a sigh of despair, "When he cries, he reminds me of my daughter."

The colonel was deeply interested in anthropology and archaeology and in classical literature, and these interests he passed on to Charles during their walks in the quiet of the woods. Many years later, on a Christmas night, when Charles was a hermit in the Sahara, he sat with some soldiers, elbows on table, by the light of a paraffin lamp, talking of his grandfather and the peace of these woods. But the age difference was too great, and when the child needed positive teaching about the Faith, he did not receive it in the Lycée of Nancy where he studied, nor from any particular priest, and above all not from his grandfather, who, though charming, was a dilettante. The insecurity in which he lived began to influence his character.

One incident reveals Charles at his most diabolical. One day he built a fine fort in the garden, complete with drawbridge, bastions, crenellated towers and look-out posts. His cousin, Marie de Moitessier, eight years older than himself, thinking she would please him, put small potatoes on top of the walls, no doubt to represent cannon balls, and little lighted candles. When Charles saw this, he thought he was being laughed at; this he simply could not endure, in a world where he imagined there was no stability in Faith, and no one to love him. He stamped on his fort and destroyed it completely. Then he took the potatoes and, that night, put them in everybody's beds.

He was passing through the crisis of adolescence, and these attacks of fury showed that his energies were unemployed. He was at the centre of a dynamism which remained mysterious to an entourage not endowed with much perspicacity. No wonder he had attacks of claustrophobia. He felt as though his family lived in a hot-house, and he could not breathe the rarefied and scented air—he was smothered. He felt removed from the realities of life. Deprived so young of the love of both mother and father, he was unconsciously seeking the tenderness of the great Lover of mankind. The Moitessier family with its surroundings of material comfort, its financial stability, its heavily over-furnished and richly upholstered drawing-rooms, all these must have sickened a lad who was destined to such great things. His was the vocation of a solitary hermit filled with a deep love for all mankind.

Charles's alarming paternal aunt, Inez de Foucauld, who in 1842 at the age of twenty-one had married the eccentric bourgeois, Sigisbert Moitessier, twenty-two years older than herself, had probably accepted her husband for his great wealth. There is nobody more snobbish than a woman who thinks she has made a *mésalliance*. She seems to have spent her life making up for it. The Ingres portrait in the National Gallery is rather terrifying, and we can understand why Ingres was afraid of her, just as her husband was too. Ingres spoke of that "divine face, that terrible and beautiful head". The eyes are entirely expressionless. In that portrait she appears a richly bedecked woman without a soul. And yet she was officially a practising Catholic. Of course, in good society in that era, it was fashionable to be a devout Catholic, because it was a legacy from the *ancien régime*. Even the new devotion to the Sacred Heart had a somewhat aristocratic tinge about it, for it had been brought to Versailles in the first place by Queen Marie Leczinska, wife of Louis XV. It was at Wissembourg when he lived there as a little boy surrounded by craggy wooded heights that Charles saw the two Leczinsky palaces.

Inez Moitessier was deeply conventional, and even when her nephew made a name for himself, she and the family were a little embarrassed by what they called his "originality". Her Paris house, 42 Rue d'Anjou, was so large that it could house both her daughters, their husbands and children, as well as herself and her deferential husband who always addressed her as "Madame Inez". It has now all been pulled down, but in the old days, beyond the imposing façade overlooking the Boulevard Malesherbes, there were formal flower beds and lawns, and stables for the carriage horses. It was probably in one of her elegant vehicles that she took Charles to the Paris zoo, where she did not have to pay an entrance fee, because she was a member of the Zoological Society. Charles must have enjoyed wandering through the stables among the watering troughs, watching the hurry and flurry of smart grooms, or in the gardens, chatting to the gardeners.

When aristocrats like the Duc de Broglie called at his aunt's house on Sundays, she might have been a little irritated by the eccentricities of her deferential husband. Although a vegetarian himself, he was always scolding his cook, but that was mainly for the benefit of his guests. He was a man after Charles's own heart, who liked to see him eat a whole melon or three quarters of a blackberry pie at one sitting. He was something of an endearing lunatic, for in the middle of a serious conversation, he would irrelevantly tell the assembled company, "I have seen a Negro eaten alive by mosquitoes at Vera Cruz; and when I was in New Orleans fighting a duel, I broke my sword, but none the less, I left my opponent for dead with a blow from the hilt."

Charles piped up, "But tell us your story about the dog."

"Ah yes," said Monsieur Moitessier, polishing off a dessert plate of cherries, "when I was attacked by a mad dog, I tore out its tongue with my fingers. No weapon, just as when I was set upon by a native in Africa. What do you think I killed him with?"

"A carefully rolled up umbrella," Charles chimed in.

Madame Inez was somewhat nettled by Charles's absorption in the idiosyncrasies of her husband. She loved to be the centre of attention, and all her life she had been painted and admired. Indeed, one of the statues representing French cities on the Pont des Saints-Pères is modelled from her, and there was a great bust of her adorning her own drawing room.

She was really no good to Charles, except that her contempt for his bad behaviour put him on his mettle.

CHAPTER 2

Marie

COLONEL DE MORLET, distinguished in his manners and speech, took his grandson's preparation for his first Communion very seriously and he did the correct things. He supervised the boy's first confession, and in 1872 on the 28th of April, Charles de Foucauld made his first Communion at Nancy. His cousin, Marie Moitessier, came all the way from Paris, which touched him immensely. She brought him a book which he treasured and which was to influence his whole life—Bossuet's *Elévations sur les Mystères*.

The great Bossuet, although accustomed to the glories of Versailles, speaks with sweetness about Bethlehem being the true House of the Bread of Life, and it is this Bread which God gives to the poor in the Nativity of Jesus. If the poor share His poverty with Christ, they will know true riches. When Bossuet leads us to worship Our Lord in the crib at Bethlehem, he exclaims, "Enter in possession of the throne of Your poverty. The angels will come to adore You there." All this was to surround Charles in later life as was the beautiful 111th Elevation when Bossuet addresses stargazers:

"Imagine a tranquil and beautiful night and a pure sky, lit up by all its fires. It is on such a night that David looked at the stars, for he does not speak of the sun.

"In this Psalm he sees only the beauty of the night, he rejoices in a sacred silence, and in the darkness contemplates the gentle light which the night bestows on him, and from thence he raises his soul to Him who alone shines among the shadows."

When he describes the three kings adoring the Holy Child, Bossuet says: "What is the incense of the Christian? Incense is something which is exhaled, and is only effective as it vanishes. Let us exhale ourselves before Almighty God, losing ourselves entirely." In a passage in the twenty-second Elevation he says, "Let us grind down by fasting and prayer that which is alive in us." Many years later, these meditations were to have their delayed effect on Charles, especially the tenth Elevation in which Bossuet says: "Look at this Divine Carpenter with His saw and His plane, hardening His tender hands by the use of instruments so rough and so coarse."

But he is at his most sublime in the eighth Elevation, which is in the best tradition of the highest mystical writing inspired by the Canticle of Canticles. It is about Our Lord as the Spouse of the soul:

> "He has espoused Holy Souls whom He has called to the company, not only of His kingdom but of His royal bed, overwhelming them with gifts and with chaste delights; rejoicing in them, giving Himself to them, lavishing on them, not only all that He has, but also all that He is, His body, His soul, His divinity, and preparing for them, in a future life, an incomparably greater union. . . . I have washed you, I have adorned you, and I have spread My mantle, My covering over you, and you have become Mine. *Facta est mihi*. Bride, take heed of His holy and inexorable jealousy, do not divide your heart, do not share your heart. . . . There then is the character of Jesus. He is a Spouse, tender, passionate . . ."

One little book, and it can mould thousands of lives throughout the world. In the letters of Herbert, Cardinal Vaughan, to Lady Herbert of Lea, written between 1867 and 1903, he said that "every Christian woman is a mother, a spiritual mother, and the holier she is, the most truly is she one". These words perhaps put in a nutshell the relationship between Charles and his cousin Marie, which has been the subject of much idle speculation. Indeed one biographer goes so far as to hint that it was a muted human love, and wondered whether they would have married, had the death of Marie's husband occurred earlier in their lives. One returns again to Cardinal Vaughan writing to Lady Herbert: "Let us both give Him our hearts in no common and perfunctory manner: our truest and happiest love will be to help each other to love Him." This is what Charles and Marie did for each other.

The photographs of Marie show a very lively young woman, with her hair coiled at the nape of her neck. Her nose and chin are determined. She truly loved her lonely young cousin and was the first to realize that he had a soul with spiritual longings. It is useless to speculate as to whether she would have been happy had she married this younger cousin. Divine Providence had a singular vocation for Charles which he had to discover step by step, and Marie helped him to respond to it and to live it out. For long years she never failed him. One of her best traits was that, even when he was living a wild life, she never lectured him. When her mother, Charles's Aunt Inez, was sending him reproachful and furiously angry letters, Marie wrote to him very gently and sweetly. In fact it was she who, by her example, inspired Charles with the idea of the forceful influence of a silent presence. He grew more and more impressed by the beauty of her character. It was because she was a girl, and then a young woman deeply rooted in God, that her own confessor never forbade the correspondence later on, and his Trappist superiors, with admirable understanding, were never puzzled by the effusiveness of Charles's letters to her when he was a novice.

Charles's uncle, Sigisbert Moitessier, had bought a country house at Loüye. It had formerly been the home of the Comte de Dreux. Charles was invited to stay there in the summer of 1866; and in 1869, when he was eleven, there was a party on August 19th to celebrate Marie's nineteenth birthday. He saw a great deal of her then. She was studying Italian and he was allowed to join in the lessons. His other cousin, who married a de Flarigny, was a great linguist. Charles was never to forget Loüye. Marie took him to visit the church there and to gaze at the statue of the Sacred Heart given by the Moitessier family. This statue was to impress itself deeply upon his imagination. Marie knew that the motherless boy loved long walks, and she went with him. He would tell her how his grandfather used to take him for walks in the woods of Saverne in Alsace. "You know, Marie, I love solitude in places like these. Solitude makes me think, because it brings peace and silence. Listen to the wind here at Loüye. In Saverne I only heard birds singing and the hum of insects. I felt very happy in those days." They went on walking in silence, and then

Charles told her of his memories of Queen Marie Leczinska at Wissembourg.

Marie said, "Oh yes, it is a little through her that France came to love the Sacred Heart, because it was a devotion of the royal family. And it was handed down to Louis XVI and his martyred sister, Elisabeth."

"Did you know," added Marie, "that Louis XVI made a vow that if he escaped from the hands of the revolutionaries, he would dedicate his kingdom to the Sacred Heart of Jesus? How I should love to go to Paray-le-Monial on one of those pilgrimages."

And Marie would speak to him about the immense love of God which is revealed in this devotion. "Remember, the heart is the very person of Jesus Himself. His love is His whole being. Great saints, even intellectuals like St Thomas Aquinas and Pascal have come to the conclusion that truth can finally be reached only by love. You see, Charles, whereas human things must be known before they are loved, Divine things must be loved before they are apprehended."

After a while, she said: "How good to think that English pilgrims are coming over to Paray-le-Monial. There was a pilgrimage led by their Cardinal Vaughan, and someone who saw him was greatly moved by his expression, which was the epitome of love.* I hear that there's a certain Abbé Huvelin who put in the preface of a spiritual book that preachers and confessors neglect this devotion of the Sacred Heart of Jesus. The essential thing is to speak of the love that one owes to Our Lord."

"Perhaps," said Charles hopefully, "we could make a family pilgrimage to Paray-le-Monial. We could all go together in two carriages, and spend the night on the way with friends, and then you could tell me more, my dear Marie."

But sadly, after this short idyllic interlude, on April 11th, 1874, his cousin Marie married the Vicomte Olivier de Bondy. He was a member of the Jockey Club, the image of a Parisian *bon viveur* and a staunch adherent of the legitimate Pretender to the French throne. Poor sixteen-year-old Charles, on the brink of young manhood, felt he had been forsaken and betrayed.

One can see him wandering about Aunt Inez's Parisian house, amid the bustle of wedding preparations, getting in the way of

* Alice Meynell in a private letter which I have seen (unpublished).

florists and pastry-cooks, on the pavement, bumping into gay *midinettes*, all carrying their huge cartons for the trousseau. He felt that his beloved cousin, Marie, though still kind to him, was in a whirl, in a bustle of elaborate preparations, and naturally immersed in her betrothed. How her eyes lit up when Olivier de Bondy called with his daily bouquet of flowers!

One can picture Charles at the wedding festivities, wandering about like a lost soul, his eyes filling with tears whenever he glanced up at the white-clad bride, so joyously absorbed in her bridegroom. She was to be very unhappy with him, and her three sons, when they grew up, caused her to shed many tears. They had wild de Foucauld blood running in their veins, also they were extremely extravagant. Indeed, she had to set up trustees to protect their finances. Rather jealous of Charles, these boys even dared to call their father "a spiritual cuckold".

There are two great classic French novels of the time about an adolescent passion for a married woman. *Le Lys dans la Vallée* by Balzac, and *Dominique* by Eugène Fromentin. It is so easy to think the young a little ridiculous in these situations, forgetting that those early loves can go very deep. In the insecurity of his life caused by the death of his parents, by the troubles of the Franco-Prussian war, the move from Strasbourg to Nancy, there had always been for Charles the thought of Marie as an anchor, something stable. Now she was floating away. It would be easy to pity him at that wedding, surrounded by all the highly fashionable friends and relations of the de Bondys and the Moitessiers; too easy to picture the procession into the sacristy of the church after the wedding to congratulate the bride and bridegroom and wish them well. Marie, radiant in her cloud of tulle and orange blossom, kissed him on his pale cheeks and whispered in his ear, "Come and see us directly we come home again."

Charles took care not to tread on the many trains sweeping the nave—those long-skirted dresses which Ruskin thought so unhygienic. He was heedless of all the pretty girls whose bustled dresses were so tight that they were hardly able to sit down in the church, and whose waists were so ferociously laced that they were apt to faint at the smallest provocation. Charles took refuge in drinking as much champagne as possible. Then, when he could at last escape, he left early and walked blindly towards Félix Potin and then to Latinville, the world-famous *confiserie* just a little beyond it, and there compensated by devouring their world-famed nougats, pralines, dragées, marrons glacés and boxes of beautifully arranged candied fruits. It was in his hours of misery that Charles began to put on weight, a phenomenon well known to psychologists. Then, in spite of admiring the pretty society women in the shop, who were tasting the chocolates before they made orders for their friends, Charles found it all very tame, and decided to stroll to the Bal Mabille, which was to close the following year.

Wedding receptions in France go on until late into the night. We may imagine Charles in his smart frock-coat strolling up the Avenue Montaigne. The famous Bal Mabille had been opened by a dancing master of the Second Empire. It had begun as an outdoor ballroom for *midinettes* and shop girls and their *galants*. Then Mabille had decided to make it smarter. He increased the entrance fee, filled the gardens with wooded glades and rich lawns, planted flowers and shrubs in the alleys and installed three thousand of the new gas lamps. Then he selected an orchestra. Over the immense entrance portico, on a sort of arch smothered in ornaments, the name of Mabille shone triumphantly.

Charles watched sadly for a moment from a distance. Some young ladies were dancing the *can-can*, and the 'lions' and the dandies who were their admirers were applauding them in frenzied fashion. In his father's day, the Duc d'Aumale and the Duc de Montpensier, the sons of the King, used to come incognito, and rich men followed their example. The orchestra started a new tune, and soon the company danced the lancers—a frolic which was to be adopted in all fashionable drawing-rooms. The capers of the young ladies of doubtful repute filled the onlookers with enthusiasm, specially when one girl with a well aimed kick sent an old gentleman's top hat whirling. "Shouldn't have come to this place of perdition," Charles chortled, as he sidled to the doorway. He began to forget his troubles as he watched the frothy white petticoats revealing slender legs and the high kicks which inspired the art of Toulouse-Lautrec at Montmartre.

"Well, well," murmured Charles to himself, "this is a good place to come to when I feel down." And he vanished into the night.

Unfortunately, when his grandfather sent him to school to the Jesuits, at 10 Rue des Postes, in the autumn of that year, he soon found that the young men were not allowed to go out alone. Many years later he wrote to a friend, "At seventeen I was all egoism, all impiety, all desire for evil, I was as one bewitched." He bombarded his unfortunate grandfather at Nancy with letters forty pages long, imploring, beseeching him to take him home again. But this time Colonel de Morlet stood firm, so Charles decided to get himself sent down, and did no work at all. The good Jesuits, for whom, by the way, he kept a life-long respect, were in despair, and when they heard that he was disappearing with little shop-girls, alone, they became seriously alarmed.

Charles's letters are full of greed at this time. He told his grandfather, "You know how I love *pretzels*." He also reminded him that he was very fond of steaks roasted on a spit with vegetables, salad and water-cress. He was even becoming a connoisseur of wine: "None of that miserable Tokay, please, stinking of cork, that appears on Aunt Inez's table." When he went to have luncheon at Aunt Inez's, where cousin Marie and her husband had settled down, and where they all had meals together, he always contrived to sit next to Olivier de Bondy at table, because he had in front of him a bottle of first-class Sauternes.

The fact was that Charles lived for the holidays. He wanted good wine, five meals a day taken at home, and all outside invitations to be firmly refused. Also he didn't want his room to be dusted before his return. "In a week, Grandfather, it will be absolutely marvellous, I will be almost leaving." "Tomorrow week, at this hour, I will be with you. It is absolutely marvellous, entirely marvellous. *C'est vraiment chic et rudement chic.*"

Charles lost his faith in that autumn of 1874. By March of 1876 the Jesuits, after struggling in vain with that iron will, watching him getting fatter and fatter every day, and unable any longer to prevent his secret escapades, asked his grandfather to remove him on some health pretext. Charles was enchanted.

There were long family discussions as to what he should do. There was, of course, a long military tradition in the family. He was made to work with a tutor for the entrance exam to Saint-Cyr, the Military Academy near Versailles, and in October, in all the splendour of the autumnal woods, he entered Saint-Cyr. It is a tradition that the cadet always comes very smartly rigged out. Unfortunately, when it came to wearing the famous uniform, red trousers, blue jacket, feathered shako and white gloves, nothing would fit, and he had to wait until he got his weight down before he could begin to look anything like a soldier.

"Yes," said Charles unperturbed, "I've put some good food into this old carcase in my day. I began in my infancy at Wissembourg, which was an epicures' paradise. But it will stand me in good stead. I am like the camel who's filled his hump properly before a desert journey. In later life, I will have good reserves of muscle and endurance to fall back upon."

During the eleven months that Charles was at Saumur, he spent the sum of seventy thousand francs in the chic restaurant of Monsieur Budan. Every evening he would saunter in there at six o'clock precisely, go to a room especially reserved for him, and eat and drink for about two hours. At other times he would invite his friends and comrades. Budan, of course, was all smiles and attention since the day that the two young men had bought those bottles of Pontet Canet from his cellar. He provided all the delicacies of North-west France, oysters, fresh sardines, the white wines of Anjou, delicious game and venison. He had heard from Martin the hotelier how Charles and Vallom had asked him to reserve all the partridges of the neighbourhood, indeed, to commandeer all the available game and venison. Charles had a very sweet tooth and a particular passion for a Mont Blanc, a rich confection of grated sweet chestnut surrounded with whipped cream. Although surprisingly he never succumbed to serious liver trouble, his looks suffered badly. A photograph of the time shows him as a perfectly horrid young man, arrogant, with little pig-like eyes deeply embedded in flesh, no real sign of intelligence (though he was clever despite his gargantuan eating), and certainly not a glimpse of the radiant spirituality which shone from his face in later years. He made up for his unattractive appearance, however, by spending a fortune at the fashionable bootmakers of Saumur, and saw to it that his orderly kept his shoes and riding boots in perfect condition. Also he went to the best tailors.

Particularly, he took care of his hair: first he went to the smartest hairdresser every day, and then, finding that too much of an effort, he told the man to come to him. His dark, shining hair was combed into all the fashionable shapes patronized by the famous actors of the day. And of course he always used the right Eau-de-Cologne or the most costly Cuir-de-Russie.

At Saint-Cyr his appearance had been deplorable, but his

behaviour, at least outwardly, in the eyes of the authorities, passable. At Saumur it was the other way round. He became renowned for *chic*, combined with bad behaviour. He affected an aristocratic nonchalance which must have irritated some of his more hard-up superiors: for example, week after week, he forgot to collect his military pay, and for that fault his name was put into the punishment book and he was gated. It was even too much effort to climb into an ordinary cab after an evening's outing, so he ordered a low-slung carriage. In order to sleep late every morning, the first thing he did when he got to Saumur was to win the good graces of the head doctor who gave him a certificate to say he was unwell and therefore could not rise early.

Two escapades remain famous, for, unfortunately, they reached the ears of Aunt Inez in Paris. One morning he did not answer to the roll call, nor the next day. He had simply vanished, and the authorities finally had to inform the police. All the policemen of the Maine-et-Loire were alerted. At length they found he had been wandering about the countryside, disguised as a beggar in rags.

"But why did you do such a thing, my dear fellow?" asked the devoted Vallom. "Look, you've now lost nearly a month's leave. Was it worth it? What fun was it sleeping under hedgerows and going to farmhouses to beg for a little bread and water?"

Charles shrugged his shoulders. "I don't know what came over me, I suddenly felt hemmed in by comfort and luxury, I found I couldn't bear it any more. I was smothered by all these cushions. I sometimes feel like that when I'm at Aunt Inez's. Her drawing-room is so cluttered up that it's difficult to walk in it without falling over a footstool or plunging headlong into an urn. There's something airless about that drawing-room which doesn't suit me at all. And all her friends with their heavy wigs and bustles and long, sweeping skirts. And that cackle-cackle of small talk. The complete lack of solitude and silence."

"It sounds, my poor fellow, as if you needed to be sent to Africa. That would suit you, the Sahara, you know. The wide open spaces, the stars at night."

"And," added Charles, "I wanted to experience life in the raw. I've only got to lift a finger here and in Paris to get all I want. I wanted to know what it felt like to be a beggar at the mercy of a harsh farmer's wife and her dogs, what it was to feel hungry and thirsty."

"Well," said Vallombrosa, drinking a glass of Anjou and pouring some out for Charles, "now you won't be able to come to our little party at Tours. And we were all looking forward to your company."

At this Charles assumed an air of feline cunning. "Me, miss the party? You wait, I'll be there."

"Oh," exclaimed Vallom, "don't do anything stupid, you'll only be sent down for good and ruin your whole career."

On the night of the Tours party, Charles slipped out unseen from the cavalry school and made his way to the railway station on foot. Hiding in the cloakroom, he stuck on a false beard, and glancing in the looking-glass, congratulated himself on his complete change of appearance. Unfortunately, on his arrival at Tours (a town which is irradiated by the presence of the great St Martin, a soldier of quite another calibre), Charles was unwise enough to go to one of his favourite restaurants. There, his beard became partly unstuck, the manager called the police, who took him for a bandit and arrested him.

The fury of Aunt Inez when she learned that her nephew had been brought back between two policemen can be imagined. She wrote him a letter in which she let herself go in no unmeasured terms. What was this, a de Foucauld brought back by the police and ruining the family's good name? Charles, again confined to his room, yawned loudly. But in the same post was a letter from his cousin, Marie de Bondy. He wrote later, "You had written me a letter which did me good, which moved me at an age when I was difficult to move."

There were two more escapades. He was seen at a window disguised as a woman fanning himself, and on the next occasion he distinguished himself by throwing rotten eggs at a usurer who had complained to the authorities. The second in command of the school wrote about him, "Not a very military spirit, he hasn't got enough sense of duty." When he graduated from Saumur on October 14th, 1879, the Inspector General declared, "Monsieur de Foucauld has a certain distinction and has been well brought up. But he is empty-headed and thinks of nothing but amusing himself."

His other great friend, the Duc de Fitz-James, a descendant of our James II and Arabella Churchill, described him in those days as "a good, fat, jovial fellow". He also spoke of the brilliance of intellect which lay hidden beneath the rolls of fat. "From whatever military, scientific, historical, geographical work or novel he read, he knew how to condense and filter all that it was necessary to remember. . . . When it was his turn to give an address, in an hour and even less, he had prepared his subject and developed it in the most instructive fashion. And what amused us all, was when our chiefs used to say to him, 'That is very good, I see that to have mastered your subject in this way, you must have worked very hard.' "

Another officer has written of him about that time: "Very sluggish, having an answer for everything without losing his head. He disarmed the authorities when they reproached him for being the leader of our pranks. He would arrive looking very correct and well disciplined. It was all very well for us to wish to be severe, the stiffest members among the authorities would finish by laughing at his excuses and his humorous explanations, excuses which were respectful and put across so calmly . . ."

Nevertheless he passed out eighty-seventh out of eighty-seven, and thus finished his career at Saumur.

CHAPTER 3

The Army

NAPOLEON I had sent the cadets away from the special Imperial Military Academy at Fontainebleau in 1808 because he thought that the proximity of the court would bring them too many dissipations. And so they went to Saint-Cyr, that ancient royal house which Madame de Maintenon had been given by Louis XIV for the education of two hundred and fifty impoverished girls from noble families. The memory of the great Louis XIV was ever recalled for them at the entrance, where shone a sun, the royal sun, surrounded by the motto, "They take instruction in order to conquer."

On his first morning, Charles was roused from deep sleep at early dawn, by the bugle blown on the great staircase. He was stretching at his ease in his night-shirt, and rubbing his eyes, when a friend said: "Hi, you, hurry up. No good going off into day dreams. In half an hour you've got to be washed, dressed, all your bedclothes opened up, and all your things in order."

"I hate to be hurried, I am used to a quiet life."

"Well, why the Devil did you decide to go into the Army, then? Get a move on. Come on: scuttle."

In half an hour, looking rather untidy, Charles was drinking a large bowl of hot coffee in the refectory.

Charles enjoyed the riding near the woods of Satory, immortalized by many a royal canter, and he enjoyed Marly with its forest of high trees so well loved by *le Roi Soleil*. And always in the distance, barely two or three miles away, the glorious Palace of Versailles, with its gardens and park designed by Le Nôtre, its cascades and fountains and flower beds and huge urns and statues. Versailles, beautiful at all seasons of the year, is loveliest in October. Général Waygand has written in his memoirs, "I remember the impression of my first night at Saint-Cyr, when for the first time, in the courtyard I heard the curfew being sounded, with its melancholy notes."

Weygand also speaks of "a little edifice with a welcoming air about it, the infirmary. You reach this paradise by a shaded alley which rose gently. To go to the infirmary was to climb into paradise. There, in fine white sheets, we only had to give ourselves up to the attentive cares with which we were overwhelmed by the nuns, the guardian angels of this place of repose. . . .

"On the last day of the month, in our white gloves and wearing our swords, we would go to the office to collect our pay. . . ."

They all basked in one splendid luxury—riding. For a real cavalryman, the horse is a boundless source of satisfaction. A manoeuvre, even an uninteresting one on a long, monotonous road, is agreeable on a good horse. Once he has finished work, he can seek the shade of the riding school, watch the training of horses, or he can ride aimlessly, his reins slack, looking at men working in the fields, in communion with the beauties of nature.

All that was well calculated to please Charles, who remained as dreamy as ever. In spite of being surrounded by enthusiastic young men who were filled with the spirit of revenge for the defeat of 1870, he worked as little as he could. His depression, no doubt about Marie, continued to show in the neglect of his person. His report on his appearance was bad, whereas his moral conduct was judged to be perfect. In his free time, he dipped idly into his favourite Greek and Latin authors. He always kept a specially bound copy of Aristophanes in his pocket. "Come on, then," said one of his friends, "read us a little of your precious Aristophanes."

Charles gave an idle, good-humoured laugh and opened a page at random. "Listen to this:

" 'Come to the banquet, come quickly, armed with your basket and your wine measure; it is the feast of Dionysus and he invites you to it. But hurry, you delay the banquet. All is ready—tables, cushions, carpets, crowns, scents, delicacies— the courtesans are there—the pancakes, the cakes, the sesame breads, the tartlets, the dancers, and the song "Belovèd Harmodios, ah . . . no, thou art not dead" . . . But hasten.' "

But in spite of his apathy and even of his unbelief, Charles was one of the first to sign his name to a loyal address to the newly elected Pope Leo XIII. Not only did he sign, but he got others to do so as well.

The chaplain of Saint-Cyr, the Abbé Lamusse, used to ride at the head of the battalion when they crossed the streets of Versailles, and would tell the young men about his campaigns in Mexico. But he seems to have had no influence on Charles. Of the 800 pupils, only 400 were practising Catholics, and de Foucauld was not of that Christian élite which for the last sixty years had been the backbone of glorious Saint-Cyr. The Abbé Lamusse said of him, "He was independent, and the discipline of the school weighed heavily on him. He felt the effects of this and he was not very sociable, even a little moody. Far from being a saint, he was a free-thinker."

A fellow Saint-Cyrien said, "Amongst those of us who were mad devils, Foucauld was conspicuous by an incredible physical apathy. His idleness, however, had something special about it, and that singular indolence always appeared to me as if it were hiding an original mind, not lacking in *finesse*."

Another comrade added, "I have kept the memory of a charming comrade, distinguished, a little distant." A fourth noted, "He appeared to me reserved, talking very little, rarely laughing." Finally, there is the inestimable testimony of the great Général Henri Laperrine who said, "Charles de Foucauld neglected his studies at Saint-Cyr, trusting to his lucky star to get him through examinations: a man of letters and an artist, the time left from his military obligations he spent strolling around, a pencil in his hand, engrossed in Latin and Greek authors."

But in spite of having all the characteristics of a young man who lived in his own private world, he still had a heart of gold. As his cousin Marie de Bondy was now spiritually far away from him, all the affections of his heart poured out on to his sister, his dearest Mimi. He often wrote amusing letters to her, including the classic, rollicking letter about the geese of the Capitol who warned the Romans by their cackling.

He also wrote to a cousin from Saint-Cyr on June 18th, 1878:

"I intend to stay near Mimi during my holidays, I shall spend them therefore entirely at Loüye, save a few days when I will go to Nancy in October. In several days she will go to Loüye. I am very glad for her sake: it's been three years since she's been to the country, and the fresh air will do her good. However, she is very well and looks fit."

He wrote her the most entertaining letters. He told her about the stag beetles that were the craze at Saint-Cyr. His neighbour kept three: "The docile creatures can be taught to draw carriages made of paper, run races, do gymnastics." He enjoyed his quiet holidays at Nancy where he was rather solitary. "This solitude has nothing disagreeable about it, when one comes from Saint-Cyr, where one has more friends than one wants."

And then on February 1st, 1878, the next great blow fell. He was hurriedly called to Nancy, for his grandfather, Colonel de Morlet, was dying.

From then on, Charles de Foucauld became a libertine. The tenderness which he had felt for his grandfather had restrained him on the brink of the worst excesses; but now he felt free to go to the Devil. The military reports about him complain of his inattention, untidy bunk, bed ill-made, appearance bad, dirty trousers, hair too long. Indeed, he showed all the signs of a real disgust for living, he who had so much enjoyed looking impeccable. He appears even to have taken a private flat in Paris in the Rue de la Boëtie, no doubt a rendezvous for the many mistresses of the lower classes whom he had collected here and there. He also entertained his soldier friends in this flat.

And then came the next disaster from the point of view of his spiritual life. On September 15th, 1878, he attained his majority and was able to take possession of his reasonably large inheritance, and from then on he seemed filled with an almost fiendish fury for living.

However, in spite of all these reverses, Saint-Cyr and its training was to have a deep influence on him for the rest of his life. Even when he became a hermit, a brother officer wrote of him, "He still has all the qualities of a cavalry officer." The habit of order inculcated in those early days was to reappear in later life in the desert, and the great Laperrine commented. "His packing is a miracle of neatness. He'd make a sailor jealous."

Général Audié, a fellow comrade, wrote of him:

"I still see Foucauld with his lustreless complexion, his regular features, his fine black eyes sunk in their sockets, his speech measured; he spoke in slow sentences without any special brilliance, while Vallombrosa (his great friend) had a mobile face, a much warmer and livelier temperament, ardent speech. Quite often they discussed the way they would spend their free time in Paris on Sunday. I can still hear him asking our comrade Gouyon de Beaufort if he were going out the following Sunday, and as this one explained that he had to prepare his leaving exam which would open the cavalry school to him, Foucauld was trying to induce him to come, saying to him, 'Take your books with you and we will swot together at my place.' But as Gouyon still remained refractory, Foucauld finished up by saying, '*Mon cher*, you are a complete idiot and you will always be an unlucky conventionalist, an unfortunate scholar. Well, since you do not want to come, I will profit by getting myself in trim during this heat wave. Either I'll work or I'll sleep, but it's I who'll get into the cavalry and you who will be left high and dry.' In effect it was Foucauld who won his spurs and Gouyon ended up in a foot regiment."

At last Charles passed his exams, and to his great delight was sent to the famous cavalry school at Saumur on the Loire. I had the privilege there of seeing the large old-fashioned punishment book in which Charles is mentioned so often. He missed many days of leave by his escapades. Proust has said of the cavalry school:

"It is at once aristocratic and military, set in a broad expanse of country over which, on fine days, there often floats into the distance a sort of intermittent hum of sound which indicates the movement of a regiment on parade, so that the very atmosphere of the streets, avenues, and squares has been gradually tuned to a sort of perpetual vibration, musical and martial, while the most ordinary note of cartwheel and tramway is prolonged by the silence in vague trumpet calls, infinitely echoed, to the hallucinated ear."

Charles shared the now famous room 82 with the delightful Antoine Duc de Vallombrosa, tall, slender, handsome, impetuous, a great contrast in his passionate oratory to the sulky, quiet-looking Charles. Antoine de Vallombrosa started his career at

Saumur by this astonishing declaration: "Charles, I want to give you a royal gift, my friendship, entire, confident, final. . . . In exchange for this friendship, will you give me yours on the same terms?"

And Charles did. And when he became a Trappist he wrote to him, "My old friend, you to whom my heart has remained so warmly devoted . . . you know my affection for you, neither time nor absence has changed it."

The two young men shared a taste for epicurean food and a wild life. Nothing in their behaviour could make one foresee that both were to die violent deaths in Africa. It was with that kind of young man in mind that Balzac had written, "He who has a lively appreciation for the pleasures of this world, is sooner or later drawn to taste the fruits of Heaven. Did not the Lord himself say in the Bible, 'the tepid man I will spew from my mouth'?"

Taking a glance at the cold austerity of Room 82, the two young men at once set out to the Saumur shops to buy all kinds of things to make it habitable—pale pink toile-de-Jouy to hang on the walls, an armchair or two and some comfortable cushions, a few knick-knacks from the antiquaries—and finally they hung up on the nails on the walls their military headgear and their swords. Then they laid up a provision of food and wine, plates and glasses, and before long the place became the rendezvous of anyone who liked good jokes and tall stories and a choice glass of Pontet Canet, the two young men having bought up a large supply from the restaurant Budan for eighteen thousand francs. "And now, some *foie gras*," cried Charles, who had a passion for it—no doubt because he came from Strasbourg.

Said Vallom, as he was nicknamed, "If you go on gobbling *foie gras* at the rate that you ate it at Saint-Cyr, my good fellow, you'll never get your figure back. I shall never forget that funny clicking noise which I used to hear in our dormitory in the middle of the night. It was your spoon scraping against the *foie gras* tin, which you ate peacefully in the small hours. You must have a digestion of iron."

CHAPTER 4

Africa

BETWEEN October 1879 and November 1880, Charles was transferred first to Cézanne, which he found boring, and so he asked to be moved to Pont-à-Mousson near his native town of Nancy where he had many friends. During his leave days, he would sometimes dash back to Paris to his flat in the Rue de la Boëtie, near, but not too near, Aunt Inez. In this little *pied-à-terre* he spent his mornings among his ancestral pictures and his precious, beautifully bound books, surrounded by the luxury without which he could no longer exist, in spite of the beggar escapade. He does not seem to have frequented his family in the Rue d'Anjou very much during that time; Marie de Bondy was busy looking after her growing family of three boys and a girl. Moreover, he found his aunt's Sunday afternoon receptions tedious, and his other cousin a blue-stocking. Here in his own flat he could do what he liked, receive whom he liked. He went to luncheon in a fashionable restaurant where the waiters greeted him with flattering respect. This experienced gourmet in his smart uniform believed with Brillat-Savarin that "to eat is a necessity, but to know how to eat is an art".

So here, in Paris, Charles knew all the specialities of the most famous restaurants, the *suprème de volaille aux truffes* and the Château Latour of the Maison Dorée, the game imbedded in mushroom purée and the iced champagne of the Café Anglais which was reserved only for special clients. Who could have predicted the terrible fasts of the young hermit, of the Trappist who believed, like St Athanasius, that "fasting is the food of angels"? And here he entertained his mistresses, many creatures who came and went and left no trace. He was not very attractive to look at in those days, so probably they only clung to him for what they could get, for he was very generous. He warned them beforehand, "I rent by the day, not by the month."

At Nancy he took a flat, but there he refused to receive his mistresses, for he said, "Here in this garrison, Mimi, Lucienne, Albertine, anybody you like. A fox is a foul beast, but even he does not sully his earth nor does a de Foucauld his family." In Paris he would make provisions for his Nancy parties and buy all sorts of things he could not get in the provinces. He ordered some magnificent writing-paper headed by a Vicomte's crown—not quite as splendid as the ducal crown of his friends Vallom and Fitz-James, but still, something. He spent money lavishly without counting, would never ask for change when he paid a bill or gave his fare to a cabby. He bought an English dog-cart and a high-stepping horse. He was always accompanied by a well-trained, well-groomed footman. He would invite his friends in turn to go out with him, either in the town or to the surrounding country. When they came back, they would always find in his flat delicious *foie gras* sandwiches and the best Rhine wine, served by impeccable orderlies. Then they would all play cards and sing and make a terrible noise, and in fact the neighbours began to complain and the police were soon on his track. Complaints were made to the commandant. His superior's words were characteristic; he thought him very youthful, lacking in firmness and enthusiasm, with an indolent character. But he did grant that he had good judgment.

His regiment was the 4° Chasseurs d'Afrique. Quite soon his colonel had another cause for complaint. He and his wife were giving an evening reception for all the pompous dignitaries of the provincial neighbourhood, but they found to their dismay that they could not get a single cab to come and fetch their departing guests. When one of the cabbies was questioned, he replied, "Well, you see, sir, Lieutenant de Foucauld is also giving a party and he has commissioned all the cabbies of the town to drive round and round until he calls for them, so we're none of us free. We can't afford to miss the chance of such a good tip."

Charles was so reserved, and knew so well how to assume a mask, that none of his contemporaries at the time guessed that underneath all the gaiety, the mad prodigality, he was suffering from the deepest depression. Speaking later of his parties, he says: "I felt a painful sensation of emptiness, a sadness which I had never experienced before, and this sadness fell upon me every evening, the minute I had gone back alone to my flat; this depression left me dumb, overcome, during what people call festivities. I organized them, but when the time came, I felt I could hardly speak and I was overwhelmed by an infinite disgust."

It was here at Nancy that Charles acquired a new mistress, two years older than himself. In spite of his "I rent by day" warning, she spent quite a long time with him. It is not clear whether she was a young, fresh peasant girl of the neighbourhood called Marie, or a dancer from Paris called Marie Cardinale, mentioned in *Les Petites Cardinales* by Daniel Halévy. Anyway, she had several good qualities, she was genuinely attached to Charles, knew how to charm him out of his glooms, and looked so much like a gentlewoman that, when he carried her off to Africa, he was able to pass her off as the Vicomtesse de Foucauld: he would never have done this had the girl looked common. No doubt she knew how to dress, she appreciated the furs and fine jewels with which her lover loaded her, and she had a natural distinction which could deceive the unknowing. She was dark-haired and very gay. He nicknamed her Mimi, in spite of the fact that his sister shared the same name.

It was for her that Charles gave one of his most original winter parties. The Meuse was frozen over; he invited all his guests to meet him in a field at night, and there, to their amazement, they found that red lanterns had been lit on every tree. The river was floodlit, sledges and skates were provided, there were torches and fires blazing everywhere. And then the supreme surprise, a sleigh carved like a swan was drawn up, and into it Charles lifted Mimi wrapped in sables. Then the orderlies brought up a buffet table on which were caviare and *foie gras* and truffled ortolans. Also, two specialities invented by Charles, coffee brewed with old kirsch instead of water, and his favourite chestnut mousse frozen into an ice cream and covered with hot chocolate sauce. Mimi looked a picture, with her rosy cheeks and glowing eyes. The young men cheered, and then by the glow of the punch flaming up in a huge silver bowl, Charles gave the toast: "To the honorary colonel of the Fourth Hussars, the Ice Queen Mimi."

How much one is reminded of a passage in the confessions of St Augustine when he says, "I only strove by my excesses and vanity to appear a charming and agreeable man, and I fell into the net of love, where I wished to fall and be caught.'

Is it surprising that his friends should idolize him and be unable

47

to see beneath the mask? The Duc de Fitz-James, who knew him at Pont-à-Mousson, said of him that his tact was perfect and that he was most considerate. He dazzled everybody by his vast intelligence and his prodigious memory. He seemed always to be in good spirits, but prompt to fight a duel. Another friend told how, when he played cards with a hard-up brother officer, he always arranged to lose the game, and as at Saumur, no doubt many of the improvident were discreetly helped out of financial difficulties, assistance being offered in such a way that there was no humiliation involved.

Then the regiment, the Chasseurs d'Afrique, was sent to Africa. "Of course you'll come with me," Charles said to Mimi. And without caring a fig for anyone's opinion, he ordered a ticket for her at Marseilles in the name of the Vicomtesse de Foucauld. Mimi went ahead of him, and appeared to have played her part so cleverly that even the colonel and his wife were taken in for a time. On board ship she was invited to eat her meals at the captain's table. Everybody was all attention, impressed no doubt by the title, the furs and the expensive luggage. So in December 1880 she landed at the port of Bone, which was the ancient Hippo of the great St Augustine, though Mimi was the last person to be aware of this fact. She was to furnish a house for them both. Charles followed quite soon afterwards, so that he was alone when he made his first encounter with Africa, when Africa took him into her fierce, burning embrace, the memory of which was to mark him for life.

Africa! One is stunned by the scorching sun, the dazzling light. The Sahara symbolizes eternity and awakens in the breasts of men a love of the eternal verities. The law of Africa is silence. Just as the monk keeps silence in his monastery, the desert keeps silence in its white cape. Great things are wrought in souls in Africa. It was in Africa that, on a never-to-be-forgotten day, the unbeliever Psichari realized beyond any shadow of doubt that eventually he would become a Catholic. As he lay awake under the stars, he felt a strange well-being, almost as if he were in an ocean of eternal beatitude. De Foucauld himself was to write later, "On such nights one understands the belief of Arabs in the mystical night, when the skies open and angels float down to earth . . . and all creation bows down humbly in adoration of the Creator." And the sunsets which heralded those nights! De

Foucauld marvelled at the wonderful tints which greeted him as he came up out of his tent. The sky was painted in unaccustomed colours, with the translucence of pale green water, or the delicacy of Chinese roses, or the depths of the sea in the gulfs of Brittany. At that moment the plain appeared of a prodigious immensity. Charles must have felt like Psichari, the agnostic, who wrote, "You cannot imagine what it is to live for three years in a country where everybody prays. It is there that I experienced my first hours of true solitude. . . . In that dead land where man had never fixed his dwelling, I seemed to leave the ordinary horizons of life, to go forward trembling, head spinning, to the very brink of Eternity." In the desert, Psichari discovered in his heart great unexplored vistas. In his dereliction he at last saw a Master.

Charles must have forgotten his mistress entirely when, at the call of the Muezzin at the top of the minaret "*Allah Akbar!*" five times a day, men would throw themselves from their camels and horses, and with white robes floating, bow their heads to earth and worship Allah, regardless of who was looking on. Did this libertine, who had not been inside a church since the age of sixteen, then turn his mind for a moment to Christ, who, in the words of the Catholic litany, is the "Door of Heaven" and "the Desire of the Eternal Hills"? He confessed later that he was profoundly shaken by his first encounter with Islam.

The Spanish mystic and Doctor of the Church, St John of the Cross, saw the desert as a state or a condition of the soul. In his wonderful classic, *The Ascent of Mount Carmel*, his mountain is a symbol of the Sahara. The desert draws some men in a mysterious manner, as if they felt the compelling presence of a friend. In this way the desert is exacting. Primarily, it makes a man realize his nothingness, his wretchedness. Charles could have exclaimed with Psichari, "I might have been a drawing-room man, a witty man, a fastidious man. O blessed be Africa which has saved me from such a destiny. . . . From morning till night I will bless thee, O Africa, venerable virgin . . . who alone has remained pure. . . . The silence is also the master of love. It is in the desert that God speaks to man. The book of Hosea says: 'I will lead him into a desert place and I will speak to his soul.' "

When at last Charles reached Mimi and the house she had prepared for them both, he must have seemed slightly strange and lost, as if he were absorbed in a secret dream which she could not share.

But the disagreeable realities of conventional life were soon to close in upon the guilty pair. The truth dawned upon the authorities that Mimi was not the Vicomtesse de Foucauld. Far from it. The colonel was incensed and affronted. He realized that he and his wife had been made to appear ridiculous. In March 1881 he summoned de Foucauld to appear at his office. His face was grim but determined; he came straight to the point. "Lieutenant de Foucauld, the private lives of the men in my regiment are not my concern, but when they create a public scandal, that is quite a different matter. I won't have the good name of the regiment slandered. You have done an unpardonable thing in passing off your mistress as your wife and calling her the Vicomtesse de Foucauld. I order you to send her back to France immediately."

Said Charles respectfully but firmly, "*Mon colonel*, may I point out that she doesn't come under the jurisdiction of military discipline, and that what I do in my free time is no concern of the authorities."

The colonel was furious. "How dare you speak to me like that! And you, coming from an old French family with honourable Christian traditions. No, Lieutenant de Foucauld, either you dismiss your mistress instantly, or I must ask you temporarily to leave the regiment, and retire into non-active service."

Charles gave a bow and said, "Then, *mon colonel*, I can do nothing but acquiesce to your will, and send in my papers."

He left Africa, and he and Mimi settled down at Evian, overlooking the lake and the mountains. In civilian clothes, he spent a great deal of time learning Arabic. This puzzled Mimi. Is there anything more calculated to create boredom in a lover than to be constantly in the company of a woman who is no longer a kindred spirit? It is the Hell of Dante's Paola and Francesca, to float for eternity, for ever and for ever, clasped in each other's arms. But this Inferno did not last more than two or three months. Africa had already cast too powerful a spell on Charles. She was more splendid than any mistress.

One morning at breakfast he was glancing idly through the newspaper in their bedroom overlooking the peerless lake. Mimi had been trying on a new mauve pleated chiffon négligée which had just arrived from Paris. The floor was littered with feminine trifles—silk roses, scent bottles, lace petticoats, satin mules and copies of *Le Rire*. Now she was reading aloud the rather erotic advertisements from *L'Illustration*. " 'Oriane's Dew'—used by Ninon de Lenclos for half a century: it gives to the skin the whiteness and the bloom of a camellia leaf; and the 'Rose of Cyprus' —do listen, Charles—it bestows on you the freshness of those diaphanous creatures who live on the banks of the Thames, who, one would think, had been born in the mists of the fog. Are you listening, Charles? Here is another cosmetic milk described as 'a drop of milk coming from the proud bosom of Juno, guaranteed to destroy pimples and to give your complexion all the glory of a lily'. And here is the lingerie of Madame Leblanc which is both 'angelic and sprightly'. Her petticoats are so charmingly enticing, that if a wife wore them, they would make the most unfaithful husband love to sit by his own fireside. And Madam Henocq creates enchanting spring hats with veils and gauze at the back, and in the front large tufts of wild marguerites and bunches of ribbons."

But Charles was not listening at all. He had been clutching the paper. His face had that far-away look which Mimi had noticed lately, with a sinking heart. His thoughts were miles away from petticoats guaranteed to captivate the most unfaithful husband, let alone a lover. Oh, would Mimi never stop her chattering? Suddenly, he threw down his newspaper and was true to himself, his real self.

"Listen, Mimi, my regiment, my Fourth Chasseurs d'Afrique, is off to quell Bou-Amama's insurrection. Oh, Mimi, do listen and don't hum. My regiment is going to quell insurrection in Africa. All my comrades will be in danger, and I am out of it. I must go to Paris by the next train and ask the Minister for War if he will have me back again."

Poor little Mimi! But in spite of her feather brain, she must have been endowed with that ancient wisdom of woman which knows that a man's work comes first in his life, just as Anna Karenina came to understand that Vronsky was pining for his regiment which he had left for love of her.

Mimi rang for the maids and valets to help with the packing: without a word, she bundled away all her boas, aigrettes and mules.

The War Office in the Rue St Dominique in Paris soon received the visit of this Lieutenant de Foucauld who had such a bad reputation, but who could not have been such a bad fellow after all. They granted his plea to return to his regiment in Africa. Of Mimi, no more is known—officially.

When he got back to Algeria, this habitué of restaurants at long last proved to be a fine soldier and leader of men. He bore all the hardships of the campaign with great gaiety and was devoted to his soldiers. He was kind-hearted: after a long march through the scorching desert, seeing his men panting with thirst and rushing to a well, he quickly bought a bottle of rum from the canteen girl. He came back to his men and said, "How glad I am to have my bottle to give to you."

It was during that time that he saw more of the great Laperrine who claimed a vague family relationship and who was to play such an important part in his undertakings.

It is impossible to underestimate the effect that the Army had on Charles for the rest of his life. It was a part of his preparation for his great and universal mission. As Commandant Lahuroux has written of him, "We loved Father de Foucauld, above all because he had remained a soldier, because he thought as a soldier and because he judged us all as a soldier."

Though he had been with Général Laperrine at Saumur, it was not until he saw him again in Africa that they found a common meeting ground which resulted in their lifelong friendship. No doubt a man is judged by his friends, and Charles had a gift, in later life, for associating with the cream of mankind. Henri Laperrine was two years his junior, and later Charles wrote of this great man, "Laperrine gave the Sahara to France in spite of herself and united our possessions in Algeria and our Sudanese colonies."

Laperrine was very tall, well over six foot, and very thin. His uniforms, ordered in Paris, never by any chance fitted by the time they reached Africa, but floated about him; he had piercing eyes, a radiant look, a cameo-clear profile and sensitive, aristocratic hands. He never married, for the simple reason that Africa was his bride. He came from a very large family, and therefore had little private income. He was so proud that he always refused the hospitality which he could not adequately return. He had all manner of eccentric and rather endearing habits; he was loved by his men. When a fire was lit on cold African nights, he would lift up his coat-tails to warm himself and laughingly explain that Marie Antoinette's daughter, the Duchesse d'Angoulême, had set a precedent for this behaviour.

When Laperrine met Charles again in Africa, he noticed that the *gros bon réjoui*, the fat jolly fellow he had known before, had completely changed. All that remained was his little pocket edition of Aristophanes and his taste for an expensive brand of cigars made especially for him. He would smoke no other. When the two men discovered that they were vaguely connected, this put their relationship on a friendly footing at once.

Like all great men, Laperrine knew how to recognize gifts in others. He took in the look of the changed de Foucauld, and when, much later, he was appointed military commander of all the Saharan oases, he asked him to come on an expedition with him, far into the southern desert, into the Hoggar. He understood the Moslem mentality and realized how shocked they would be by some of the officials and soldiers sent from France, who seemed to have no thought for religion and who went drinking and womanizing. He understood that a *marabout* or holy man would have more impact on the Moslem mentality than anyone else. The sermon preached at his funeral service puts the man in a nutshell: "Like all those who came near him, I was struck by the noble simplicity and the goodness of his soul which glowed on his tranquil countenance; and if he was not ideally handsome, as my intimate friend Père de Foucauld used to say, speaking of his young friend of Saint-Cyr, 'the habit of meditation and of recollection in the desert had given him, even in his radiant smile, something grave and sweet'."

Africa had seized these two men's imaginations, and they both realized that they could do great things through Africa, for she was a symbol of eternity: she would give the beautiful, the true, and nothing less. As they were gazing at one of these splendid Sahara sunsets together, an Arab came towards them, and, making a sweeping gesture towards the horizon, with transfigured face said, "God is great!"

The Sahara was the first stage in God's training of Charles for his eremitical and apostolic life. He was prepared by the solitude of the wastes. Other famous men in history had submitted to this law of the desert—Moses, St John the Baptist, St Paul, St Bernard. The desert is the scene of temptation; it is also a place of preparation. Did sensuality begin to tempt Charles again? They say the flesh disappears only ten minutes after death! St Augustine wrote after his conversion, "But those vanities, my sometime mistresses, shake me by my fleshly robe and say in whispers, 'Are you sending us back? What, do you mean that from now onwards we will never see you again?' " And the young St Benedict, father of Western monasticism, the founder of an immense religious family, when he ran away from his parents in Rome and even from his old nanny, went and hid in his desolate cave of Subiaco, the most deserted place surrounded by hills, and there the Devil of lust was waiting for him. Temptation nearly smothered him. He had done violence to his senses by his austerities, and the body began to rebel, so much so that he was on the point of leaving his cave to seek out a woman in Rome whose beauty had struck him in the old days and the memory of which haunted him ceaselessly. Several years later, Charles was to find *Les Moines d'Occident* by Montalembert, and he read how at this juncture young Benedict had thrown himself naked into a terrible thorn bush, until his body was one livid wound and he had extinguished for ever that fire which burnt him even in his desolate cave.

The solitude and silence of Africa were Charles's introduction to a life spent listening to God and doing His will. He wrote, "One must cross the desert and sojourn there to receive God's grace." St Augustine wrote, "Let my soul impose silence on herself. And in this universal silence may she listen to the Word which speaks eternally, but which the clamour of creatures often prevents us from hearing."

St John of the Cross speaks often of the desert. It fills the soul with an ideal of nothingness, *nada, nada*, of denuding and stripping which is the antechamber to the contemplative life. The desert imposes humility on the man who sees it for the first time. It makes him understand his own nothingness, his own misery; and then he realizes that silence is the language of love. In a famous page, Louis Bertrand, speaking of the desert, has said, "Even the vilest soul receives the reflection of a certain nobility from it. No cloister is like the desert, not only to sever all attachments between you and the world, but to make you feel your dependence, and at the same time to restore you to yourself. . . . It is impossible to live in those hostile and splendid immensities without withdrawing into yourself, and without trying to escape from yourself and reach out beyond. The desert forces you to think."

Prayer and meditation are the only fruits of that land without shade and without water. Those extraordinary sunsets of Africa began to pull at Charles's imagination. It was as though the whole horizon were on fire with scarlet flames, and then, when the ardent furnace was extinguished, the sky melted, softened into a rich turquoise tint fringed with rose, until little by little all the colours grew pale and mingled with the night.

CHAPTER 5

Morocco

WE can imagine the anger and shock experienced by Inez Moitessier and her family when, in 1882, they received the news that Charles wanted to give up the Army, because he was planning to explore Morocco. Marie de Bondy said not a word, for she believed in him, but Inez struck quickly and hard, and in June of that year she appointed a judiciary council which would keep a hold on her nephew's finances. He had already squandered far too much of his fortune. This expedition to Morocco was looked upon as one of his new vagaries. Charles was summoned back to France to discuss his nonsensical plan with his family.

The first thing that struck them was the complete change in his face and even his figure. He had become slender, and a photograph of the time is in great contrast to the earlier one taken when he was still at Saumur. The soul was beginning to fashion the flesh, in the manner of which St Thomas Aquinas has spoken. His whole air was manly and determined, the sensuality seemed to have gone, the eyes were brilliant and black and alive. Although the complete transformation made him more attractive to women, he was too busy preparing to be the first European to explore Morocco to think very much of his old flames. He agreed that his cousin, Latouche, should look after his financial affairs and give him a small allowance every month, just enough to live as a poor student in Algiers and to study at the great library there. The soldier that he had been trained to become now developed fully and could be seen at his best in his gift for organization. He had spent a small fortune in the four years since he had been the master of his own money, but now he agreed to live on 350 francs a month, and out of this to pay for his Arabic lessons. Later he was given permission to buy various necessary instruments like telescopes and quadrants.

He arrived in Algiers with the intention of spending nearly a year there; Algiers, where the air is golden with mimosa and where the shoals of beautiful flowers—asphodels, white hellebore and blue myrtle, multi-coloured anemones and orchids—entranced this man who had been brought up in fields and woods in the Vosges country. Charles had an introduction to McCarthy, the librarian of Algiers, who was most anxious to help this young Frenchman who was going to do what he himself had always longed to do, explore. McCarthy was very thin and brown, a dry, alert man who took no more care of what he called his "envelope" than is sufficient to make it adequately perform the services he required of it.

"What are all those cans on your desk?" asked Charles.

"Oh, pathetic, isn't it?" laughed McCarthy. "I've held them in readiness for my voyage to Timbuctoo, and they've been waiting there for twenty-five years, with biscuits inside. But all that is dreams, dreams. And now, *cher Vicomte*, here comes the reality; you're going to do what I couldn't. Don't hesitate to call upon me. I will be at your service for as long as you require."

At long last Charles finished his studies. From June 25th of the year 1883 until May of 1884, Charles explored Morocco. He hired the services of a Jew called Mardochée who had had a very unfortunate life, but who would be invaluable to Charles by passing him off as his own son and making arrangements. With characteristic fortitude, this fastidious young man, who had spent much of his life at the barber's, grew his hair and side whiskers and decided to disguise himself as a very dirty, ragged Jew, so that he would not be noticed by the Arabs, who despised Jews and their practice of usury. Charles was not only going on an adventure, he wanted to make a serious contribution to geography in the service of France. He wanted also to restore his reputation in the eyes of his family, who thought so ill of him— all except his cousin Marie. He bought instruments which included a compass, a sextant, a chronometer, a theodolite, barometers and hydrometers.

When it came to Mardochée, the Jew who was to accompany him, his cousin Latouche became a little alarmed and asked for more information about him. He wanted to check the Rabbi's suitability, for he thought his cousin Charles was a dreamer, completely devoid of the practical sense indispensable to a man of adventure. This is how Charles Pichon describes Mardochée:

"He is a man of about sixty years old, very bent, dressed in a garnet-coloured caftan falling to his feet and held in by a black belt. Over this hangs a coat of blue cloth which sweeps the ground. This Syrian costume has been beautiful, but now it is stained and torn and full of holes. The left hand holds a rat's-tail file, the right hand is continually picking his hooked nose, which seems to hide cunning and to exhale an atmosphere of misfortune. The face under the red cap and the black turban is smothered in hair. The lip is fairly good, but drawn down into a bitter expression. The scowling brows, the nobbly cheek-bones quiver with some strange anxiety. . . . As to his great forehead of Eternal Father, it is engraved with more wrinkles than a ploughed field in April. . . . And yet, from these features which speak of the Exodus and the end of the world, there glows a sort of light. Between the wrinkled eyelids, red, thick, glitter two clear eyes, two extraordinary eyes, wandering, dancing, like those of children, alchemists and poets . . .'

Charles began by asking him how he had lost the fortune he had amassed by commerce; it seemed the desert had once been furrowed by countless caravans of his, bringing produce from Morocco and the Sudan. "Envy," wailed Mardochée. "My immense prosperity excited the jealousy of my own brothers and the rapacity of a tribe of Arabs."

"I'm told you nearly lost your life at their hands. What happened to you, my friend?" asked Charles kindly.

"Well, I'd decided to leave my family, which had seized my inheritance in my absence, convert what little remained to me into gold powder, seal it in small packets, and return to Morocco. On swift camels, I was accompanied by a Jew, a black slave, and a reliable Arab called El Mokhtar. What a mistake I made, not to accompany a large caravan, which is much safer! One day, as we were nearing our journey's end, El Mokhtar noticed fresh traces of a great troop of camels, and we at once scented danger. So, quickly we disguised ourselves as Moslems, and hid my precious gold powder at the foot of a gum-tree. The black slave was sent out to reconnoitre. Suddenly he rode back, making violent warning signs. We rushed to our camels. Too late. In a moment we were choking in a cloud of dust, El Mokhtar was shot in the head and fell down dead; before we could blink an eyelid we were surrounded by sixty menacing Arabs. Without a word, they ripped open our luggage, and then stripped us stark naked and searched every seam of our clothing. The Arabs, furious at finding no treasure, brandished their arms, and pulled us about, drew blood and yelled at us. Unhappily, the little black slave lost his head when he saw us being pricked with swords and blood flowing, and confessed that we had hidden something at the foot of a gum-tree. The Arabs rushed to it, and with howls of glee, they dug up and seized my gold. I was ruined. They killed one of my camels and ate it, there and then, to celebrate. And then, for two mortal days, dying with hunger and thirst, I was made to weigh my gold, my very own gold, and divide it into sixty equal shares for the Arabs. Finally, we only saved our lives by making out that we belonged to a tribe they knew, Regibats."

"Were they eventually caught?" asked Charles.

Mardochée chuckled with unholy mirth. "Their exploit brought them ill fortune. When the head of the Regibat tribe—a valiant man who rode a white camel—when he heard they had so mal-treated members of his tribe, he cursed them soundly; I can still see him, with his foot in its rich laced boot, resting on his camel's head. He cried, 'May God burn your father and your ancestors.' The curse worked; soon after, most of them were killed on a subsequent raid. Twenty years later, the Sahara was still talking of this disaster in hushed, horrified whispers."

Charles eyed him closely, and wondered whether this adven-ture had made him lose his nerve.

De Foucauld was to have long tussles with this Mardochée, whom he only took because he said he knew Morocco inside out. Unfortunately, unknown to Charles, Mimi his sister had written to Mardochée, promising him large sums of money if he brought her brother back safely to Algiers. Naturally, Mardochée's only aim was to escort de Foucauld back to Algiers without delay, and to cash in on the promised sum. For fifteen days the two of them raged at each other, and Charles's heart sank when he realized that Mardochée wanted to deviate from his original itinerary and delay him all he could. He realized Mardochée was both cow-ardly and lazy: "He does nothing but whine and sometime just bursts out weeping. On the road he complains of the sun or his mule; in a town he grumbles about the fleas and bugs, and that the water is tepid and the food poor."

It is impossible in a short space to go into detail and wander from place to place through the lesser and greater Atlas Mountains with the two men, but as the *Reconnaissance au Maroc*, which Charles wrote when he got home, is in the form of a journal, it can be dipped into at any point. Let it briefly be said that Charles mapped 1,406 square miles, of which only 430 had been previously known. He determined forty-five longitudes, forty latitudes and 3,000 altitudes. He took his notes in the palm of his hand, in a tiny notebook, and spent half his night copying them out properly. He felt he was at long last blossoming out into glowing fulfilment. He was quite determined to overcome all the difficulties, all the great dangers and discomforts. To his family he had written, "When one leaves, saying that one will do a certain thing, one must not return without having done it."

Some of the passages in his journal are almost rapturous. He was never to love any part of the world more than Morocco, and he spent a great deal of his life regretting that he could not return. There are pages in which he describes fresh gardens, wonderful nights and strange peoples. Nothing escapes him, he seems to have been a born observer. For example, the adornings of the women who paint their faces and are covered with huge necklaces of amber and coral, and with bracelets, brooches, diadems, earrings, and other voluminous silver ornaments. Of some other women, he says that they are pretty, distinguished in their youth by great eyes full of nobility and expression, with open and laughing countenances and graceful movements.

"The women of the nomad tribes . . . are beautiful, for the most part . . . they have nobility, regularity; their skin is extremely white, at least the skin of their faces and arms; for the habit of wearing indigo blue clothes, coupled with that of never washing, gives their bodies dark and bluish tones, different from their natural colour."

He becomes lyrical again when he describes gardens.

"There are varied trees, but palm trees more than any others; under their shade, the ground, divided into squares, disappears under maize and millet, grass and vegetables. A multitude of canals water these rich plantations; here and there great

basins are filled to the brim with water. This luxuriant vegetation, these superb trees which cast a thick shade on a completely green earth, those thousand canals, that admirable sky,
those rich and laughing delights of nature, which, in the midst
of a most desolate countryside, make dwelling here full of
delights, all are found as well in the other oases. . . . Such are
all the places where we see the date palm flourishing; in all
of them, the same freshness, the same calm, the same abun-
dance; charming spots where it seems that only happy people
could live."

At one point things were not so pleasant. They were nearly
captured; Mardochée and he were seized by the neck by some
horsemen. "When we said we were from Marrakesh and subjects
of the Sultan, they were delighted because we would be held as
hostages to release some of their own prisoners."

Mardochée and Charles were put into irons. But when their
slave came up, seized the Sheikh's bridle, and announced that
they were under the protection of his master, Sultan Sidi Hemed,
they were allowed to pass without even paying toll, because of the
prestige of this Sultan.

Charles was bowled over by the beauty of the sky when once,
at ten o'clock at night, he arrived at an oasis.

"Here, no more danger; we ride slowly across a thousand
canals amongst great palm trees, of fantastic aspects, whose
branches, silvered by the moon, cover us with heavy shade . . .
the moon shining in the midst of the cloudless sky glows with
gentle clarity; the air is soft, not a breath of wind. In this profound calm, in the midst of this fairy-like place, I reached my
first stopping-place of the Sahara. On such nights, one understands the belief of Arabs in the mystical night, when the skies
open and angels float down to earth. All creation bows down
humbly in adoration of the Creator."

He is interesting when he speaks of the date honey made by
the nomads. The dates were kept in great earthenware jars and
produced a sweet liquid when crushed.

It is no wonder that, twenty-eight years later, Charles confessed, "I have a passion for Morocco." Incidentally it is really

surprising that he was able to concentrate at all, when he had such continual trouble with Mardochée, who, being paid by the month, and seeing that Charles was determined to go on, now had one great aim and that was to go slowly, whereas Charles wanted to go quickly. Unfortunately, Charles could not do without him; all the material arrangements were left to him and he had to explain the purpose of the journey to the suspicious natives, arrange the escorts, find sleeping places for the night, and food.

In the midst of all his scientific observations, so accurate that they have been used in a handbook for the Army, Charles continued to be observant about the natives and overjoyed at the beauties of nature. This is what he says about the nomads.

"The law of the strongest is alone respected. There are no quarrels and bargains as with the oasis dwellers; on the other hand, thefts and murders are more frequent. You are only safe if you place yourself under the protection and perpetual care of a man, or a tribe.... This is a temporary guarantee of safety, created especially for travellers. A written certificate says that the man asking for protection has sacrificed a sheep on his threshold."

Charles speaks of the character of the Moroccans.

"Everywhere an extreme covetousness prevails, accompanied by theft and lying in all its forms. Highway robbery, armed attack, are looked upon as honourable actions. Their morals are dissolute. The Moroccans are not very much attached to their wives, but have a great love for their children. Their finest quality is their devotion to their friends.... This noble sentiment makes them perform the finest actions. In Bled es Siba, there is no man who has not many times risked his life for his companions, and for guests of only a few hours. Their generosity is shown especially by their hospitality, and this is not the particular characteristic of any one group.... Needless to say that those populations who pass there, armed to the teeth, are brave."

He tells us also that he has never heard of an example of Moroccan cruelty.

When he reached the lesser Atlas mountains, he described dawn on the banks of a river.

"The river bed, usually deserted, was then most gay and animated. . . . At break of day, multitudes of fires are lit along the two river banks, piercing the morning fog: the first meal is being prepared in silence. Then all leave their bivouac and they begin working; little by little the mists rise; below the slopes of the left bank, still of a sombre violet colour, the sun lights up the river, and the sands are tinted in gentle rose: life springs up again; the river swarms with people: the labourers cross it in all directions: one hears nothing but the neighing and roaring of animals and the cries of the drivers who goad them on."

He is interesting about the methods of highwaymen.

"One or several individuals, well known for their audacity, announce that they will undertake a raid, and they appeal to men of good will to join them. They collect horses and camels, but many go on foot. The young men of the tribe forgather, sometimes numbering four to five hundred. Sometimes they go far, provisioned only with dates. They install themselves with their camels near water, and each day they send out horsemen to reconnoitre. If a convoy of travellers is sighted, they dash back to announce it. They seize their prey and fall upon their merchandise. They strip the men. If they are from far, and if they are Jews, they send them back naked but alive, but if they come from near, for fear of reprisals, they kill them in order to preserve secrecy.

"They get a holy man to pray to God for the success of the expedition, and they reward him with a share of the booty! If they are not successful, they call him a bad *marabout* and reproach him."

Great caravans of several hundred had nothing to fear. They were armed, and therefore these brigands dared not attack. They crossed the Sahara each spring and autumn.

A certain Dr Lenz kept highwaymen at bay, because he could fire a hundred and fifty shots from his gun without reloading.

Some of these men had weird ideas about Christians. They

looked on them as magicians, and was it true that they ploughed the sea?

The sight of Moroccan avarice disgusted Charles: "As for myself, I chuckle to see these wolves biting each other."

On his return journey, on January 14th, he noticed women dressed in white wool and wearing on their heads veils which were a speciality of the district: they were made of rectangular black wool, with black tassels at each corner. They covered their faces with them directly they saw a man. 'They show great modesty. If one meets them on the roads, they stop, look to left and right or remain on the side of the path with their faces veiled and their backs turned until one has passed."

Charles is quite rapturous about figs, grapes, pomegranate trees, apricots, peaches, apples and quinces, and on January 17th he saw almond trees in flower for the first time, and gorse.

The gift for drawing which he had inherited from his mother and fostered by the special drawing lessons he was given as a small boy, now stood him in good stead. On April 15th he made in his journal a lovely drawing of a palm tree. He describes a wonderful garden,

"full of fig trees and trees like tamarisks, and pomegranates, all crowding together, mingling their leaves and casting a thick shade on the ground; above them all sway the high fronds of the date palm. Under this dome is a carpet of greenery, for there is water and fertility and they are a hard-working race. Near the cereals and the fruit trees are tunnels, ornamented with vines, masonry pavilions, places of rest, where one can spend the hot hours of the day in shade and freshness."

He tells us of a certain man who was obliged to protect him on his journey, otherwise he would have to pay the community an indemnity of five thousand francs. No Jew dared venture out without this precaution. This was not done among the Moslems, because they don't betray each other, but it was considered lawful to rob or murder a Jew; so Jews must have special safeguards.

On April 26th and 27th, again his gift for drawing came in useful. He sketched a Jewess of Tadra adorned with a lofty hair style. Her veil was placed higher on the head, like a turban, and she wore huge earrings, two necklaces and an ornament on the front of her turban.

It was very hard for him to keep a hold on his finances, in spite of looking so poor and ill-dressed, and anyway, suspicions had been aroused several times because his face betrayed that he was a Christian. On May 6th he had to pay toll several times instead of once, because he was stopped by several hordes of bandits. They demanded one franc per beast and per person. When he complained to the second armed band, they replied "You won't pass without paying toll. You've been cheated by the others before." And as Charles and Mardochée were surrounded by forty armed men, he had to give in. This kind of thing was the ruin of all men trying to engage in trade. There were sixteen bands of that sort between two places he mentioned. No wonder many Moroccans were pining for the arrival of the French, who would protect their interests.

At the beginning of his expedition, Charles had tipped a boy in a Jewish household called Danan to bring him hot water every morning to fill a bath tub, but unfortunately he could not indulge in this as he went along. In fact he managed to make himself look so disgusting, that one day in the early part of the journey, when he was crouching by a wall with Mardochée, gnawing black olives, he saw some of his own fellow officers pass by. He heard their sneers and saw their contemptuous looks, and even overheard one of them say, "Look at that little Jew over there, eating olives. Doesn't he look like a monkey?" No one had recognized him. And the same thing happened at Mogodar where he arrived on January 28th, on his return journey. He went straight to the French Consulate and said to a Jew who was secretary there, "I want to see the French Consul and draw a cheque on the English Bank. I am the Vicomte de Foucauld, an officer in the French Cavalry." The secretary, seeing this ragged, filthy looking individual, and being acquainted with the tricks of men of that sort, would not admit him. He said to him, "Go and sit outside with your back to the wall: no one sees the Consul as easily as that!"

Charles, proud though he was, did as he was told. After a while he came back to the Jew and said, "Give me a little water and, I do beg you, show me a place, a corner where I can undress and have a wash."

Zerbib the Jew peered through the keyhole. To his amazement he found that this vagabond carried a quantity of instruments hidden in the folds of his rags, so he decided he had been mistaken; perhaps he was a Vicomte after all.

When at last Charles saw Monsieur Montel, the Chancellor of the Consulate, he had the disagreeable surprise of learning that none of the letters he had addressed to his family in France had reached the Consulate during all those eight months. Quickly he wrote to his sister Marie to reassure her. He told her he had not been ill and that he had run into no danger. That was not exactly true, for on one occasion he and Mardochée had spent a very disagreeable two days. He had been pulled off his horse by the armed band that was supposed to protect him. Unfortunately he had not got his revolver handy. He was robbed of everything except his instruments and his precious notes, and then for a day and a half, he overheard the brigands discussing whether he should be killed or not. He even had to sign a note certifying he had been well treated!

At long last, he returned to Lalla-Marnia. He was refused admission to a hotel by the ostler, who left him standing outside in pouring rain, asking hopelessly for food and a room. The ostler told the officers who were drinking inside, "I refused him, as this inn doesn't cater for Jews or Arabs. . . . He said he would complain to Divisional Headquarters and gave me his card. Here it is. Vicomte Charles Eugène de Foucauld." The card was perfectly clean, although its owner was barefoot and in rags. Of course the young lieutenants knew him, reassured the servant, and greeted Charles with joyous hilarity. He was immediately given all he needed, and they spent a jolly evening together.

The great journey was over; he had proved his worth to his family and served his country. He had left his youthful follies behind and had at last grown to manhood.

CHAPTER 6

Betrothal

TOWARDS the end of 1884, Charles fell madly in love at first sight and even became officially engaged. The whole heart-rending story is reminiscent of St Augustine breaking with his loved mistress, the mother of his son, though, in his case, it was his mother Monica who insisted on the dismissal which to us seems so cruel. But taking a long view, one realizes that both St Augustine and Charles de Foucauld, had they been respectably married men, would not have been able to follow God's inscrutable designs for them and have gained their world-wide influence.

Charles was in Algiers and had to see a geographer, Monsieur Titre. Jean Vignand writes in *Le Frère Charles*:

"The geographer lived in a little house both welcoming and gay, just outside Algiers . . . thorn apples and roses scented the little colonial garden surrounded by tall eucalyptus trees. What gentleness, what tranquillity pervaded this peaceful house. Foucauld felt suddenly purified. That little African garden accomplished that miracle, and it was not the only one. Among the softly murmuring trees, where the tall palms sway gently in the breeze, a young girl appears, like a benediction, like a shaft of light. She is dark-haired, wearing a light dress and a large straw hat, such as are worn by the shepherds of the Djurdura. Foucauld, the very same day, begins his courtship, with the father's permission. Now he's nearly betrothed; identical tastes bring the lovers close together: the young girl paints flowers; she has a delicate talent and exhibits both in Paris and Algiers works which deserve the attention of critics and connoisseurs."

She was a deeply religious young girl. Her father was a Protestant, and after being received into the Church she had given up quite a large inheritance from her grandmother. In those days a girl's dowry was essential to marriage. Her father was no doubt dazzled by the sudden advent of this Vicomte Charles de Foucauld. He cannot have heard very much of his early youth, and himself coming from only a good middle class family, he cannot have known much of the de Foucauld aristocratic family background, their strong prejudices and their snobbery, heightened by Aunt Inez's *mésalliance*. Moreover, there appeared to be no financial anxieties connected with him. He seemed to have enough money to do what he liked, he came to his household in all the glory of a soldier and an explorer. Forty-two years later, Mademoiselle Titre, by then married to another and called Madame Doucet-Titre, was asked by the Postulator of the Cause of Beatification to give a full description of Charles. And this is it:

"August 15th, 1927. The blessed will of God.

"Oh Mary, my good Mother, ask the Holy Ghost to inspire my soul so that I may say only what will lead to the truth. Father de Foucauld, Charles de Foucauld, once my fiancé, was the love of my whole life. I am sixty-five today, I was twenty-three when I knew him, that is already forty-two years ago, and he is as close as if it were only yesterday. I picture him always as he was when he was five-and-twenty, just back from Morocco where he had made his great journey. He was in all the glow of a youth of perfect physical health. Well, very well built, neither tall nor short [five foot ten], broad-shouldered, a well-defined waist, neither too short nor too thin, very muscular, he looked on the whole rather a big man and had a great air about him. He had a very delicate skin, very lustreless, very white; also, remarkable hair, eyes and a moustache that added great charm to his face. The general impression he made was one of alertness and he was most engaging. The fine, velvety black eyes varied between infinite gentleness, untamed strength and tremendous will power: sometimes his eyes sparkled in lively fashion. He talked very well, quietly, seriously, or tenderly, ever in control of himself, never carried away, always deeply thoughtful, and without being cynical. Always perfectly groomed, never slovenly and always looking very much the officer, although he was at that time a civilian. Everybody saw all this from his appearance, and these are the things which I have tried to convey in painting his portrait.

"As for his morals, it is true that at this time he did not have the Faith, but he often spoke of it to me with regret. 'When we are married, Mademoiselle,' he said to me one day, 'I will leave you completely free to do whatever you wish in religious matters, but as for me, I will not practise, as I have not got the Faith.'

'And I feel,' I said, 'that you will be converted by me.' God granted my prayer. Moreover, from that moment we had frequent religious conversations and I kept praying for him.

As for believing in the extraordinary wild behaviour of Charles de Foucauld as a young man, I cannot subscribe to it: as with all adolescents, there was curiosity and effervescence in his character; that indeed may be true, but at five-and-twenty there was certainly nothing of the child left in him: Monsieur Charles de Foucauld returned from Morocco a serious man, more serious than many other men at forty-five.

He knew life, and, humanly speaking, he had become wise. From now on, a pure, true love could claim him; he would have been a perfect husband. And so I have pined for him all my life, and I loved him, and will love him until my dying day."

A friend of the girl, Madame Verner, wrote that only for a week could Mademoiselle Titre "enjoy the pleasure of considering herself his fiancée. Unfortunately, his family opposed the marriage and he withdrew with a broken heart, leaving behind him a great sorrow and profound regrets."

The gift that this lovely idealistic young girl made, at such painful cost to herself (for she afterwards lost her faith for a long time), was to inspire Charles with a love for chastity. That is why he was able to write a little later, "Chastity became sweet to me and a necessity to my heart. . . . It was necessary to prepare me for truth: the Devil is too completely master of an impure soul, to allow it to know truth."

However, he still considered himself engaged to Mademoiselle Titre that autumn, when he had to go back to France for a family wedding and there encounter his formidable Aunt Inez. She herself, having married a rich bourgeois, knew from bitter experience the snubs and spites which must be endured by one who married outside the charmed circle of French aristocratic society. The real aristocrat does not care very much about these things nowadays, but in the late nineteenth century in France, it must be realized that it was quite natural for Inez Moitessier to be over-sensitive to the distinction. Mademoiselle Titre had no "*particule*" to her name. The magic "de" of nobility was absent.

"Don't you realize, Charles," one can almost hear Aunt Inez saying, "that she knows nobody, absolutely nobody, neither amongst our relations, our friends nor our acquaintances? *Elle n'est pas née.* She will always be an outsider. And however well you can guide her, and even if she acquires a certain flair, you will go through many uncomfortable moments in society. One false step and you will both be ridiculous outcasts. Now, my dear boy, please don't think that all our friends sleep with the Almanach de Gotha under their pillows. But imagine my Sunday afternoon receptions. Can you picture the delicately lifted eyebrows of the Duc de Broglie when an introduction is effected between him and your wife? Can you hear your friends—Laperrine, de Castries, not to mention the Duc de Vallombrosa and the Duc de Fitz-James—whispering? Now, you can get over equivocal breeding if you have a large fortune and can entertain, as with Boni de Castellane's wife. But look, you have to face the fact, she's given up her fortune for her faith and you've squandered yours to such an extent with your follies, and of course your Morocco expedition, that you couldn't possibly set up a proper household, either in Paris, or in the country. It would have to be some quite small flat, and that not in the best quarter. And only half a dozen servants; and no horse and carriage. And then, look at the insecurity in which the poor girl would live, quite apart from her social embarrassment. How does she know that you won't be rushing off to Timbuctoo at any moment?"

His talks with Marie de Bondy influenced him more deeply. He had loved her for so long, ever since he was a small boy, and when she had married Olivier de Bondy, he had felt the loss so deeply, that he had lost his faith and started going to pieces. Was it possible that Marie de Bondy felt a little pang of jealousy that any other woman apart from herself should influence this beloved cousin? Or was it possible that Charles was incapable of full human love? He had turned to Marie so often, and had almost consoled her for the unhappiness of her own married life, saddened by her husband and her three unruly sons. It has been said of her that she had "a head of ice and a heart of fire", and there was certainly great force of character. But it is quite certain that she and the Abbé Huvelin were the only two people who had a strong influence on Charles's life.

Marie was a woman of few words. That silence of strong characters can be devastating. Perhaps Charles saw in a flash how greatly she depended on him. Anyway, he says himself that he needed to be saved from this marriage and that Marie saved him. If he had really loved the girl, nobody could have swayed him. He went back to Algiers in the spring of the following year, and brought the engagement to an end. The unfortunate girl lost her faith and never saw him again until three years before his death, that is, twenty-eight years later. She ran across him in the streets of Algiers, with the red heart on the breast of his white habit. One can imagine the poignancy of such a meeting. And when she told him that she was now no longer a Catholic, and he realized that it was through him, he went to pray for her particularly at an especial shrine of Our Lady, and his prayers were answered.

Those terrible exigencies of Divine Love! On the day the engagement was broken, as she saw his form retreating through the garden which had known such bliss for her, how was she to know that in the following century the Little Sisters and Brothers inspired by her Charles were to penetrate into all the regions of the earth, as far as Alaska, working in prisons and in factories, breaking away from all the old forms of religious life, and meeting the needs of the most destitute of God's children? Pope Pius XII has said that Charles was really the saint for modern times. And this heart which had been obliged to withdraw from one human breast would soon open to a universal love for all mankind, particularly the sick, the poor and the unwanted. Charles had a will strong enough to oppose all his relations, had he wanted to. One can explain this puzzling story only by realizing that some unseen, inexplicable force was driving him on. But all this strain left its mark on him. When he returned to Paris, his friend, the explorer Duveyrier, spoke of him as a man "stricken in his affections".

Jean-Francois Six in his *Itinéraire Spirituel de Charles de Foucauld* entirely forgets to mention that his fiancée had a great influence on his spiritual life. He omits her name. And yet, it was no small thing to inspire a dissolute and selfish man with a love for chastity, thus preparing his receptivity to the things of God. So, wounded by an unfulfilled human love, now devoted to chastity, and having by his hardships and sacrifices at last attained maturity, Charles returned to Paris. But not to the old life. He never mentions his past haunts or companions.

In April 1885, he had been awarded the Gold Medal of the French Geographical Society, but as he was away at the time, it was his brother-in-law, the Vicomte Olivier de Bondy, a man of the world, who received it by proxy. There was a misunderstanding about identity among the members of the audience, for they mistook Olivier, that pillar of the Jockey Club, for Charles, and kept murmuring, "How pale and wasted he looks, what he must have been through." And this certainly was not so!

In 1886 Charles returned to Paris, and wishing to be near the family house at the corner of the Rue d'Anjou, he settled in a tiny flat in 50 Rue de Miromesnil; it is believed to have been on the ground floor.* It was very small, but contained all the things he loved, his family portraits and little treasures to which he was attached. Also there hung on the walls his sword, his military caps and shakoes. He had a manservant who slept on the top floor, that disgraceful bedlam of Paris houses. One thing Charles's flat did not have, and that was a bed, for at night he would roll up in a white cape and sleep on the floor. He had acquired that habit in the desert and now could never give it up. Three or four nights a week he changed into full evening dress and went to dine at his aunt's, Madame de Moitessier's, ten minutes' walk away. During the day time, he refused all social invitations. By now, he could have become the lion of Paris drawing rooms, but, instead, he went on correcting his *Reconnaissance au Maroc* which was to be published two years later in February 1888, and which won him universal acclaim.

When he wanted a little respite from his work, he did a strange thing. The great philosopher Pascal, at his life's end, used to wander into many Paris churches for a while each day, but for a different reason. After his night of vision, Pascal saw. Charles de Foucauld groped. He went into one Paris church after another, and, sitting there or kneeling in some dark corner, he would pray this impassioned prayer: "O God, if you exist, let me know it."

* The street has altered very much since my day, and I spent hours questioning local shopkeepers and the curé of St Augustin.

He must have gone to the Chapelle Expiatoire in the Avenue de Friedland, near the Etoile, which in those days had perpetual Exposition of the Blessed Sacrament and was always filled with worshippers. Or he would go to one of the most holy places in Paris, the chapel of the St Vincent de Paul nuns in the Rue du Bac, where a completely obscure and as yet unknown, uncanonized, little nun had recently seen a vision of Our Lady. Perhaps he wandered further afield to the Picpus convent, situated in the burial ground of the victims of the guillotine, where the order of nuns had been founded to pray for the souls of the departed, and where, too, the Blessed Sacrament was perpetually exposed. Or he went to the newly built basilica dedicated to the Sacred Heart on the top of Montmartre; and there he would naturally recall all that Marie de Bondy had first told him when he was a boy, in the parish church of Loüye, about this solemn devotion. And of course he always saw a picture of the Sacred Heart on her table, which influenced him greatly. Then, walking along the Rue du Faubourg St Honoré, he would drop in to the historical church of St Roch, one of the most poignant and interesting of all Paris churches. (When Queen Marie Antoinette was being led to execution in her tumbril, she passed that church, and the painter David made a cruel sketch of her. That is the only place where her eyes filled with tears, for a small boy blew her a kiss.) Then, on the tiny island near Notre Dame, there was St Louis-en-l'Isle, and there Charles would kneel, perhaps near the holy water stoup, which recalled Louise de la Vallière, the penitent who entered Carmel.

Nearer home, there was the fashionable Madeleine, also commemorating a famous penitent, whom one day he was to grow to love, for she had been near to Christ. Lastly there was his own parish church, the hideous St Augustin. There he would go most often, because it was the nearest to his flat, and there surely he must have been seen by the most famous spiritual guide of France, the Abbé Huvelin, who was his cousin Marie's confessor and director. This priest, with his piercing insight into souls, could not fail to notice the pale, strange, handsome young man with his strained look of yearning.

Very soon the Abbé was to come into Charles's life. He is so remarkable, so lovable, that he really deserves a book all to himself.

CHAPTER 7

The Abbé Huvelin

THE Abbé Huvelin must have heard about Charles from Marie de Bondy whom he had guided since 1876, two years after her marriage; his care for her was to last for thirty-four years. She wrote to him, "It's a long time now since you have upheld and consoled me, but on the first occasion, you made me cry a lot." A distinguished ecclesiastic of Paris had called the Abbé Huvelin "the foremost priest of France". As Charles used to get up very early in those days, perhaps he caught glimpses of the Abbé saying his Mass, which, it has been said, was his most beautiful form of preaching. All his inner life shone out in spite of himself. Through him, Calvary was present. Years later, Charles was to write to Marie, "You have put me under the wings of that Saint and I remain there. You have carried me by his hands." Perhaps Charles had even come across him along the Boulevard Malesherbes, when the rain was pouring down in torrents or snow was on the ground, struggling to get to one of his sick parishioners, or bringing Viaticum to a dying child. His tall, broad-shouldered figure was well known; he walked in haste with his head well forward, and when serious illness finally struck, he had to cling to the wall so as not to fall over. The glance of his dark blue eyes would sometimes light up as with an inner flame. His dark hair, unkempt and bushy, framed a high and noble forehead. He was always correctly dressed in a *soutane*, but his clothes were not carefully put on and his neckband was always awry. His glance struck people most—it radiated purity, kindness, intelligence.

As a result of youthful austerities, nature took her revenge and he lost his health. He was riddled with gout and afflicted with intolerable headaches. The ears and the heart also suffered. That terrible martyrdom lasted twenty-nine years. When the Curé d'Ars was about to meet some great sinner coming to his confessional, he was most particularly attacked by the antics of Satan; likewise, it is remarkable that often the Abbé Huvelin's sufferings corresponded with periods when souls under his care were being threatened. When he preached, his face became red and swollen, and it was obvious, as he leaned all twisted up on the edge of the pulpit, that he was trying to master his physical agonies. In his young days, at the seminary, at night he had been in the habit of lying down on the floor of his cubicle fully dressed, with his arms stretched as on a cross. For nourishment he took only water and a little salted bread. During recreation, every evening at five o'clock, he would go to Benediction in the chapel of the Benedictine nuns. Even if he rode on the top of a horse bus, he would preserve his solitude. He saw nothing of Paris, for he was absorbed in a book. Some of his free time he spent with other members of the St Vincent de Paul Society, trying to help the sick and the poor, and climbing dark, shaky staircases which led to disgusting attics. Another of his delights was to spend some time each morning in the church of Notre-Dame-des-Victoires in the Place des Victoires, near the Bibliothèque Nationale, which St Thérèse of Lisieux was to visit with great joy before she went to Rome with her father prior to becoming a Carmelite. The Abbé Huvelin is one of the few priests who ever confessed to human love. (The Jesuit Père de Ravignan was another.) He wrote of it to a friend, a fellow priest, in veiled language explaining that he had remained for some time in France, instead of returning to Rome: "I have been kept back by someone in my family of whom I have spoken to you and who is very dear to me . . . I have followed my heart . . . the bewitchment, the spell of a tenderness which was too lively and too human."

He was made vicar of St Augustin in 1875, the year before Marie de Bondy's marriage. He lived in a flat in the Rue de la Borde, just opposite, looked after by a grumbling, disagreeable housekeeper called Louise, whom he treated very kindly, and in the company of a comfortable and understanding cat who was to become famous and whom he loved very much. The cat always sat on his knees. The priests of St Augustin, like those of the near-by Madeleine and St Philippe du Roule, catered for high French society; but the Abbé Huvelin preached at the six o'clock Mass which was attended by the servants of this smart district. And then at eight-thirty on a Sunday morning, he would give his famous lectures for men only. Unfortunately, he could not prevent women from hiding behind the pillars or from slipping in and taking notes. These lectures were indeed remarkable, for he was a brilliant scholar, with an arresting style. For example, those from 1875 to 1876 treated, among other things, of Gregory VII, the Inquisition, the Lateran Council, St Francis of Assisi, St Dominic, the spirit of the Middle Ages, the Albigensian Heresy. The programme from November 1879 to June 1880 is riveting and included Bossuet as a preacher, the Abbé de Rancé, the Trappists, devotion to the Sacred Heart, true and false piety, Quietism, Fénelon, then Fénelon as spiritual director, the theological question of Pure Love, and how Jansenism came to an end.

His studies as a young man had been deep, arduous, varied and prolonged. He was one of the few French priests to have studied Greek, and thus his vast mind was able to see the link, that prophetic link, between the ancient pagan philosophers and Christianity. For example, Plato was familiar to him, and he loved to speak of this half-prophecy of the philosopher: "If wisdom took flesh, what love it would draw from the human heart." The style of this cultivated man was full of finesse and charm. For example, this passage on his favourite abbé:

"The Abbé de Rancé had a charming hand ... which he was not unwilling to show off. He had fragile health, but one of those delicate healths which endure a long time: it is forged in steel, it is slender but it is of steel, it is something supple, nothing at all... Look at a cat's paw, it is nothing at all, and then see this animal when it's angry; it becomes animated: the paw stiffens, the claws become extraordinarily strong. You are astonished that such a lithesome little thing which you could control a moment ago should now have become something so powerful and should also seem to have iron nerves. Well ... that was the style of the Abbé de Rancé."

And here is another endearing example which again showed his love of animals.

"Madame de la Sablière writes to the Abbé de Rancé, he tells her to unite the roles of Mary and Martha, and she goes to live with sick persons. Madame de Sévigné tells us about her visits to the Hospice for Incurables; it is very interesting. She weeps as she loses a bird (I understand her desolation, a bird who had held converse with La Fontaine); she asks the Abbé de Rancé if she may have another, he allows it because of the partridge loved by St John."

The Abbé Huvelin had a special predilection for preaching to Christian mothers. St Augustine said of his mother that one felt the presence of God in her heart. The Abbé said that the art of being a mother is the art of being a Christian woman. He said also, "If I were to write the martyrology of holy women, I would put at the end of the page several points for the husbands who have suffered from this proximity; for sanctity is a predominating thing, and can produce a disagreeable contrast."

The Abbé wrote to some mother, "I pray for you; and in the morning at Mass, I add to the drop of water in the chalice all the tears of mothers."

He could be cutting, caustic when necessary, and once said something devastating, which must have had the desired effect, for he revealed the naked truth to a very pretentious soul by saying, "If one were to wring you out, you would be like a death shroud—only a few drops of water would ooze out." He also had a thorough distaste for souls who went in for a lot of ostentatious piety, but were lacking in generosity.

The Abbé Huvelin caught sight of Charles, day after day, struggling in interior torment, and having, no doubt, heard a little of his wild life from Marie de Bondy, he thought to himself, "In an impure heart, just as in a soiled vase, everything becomes bitter, and truth cannot penetrate."

There was always a queue outside his confessional. He said that he wished to look at the sinner with Christ's own glance and to pour into his soul all possible good. His direction was full of light; just a few words which went straight to the point; he was brief, precise, and he always put his finger on the sore place. With him, it was not necessary to explain anything, his word illuminated like a streak of lightning. He was almost a prophet, for he knew everything, and you felt yourself understood in his presence, indeed, not only understood, but invaded through and through. He consoled by his very understanding of all manner of human griefs.

He was good to all kinds of women, not only the pious and those in high society, but those of dubious reputation. There was Theodora, a famous dancer at the Opéra, who had no doubt caused pious eyebrows to be raised, and there was a little whispering as she came out of his confessional, for she was regarded as a *demi-mondaine*. Her elegant gowns shocked the other ladies, and the Abbé Huvelin, to avoid any false scandal, suggested that she should come to him more simply dressed. She replied, "What is the matter with my appearance?" Puzzled, man-like, he tentatively suggested: "Perhaps your earrings?" She took them off at once—they were of great value—and begged her Abbé to give them to the poor in the parish.

He must have shared with the Curé d'Ars that privilege often characteristic of holiness, of being able to penetrate into a conscience. But he had to pay the price for the terrible confidences whispered in his ear. Sometimes he emerged from his confessional with an agonized look, caused, doubtless, by the confession of some grave sin, or of relapses into sin.

He particularly understood conversion and penitence. When speaking of his dear Trappist the Abbé de Rancé when he was young—and one must remember that in his youth the Abbé Huvelin had himself wanted to become a Trappist—he wrote, "What did he lack in the midst of all these joys? Because everything disgusted him, God was lacking to him. God—whom he felt the need to love. That is the foundation of the conversion of the Abbé de Rancé."

How well he could have understood Charles's attack of depression after the party he had given at Pont-à-Mousson, when he had returned alone to his room, feeling the emptiness of all things. Here is what the Abbé Huvelin said about this kind of state:

"Colonel d'Albergotte was a very distinguished officer. The day after the revel of which he had been the leading spirit, he wrote to the Abbé de Rancé to beg him to receive him at La Trappe. What had happened? 'Ah!' . . . he had said to himself, 'is that all the world can give me? My mind went over all these carousals which could not bring content to my soul, and I saw that God was calling me.' Society is also a preparation to conversion. But it is not yet that mysterious blow which makes the tree fall on to God's side; there is in a conversion something divine . . . impossible to explain."

How well Charles knew that feeling of the emptiness of society, when he himself had been overcome by his dreadful depression. In some young people, that search for God can be agonizingly painful. For example, the youthful Jacques Maritain and his wife, Raïssa, when they were agnostics, had both reached the point of wanting to commit suicide, if they could not find the truth. They were guided in their search by their love for one another and their philosophical studies together at the Sorbonne, and finally by Léon Bloy. Charles was led, first by the almost ferocious impact that Africa had made upon him; then, by his new-found love for chastity which he says became sweet to him. Even his face and his glance had changed. His friend, the Duc de Fitz-James, spoke about that penetrating look of his, reflecting an indefinable expression, a kind of absence in which his thoughts were elsewhere. But the third, most important element in his conversion was his cousin Marie de Bondy whom he now saw nearly every day, since she lived so near; and he appreciated the way she and the whole family accepted him and never pried into his private life. The women of the family, at any rate, were intelligent, and professed Christianity wholeheartedly. But Marie he called his "terrestrial angel". Her beauty of mind and heart drew him to the truth. He said, "Since she is so intelligent, the religion in which she believes so firmly could not be a misguided enthusiasm."*

Later Charles was to write a meditation addressed to Our Lord, in which he speaks of the mysterious perfume of Marie's virtue. She did nothing active. Indeed the heart of her influence on her cousin consisted in this silent presence.

When he became a Trappist, Charles wrote, ". . . You will not refuse me what He permits, me, unworthy as I am, who am devoted to you with such great respect. Who was it brought me back to God? Who gave me to Monsieur l'Abbé? The first religious book that I read again, it was you who gave it to me, it

* Dean Inge once told Oxford undergraduates that three things could lead a man to God: love between man and woman; the beauty of nature; mystical prayer.

was you who took me to the Trappists, you made me know the Heart of Our Lord by the picture on your table; by the name of the Magdalene, my patron saint." When he left her, as he thought, for ever, he wrote, "I have lost infinitely more than St Bernard, I have lost as much as it is possible to lose." In the same letter he says that Our Lord had commanded him to place her always first in his prayers.

The Abbé Huvelin occasionally dropped in to the big house in the Rue d'Anjou, but one cannot imagine him remaining for dinner. One wonders if Charles overheard him say one day, in a drawing-room to a society woman, "Long ago, I found the secret of happiness."

"What is that?"

"To do without joys."

In 1886, one evening towards the end of October, Charles was with the family; the children were playing around before bed time, and one of the girl cousins said to Charles, "I hear that the Abbé Huvelin will not be continuing his lectures; I am very sorry about that."

"I am, too," replied Charles, "for I was hoping to attend them."

Nobody commented on this surprising remark. Several days later he said very seriously to this same cousin, "You are fortunate to believe; I search for light, and cannot find it."

The next day, which was some time between October 27th and 30th, Charles rose very early, in fact he left his flat without his *café-au-lait*. How well one remembers those late autumn days down the Boulevard Malesherbes. The leaves have fallen from the chestnut trees, and there are no elegant carriages about, just menservants in black and yellow striped waistcoats polishing the bell-pulls of smart doors; the old rag-and-bone man is crying out his sinister note, the devout (who abound in Paris churches) are going up and down the steps of St Augustin for early Mass. In the Catholic Faith, October is a month dedicated to the angels, and Charles's guardian angel, who had for many years carried out his discouraging task, rejoiced to see his spiritual son climb up those steps, push the old leather doors, and go into St Augustin. But this time, instead of slumping down in a chair behind a pillar, and repeating over and over again his agonized prayer for light, Charles went to the Abbé Huvelin's confessional.

Charles did not kneel down by the little grille, but stood up, leaned forward and said:

"Monsieur l'Abbé, I haven't got the Faith; I have come to ask you to instruct me."

The Abbé Huvelin gave him one of his quick, piercing glances, one of those glances which saw into the depths of a man. Moreover, long experience had taught him to believe the words of Isaiah: "If you do not believe, you will not understand." Likewise, if Charles did not courageously risk the painful experience of confession, he would be lacking in faith and, like St Peter, sink into the waves of the sea. But he obviously had faith. Love would come. And he would walk on the waters towards his Lord, in all the beauty of His shining on the sea.

So the Abbé said, "Kneel down, make your confession to God: you will believe."

"But I did not come for that."

"Make your confession."

And this independent, headstrong young man, who had never obeyed anybody, realized in a flash that the light of truth could come only to a cleansed soul. He knelt down and confessed all the sins of his life.

The priest gave him absolution, then, as he saw him rising from his knees, he said:

"Are you fasting?"

"Yes."

"Go and make your Communion."

And so, amid the jubilation of the angels who rejoice when one soul returns to the Father, Charles went to the Lady altar and made his Communion, the first for many years.

Cardinal Manning in his precious little manual, *The Love of Jesus to Penitents*, says:

"There is still one more token of His compassion in the Sacrament of pardon, and it is the fervent desire with which He desires to absolve us of our sins. He loves every several soul with all the love of His Sacred Heart, and His whole heart is bent at every moment on the salvation of those that are lost. . . . He seeks out such a soul by His preventing grace. He surrounds, encompasses, envelops it with lights, inspirations, impulses, attractions of His love and power. Even when we are unwilling to come to Him, He is yearning to draw us to Himself."

Here was the Prodigal Son returning at last to his home. His father runs to meet him, and even before his son can speak, he embraces him. He gives him a robe, a ring, and prepares a banquet for him.

Charles said afterwards how he realized on that day that he could do no less than offer his whole life to God. Perhaps that is why he loved Mary Magdalene so much and often went to the Sainte Baume in Provence, to honour her shrine. She had sinned much and therefore was told to love much, because so much had been forgiven her. Charles felt the same.

The great St Augustine, patron of this Parisian church, must also have rejoiced, for he had gone through so many of the experiences of Charles himself. He had written, "You were always there, Lord, striking me in Your mercy and mingling the bitterest displeasure in all my evil joys; and thus You urged me to seek true happiness." The grace of conversion makes the saints act vehemently. St Gregory the Great—the Pope who sent St Augustine of Canterbury to convert England—when grace entered his soul like a lightning flash, consecrated his riches to the foundation of six new monasteries in Sicily, and he built a seventh one in his own Roman Palace on the Caelian Hill, dedicated to St Andrew, for Benedictine monks. He sold all he had to give to the poor, and Rome, which had seen the young and opulent patrician walking her streets in silken, jewelled robes, could now hardly recognize him, dressed as a poor monk.

Unbeknown to his family, to whom he did not speak of this great event for some time, Charles too was planning to embrace the Folly of the Cross. All the cousins in the house in the Rue d'Anjou must have guessed, though, because now there was an expression of such light and peace on his face.

Marie de Bondy had been very ill at the time, and was barely convalescing by Christmas. But she insisted on going with Charles to midnight Mass, where they made their Communion together at that same Lady altar. What a Christmas it was in Paris, in that year of 1886. The poet Paul Claudel was at Vespers at Notre Dame and the choir was singing the Magnificat. This is how he describes his own conversion:

"I myself was standing up in the crowd, near the second pillar at the entrance of the choir, on the right hand side near the sacristy. And it is then that the event took place which dominates all my life. In an instant, my heart was touched and I believed. I believed with such a clinging force, such an uprising of my whole being, with so powerful a conviction, with such a certitude which left no place for any kind of doubt, that since then, all the books, all the reasonings and arguments, all the hazards of an agitated life, have not been able to shake my faith, nor to speak truth, to touch it. Suddenly I was lacerated by an impression of the innocence, of the eternal childhood of God, a revelation never to be blotted out."

Claudel thought, "How happy are the people who believe. . . . But it's true. . . God exists. He is there . . . it is Somebody, it is a Being as personal as I am. He loves me, He calls me."

And thus came into the life of the sick and overworked Abbé Huvelin one of his most demanding and yet rewarding penitents, with whose restlessness he had to cope for many a year. But he never changed towards his spiritual child. He was ever tender and gracious—he who could be so impatient, rapping the floor with his stick, for example, when Baron von Hügel was late for an appointment. In an age when daily Communion was certainly not the custom in a France still tinged with Jansenism, the Abbé Huvelin advised Charles to go to Mass and Communion every day. He even received him nearly every day in his famous room in the Rue de la Borde, in whose ante-room had waited patiently people like Gounod, Pasteur, Bremond, Baron von Hügel. Indeed there was always a motley crowd awaiting his counsel, ushered in by the ever grumpy Louise. There might have been a well-known writer, a man in high society, a director of a museum, an aristocratic lady, a servant out of work or a miserably dressed working girl; or perhaps there would come the Duc de Broglie, one of the great Catholics of the day. The Abbé would receive them in an armchair which some friends had insisted on his having. (It still exists.) On his painful knees was the understanding black cat. (When he died, the Abbé refused to replace him, saying with gentle irony, "One does not love twice.") There was enormous untidiness among his papers, and perhaps on the floor a plate of food which had not been touched. A chair stood on the top of a cupboard, Heaven knows why. Louise would grumble to someone, "He spent the night on the floor, possibly with his arms out cross-wise. His bed hasn't been slept in." One is glad to think that Madame Cécile, Abbess of Solesmes, sent a novice of hers, Mademoiselle Hamon, whose health had broken down, to try and look after him when Louise retired. But he was nearly impossible to care for.

On the wall of his study was the Crucifix of Dom Eugène, his Benedictine ancestor, and then a copy of *The Last Supper* by Leonardo da Vinci, because he particularly loved the glance of the Saviour looking down with love touched with sadness, as St John leans his head against His heart. Indeed it was from the Abbé Huvelin that Marie de Bondy had first learned of this devotion of the Sacred Heart of Our Lord. The Abbé wrote, addressing Our Lord, "If the devotion of the Sacred Heart has something material in it ... You are the cause. ... Why did St Thomas touching that Heart exclaim 'My Lord and My God ...', and John reposed on it. ... The Flesh of Our Lord has a spiritualizing influence ... that Flesh cannot be separated from the Divine Person who took it ... this Heart, through which has flowed all the Blood which has redeemed us."

In his guidance of Charles, the Abbé must have spoken often of this actual need of consoling the Sacred Heart which one recalls reading about especially in the story of St Margaret Mary: this saint was greatly honoured in the second half of the nineteenth century. Charles was to write, "that Blessed Heart of which you spoke to me so often".

Through his friendship with the writer, the Abbé Bremond, the Abbé Huvelin was able to penetrate intimately into what we must call the spirituality of the French school. He particularly admired a seventeenth-century priest, Père de Condren, who honoured the hidden life of Our Lord. In him, he found a mystic who was vowed to *annihilation*—untranslatable word. He was dedicated to lowliness in imitation of Our Lord who was humiliated for our sakes. This Abbé de Condren influenced, in his turn, a spiritual son, Monsieur Olier, who refused a bishopric and consecrated himself to the poor in the most wretched quarter of Paris. About all this the Abbé Huvelin said, 'When Our Lord lives in a heart,

He fills it with His own feelings, and that heart goes out towards the little ones."

To look at Jesus Christ in one or other "of His states", is a typical expression of the seventeenth-century school of French spirituality, and it was always being spoken of by the Abbé Huvelin. Hence, Charles's growing desire to console Christ in the state of His agony in the Garden of Gethsemane, to console Him now for something which occurred nineteen centuries ago (as with God there is no time, and Pascal said that Jesus Christ will be in agony till the end of the world). There is a desire to imitate Christ who, in the love He bore this world, wished to stoop in compassion to our littleness, and indeed to do violence to the dignity of His person. The desire for reparation and imitation became a passion with Charles after his conversion.

So, that winter, he began a long spiritual pilgrimage, in which he could see only one step ahead.

CHAPTER 8

Resurrection

IN the following spring of 1887 Charles heard the Abbé Huvelin preach, and the words he said remained in his memory all his days and influenced his whole outlook on life. He said, "Our Lord took the last place so thoroughly that no one has ever been able to take it away from Him."

The Abbé also gave Charles an excellent piece of advice. He told him to write down his meditations, in order to help him to concentrate. That is why we are able to follow him step by step.

Marie's young sons, in spite of attacks of jealousy, found Charles delightful to tease, and also a most obliging cousin. Whenever they wanted any of his military gear, they had only to ask for the request to be granted. They did not realize how this alone revealed the growing detachment of a man for whom the things of this world were ceasing to matter. One cousin talked of his "delicious and continual smile". François de Bondy described him as still very sunburned by Africa, with lively gestures, piercing black eyes, usually amused and gay. His bearing was very retiring. François de Bondy was much favoured because, when Charles's book on Morocco was published, he gave his nephew a special copy in a fine binding, and inside it were his passports and certificates and various letters from famous explorers. It also contained thirty-nine manuscript pages which he could not have put into the book itself, in case they implicated other people. Charles even gave this little cousin geography lessons, which must have been exciting indeed, and ever to be remembered.

Charles records that after one such occasion, he went for the first time to Benediction at St Augustin with Marie. It was during those days that he became more and more filled with a deep love for the Blessed Sacrament Exposed on the high altar. At that time, of course, Benediction was surrounded with every kind of splendour, and the choir sang the motets *Tantum Ergo* and *O Salutaris*. Those hours of gazing up at the sacred Host in its jewelled monstrance eventually inspired him with the certainty that the very presence of the Host in the desolate wastes of the Sahara could bring blessing to the Moslems. And thus his spirituality, guided by his cousin Marie, became more and more Christ-centred. Jesus was his chief, his friend, his model, his companion. And when he eventually became a hermit, he wrote, "But to remain in my cell when I could be before the Blessed Sacrament, is as if I were imitating Mary Magdalene when You were at Bethany, leaving You solitary . . . to go and think of You, alone in her room."

All his spiritual notes reveal the heart-to-heart talks of a friend with his friend, of a soldier with his chief, of a disciple with his master. He wrote, "If I love fasting and vigils, it is because He loved them so much."

Of Charles at that time François de Bondy wrote:

"I remember very clearly this excellent cousin, so gentle, always smiling, already remaining rather in the background because of his love for humility, which resulted in my brother and I imagining that he had been put in this world solely to allow himself to be teased and to give us presents. He gave us his military equipment, so that we could act in plays with other children: we had his shako of Saint-Cyr, his battle helmet of Saumur. Then little by little, all his belongings brought back from Morocco found their way into our hands, pistols, guns, daggers, harnesses with silk tassels, and specially hooded Arab cloaks. . . . We hadn't understood for a moment that a man who gives up all his travel souvenirs so easily—and what a journey it was—this man is no longer very much attached to anything in this world."

When his book *Reconnaissance au Maroc* appeared in February 1888, it was a tremendous success. Charles could have been entertained and fêted everywhere. And of course now, having become so handsome, he could have frequented a whole bevy of new and fascinating Parisian *cocottes* of the more refined variety. But he lived very quietly, seeking out members of his own family and men who shared his tastes. He particularly liked seeing the explorer Duveyrier. The first time he called on him and was offered tea and cakes, Charles said, "I can't take any, I am keeping Lent." Duveyrier at the time was suffering deeply from a painful bereavement, because the only woman he had ever loved had just died. He had been engaged to her for a long time, but unable to marry her for financial reasons. He guessed that Charles also must have suffered through his broken engagement. But he also sensed that Charles belonged to a special *élite*, and that human love did not fit into his background.

Duveyrier's ideals for North Africa were inspired by Cardinal Lavigerie whose statue overlooks the port of Marseilles. It was he who had founded the White Fathers, devoted to the almost impossible task of converting the Moslems. Duveyrier said to Charles, "England and France have suppressed slavery in their colonies, President Lincoln has freed four million men in the United States. And yet this scourge is rampant in Africa more than ever before, perhaps more violently than before, because they feel that its reign is nearing its end. . . . It is Islam which is to blame. They want workmen for manual labour which they are too indolent or vain to undertake themselves. They want beasts of burden to carry the ivory, and slave women for their harems, which their shameful polygamy fills with hordes of these unfortunate creatures."

"How do they catch the slaves in the first place?" asked Charles.

"Bands of Arabs simply make a clean sweep in German East Africa and carry away thousands of natives. The villages are set on fire, the unhappy people flee on all sides, and the armed brigands search all the undergrowth, coming back at night with women and children bound together, and with the flocks of animals. Cardinal Lavigerie used to say that when he received news of these things by the post, he could not sleep at night. He wrote to Pope Leo XIII to point out all these iniquities to him, describing the slave markets, the forced marches of sixty to eighty days during which the Arabs simply slaughtered those who could walk no more, or left them a prey to wild beasts. If you happened to lose your way anywhere near the equator, and you were somewhere near the towns where these slave markets were established, you could easily find your way by the tracks of dried bones."

Charles looked horrified, then said, "I remember reading somewhere that Livingstone used to wake up in the middle of the night with a start, when he remembered all these horrors, and he couldn't drive away all the frightening images he saw."*

Duveyrier continued, "You know that Archbishop Lavigerie was at Nancy when he received a letter from Marshal Mac-Mahon who was then Governor of Algeria. The Bishop of Algiers had just died and Mac-Mahon suggested that Lavigerie should leave Lyons and take his place. And he replied, 'You are offering me a painful and laborious mission, an episcopal seat inferior in all points to mine.' But he accepted. Algeria has been Mohammedan for about 1,200 years, after having been Christian for more than five centuries. Algeria is the open door to a continent of 140 million souls, and it is especially there, to the centre of this still unknown and totally forsaken continent, that the light of the Gospel should be brought. Lavigerie said that it was this prospect which finally drew him. He said, 'Can you find in France any work more worthy of tempting the heart of a bishop . . . ? Oh, it is very probable that it would be pleasant to live at Lyons, but it will certainly be less hard to die at Algiers, especially and particularly because I am assured that one will have much to suffer there.'"

Abraham Lincoln once said, "God must have a special love for ordinary people, for He made so many of them." This love for quite ordinary people was not a new thing in Charles, who was to write much later, "It is in loving men that one learns to love God." It is as if he realized that in every single human being the image of God remains, and that in every soul one may discern what St Irinaeus called "the trace of the Divine Fingers".

In the days when he had been a lieutenant, there is the testimony of Eugénie Buffet, the pretty sixteen-year-old maid to the Sheriff of Mascara's adjutant. She has described in her memoirs how her master and mistress often sent her to carry fruit, plants and jam to one of their intimate friends, Lieutenant Charles de

* When Archbishop Lavigerie became a Cardinal, he went to London to address the English people. The assembly was presided over by Lord Granville and attended by many important personalities, among whom was Cardinal Manning, Archbishop of Westminster. Cardinal Lavigerie recalled to the English all their colonial glories and quoted the indignant words of Livingstone on slavery, to make them see that they must carry out his most ardent desires.

Foucauld. She wrote, "Ah, the kind, affectionate look of Charles de Foucauld, glances of sincere love and true tenderness! Alas, I went back to Oran and I never saw him again." She became an actress of local repute, then a singer, and finally died, like her father, in a hospital bed, neglected and forgotten. But Charles had been good to an obscure girl, even before Christ filled his life.

One day, in his Paris flat, Charles's manservant announced a certain Judah Danan who looked like a Jew from Morocco and who assured him he was a student who knew Monsieur le Vicomte. "Shall I admit him, Monsieur le Vicomte?" asked the valet.

Charles looked puzzled, but said, "By all means, bring him in." He greeted him warmly and then said very politely, "You must forgive me, you must have changed a great deal, but I can't quite remember you."

"Well, when I was a child in Tetuan, one fine morning two individuals dressed as Algerian rabbis arrived with an introductory letter at our house. We received them, we gave them mattresses on the floor, for they wanted to sleep on the floor."

"Ah, I remember," said Charles. "Now do sit down. I remember we used to cook our own food. My companion was Mardochée, and we were just preparing to explore Morocco."

"I loved talking to you, even though I was very young in those days. I noticed how distinguished you were. Don't you remember, you asked me to prepare a hot bath for you every morning, and each time, for this little job, you gave me twenty-five Spanish *centimes*, which was a large sum for me then."

Charles laughed. "How I enjoyed myself in those days! I remember I didn't sleep the night through, but I used to spend most of the night on the terrace of your house, watching the weather and taking notes."

"Yes, and my mama thought that we had a madman in the house."

Charles laughed. "No doubt she thought that my companion, the Rabbi, was also not very presentable. But he could be very useful if I was working on a roof with my instruments; he would prevent curious strangers from spying on me by keeping guard on the stairs, and engaging them in long conversations."

This young Danan certainly knew on what side his bread was buttered. He wrote in his memoirs:

"In 1886 I was in Paris at the School for Oriental Studies, when one evening I went to the library where I found a book called *Journey into Morocco*. Out of curiosity, I looked for information on Tetuan, and what was my astonishment and my joy in seeing at the bottom of the page the name of the Vicomte. All this happened in the centre of the town of Tetuan, at Monsieur Jacob Danan, my father's. What could have brought the Vicomte de Foucauld to us at Tetuan? By evoking the memories of my childhood, I reached the conclusion that the author of this book could be no other than the Rabbi Couvaud. I went to the publishers of the book and they gave me the address of the author. I went to that address and had myself announced as a student. They asked me to come in. The master of the house appeared. Without any doubt it was certainly my Rabbi. In my naïve manner, I said, 'Monsieur le Vicomte, look at me hard.' But he didn't recognize me, and then I told him who I was. He received the news with joy and embraced me. As I had to get back to college, I left him with regret. As I said goodbye to him, he gave me a gold piece to buy myself, as he said, some chocolate and cakes, especially urging me to come and see him every Sunday, and that indeed I did, and each time I left the house I came out richer by ten or twenty francs. One Sunday the Vicomte had no money on him, so he gave me a handful of postage stamps which I sold afterwards to my friends."

But of course Charles never neglected his own family. Olivier, Vicomte de Bondy, Marie's husband, was really fond of him and had been proud to receive his gold medal from the Geographical Society by proxy. But he found his brother-in-law's new religious "craze", as he called it, most embarrassing, and when he signed his letters "I love you in Jesus", he shuddered.

The family was to be even more uncomfortable in August 1888, when Charles came to spend some time at the Château de la Barre, in the Indre, a house surrounded by groves of trees, shrubs, lawns and vineyards. The de Bondys had their own private chapel where the village curé came to say Mass on Sundays. The Vicomte de Bondy, who was an ardent monarchist, had put blue and white fleur-de-lys everywhere, and the Royalist flag was tied with a black crêpe bow in mourning for the guillotined Louis XVI. Each member of the family knelt correctly on a red velvet prie-dieu. They were horrified when Charles threw himself prostrate on the floor, like the Arabs, and the Vicomte de Bondy had to whisper to his giggling children, "That's the way Moslems pray." Personally he thought this was quite out of place. We are not told what the peasants and servants kneeling in the background thought of the whole proceedings. But the contrast is amusing. Here was Charles immersed in reading *Les moines d'Occident* by Montalembert which he had just ordered, trying to find the religious Order which would suit him, for he realized that the world and its customs bored him. And on the other side of the picture was the conventional de Bondy family, trying to hide their confusion.

The *Vie Parisienne*, a kind of fashionable *Tatler*, for January 6th, 1872, has a most amusing article called "A Winter Day in the Château", which describes the sort of life led by the de Bondys. The lord of the manor, arrayed in a flannel shirt, knickerbockers and indoor shoes, has his morning soup. Afterwards he dresses for hunting. France was then overrun by wolves, and as he was helped to dress by his valet, the squire would smoke a cigar and discuss a local hunt. Then a new change of clothing. The master would wear a striped linen shirt, a waistcoat of blue silk velvet and puffed-out breeches. At midday or even earlier, the family had luncheon. It would be an intimate family luncheon, to which the children were admitted. Only one servant, and he would be sent out of the room when one wanted to talk more privately. Then the *seigneur* would go and look at the new harness for Madame's brougham which she would take to Paris in the spring months. Afterwards, he would fulfil his duty of lord of the manor, and do some sick visiting on the estate. The wife of Baptiste the farmer has fallen from the roof of the barn. He brings her a bottle of arnica and cheers her with affectionate and consoling words. He visits the Mayor and discusses bridges. Between five and six in the evening, he is locked up with his agent in his study. Then he changes for the evening, black suit, white tie, and becomes a man of the world again. Dinner is served at seven o'clock. Afterwards, the men perhaps go to the smoking-room for a while; it is not customary to smoke in the presence of ladies; then they return to the drawing-room and the rest of the evening is spent in parlour games, gossiping or music.

One feels that none of this would appeal very much to Charles. Of course the countryside was lovely, the distances had that blue tint which became violet and almost black on stormy days. The landscape was infinitely varied. There were granite rocks as well as flowering meadows. In the intervals of long hours spent alone in the chapel, Charles would go for walks, wondering what God wanted him to do with his new life. Perhaps Marie had told him some of the local legends. The Seigneur of Bouchet who had accompanied the King, St Louis, to the Crusades, one day on his return from his captivity in Egypt, went hunting on his estate. In the evening, his favourite falcon did not return when he called him; but he had seen him cross a pool and settle on a tree. The boat he was in seemed guided by a mysterious hand which at length brought him to the foot of a gigantic oak and there, in a fork made by two branches, he saw not only his falcon, but a wooden statuette of the Virgin Mary, glowing red in the setting sun under the dark foliage. The falcon flew away and came to settle on the shoulder of his master. The Crusader made the sign of the Cross, and, very moved, murmured the words *"Sancta Maria in Mari Rubro"*.

Then there was the charming legend of the young virgin Solange who would tend her flocks, spinning the while, and in the evening listen to her father reading aloud from the *Golden Legend*. Her favourite saint was the martyr, Agnes, the betrothed of Christ who kept her faith and preserved her virginity. "I will be like you, O Agnes, if I am pursued," said Solange. And it came about that a young prince, attracted by the renown of this young shepherdess, fell in love with her and knew no rest before she was his. . . . But in spite of the most seductive promises, Solange refused to leave her distaff and her lambs. The young man wanted to seize her by force and drag her on to his horse, but the young girl slipped from his hands and ran to the river to throw herself in. The furious knight sprang after her, sword in hand, and with one stroke, cut off her head. "Jesus, Jesus, Jesus," pronounced her lips before closing for ever. The miracle was so manifest that the evil lord fled into the distant country, frozen with fear and remorse.

This mystical ideal of spousal love for Christ was slowly penetrating the soul of Charles. The Catholic mystics, St Gertrude, St Bernard, St Teresa of Avila, St John of the Cross, to mention but a few, at a loss to find words to sing of the ineffable union of God and the soul, borrow the words of human love. The Canticle of Canticles is their missal, and of course the loftiest of all these contemplatives is St John of the Cross, in his commentary on the Canticle of Canticles. Charles advised his intimates to read him. Years later Charles wrote to his dear friend, Henri de Castries, "I will tell you a secret. I am brimming over with happiness. It is like a love affair"—the love story between the soul and God.

Guessing a little of what was happening in the heart of her cousin, Marie de Bondy suggested that they should all drive over to the Cistercian Abbey of Fontgombault and visit the Trappists. It was a distance of about thirty kilometres. Olivier de Bondy said laughingly as they set out, "I am sure we won't bring Charles back with us. We'll leave him behind."

It was really Marie who took the initiative for this expedition. Charles wrote later, "It is you who brought me to the Trappists." During the ride, some people thought that Marie was his mother. This simply delighted Charles who said, "The people of the Berry were not wrong, and they pleased me more than they thought in saying that I was your child." The de Bondys, who were benefactors of this abbey, were given a great welcome. A lay brother would take the children to the orchards and give them some ripe fruits, whilst the Vicomte and Vicomtesse were entertained by the Abbot, Dom Albéric, a young aristocrat with very solemn manners. And there, a most extraordinary thing happened to Charles. He noticed that the lay brother who entertained the children wore a very ragged habit, and immediately felt drawn to an Order where the Lady Poverty was held in such high honour.

The Trappists are a branch of the Cistercian Order, which was founded at Cîteaux in 1098 by Robert of Molesme, and one of whose greatest adornments and reformers was St Bernard of Clairvaux in the twelfth century. In 1664 De Rancé, the Abbot of the monastery of La Trappe in Normandy, instituted an even more severe Rule and his followers were known as Trappists, and are still today.

The monks rise at two in the morning and do not return to sleep. The fasts are long and seem to us moderns rather terrible (though a saint once said that fasts are the feasts of angels). On a meagre diet, they do heavy agricultural work in the fields. And yet they are extremely merry, and many live to a ripe old age. St Bernard, that father of 160 monasteries which he had filled with the élite of his contemporaries, used often to say, "Oh my God, what happiness you give to your poor!" They were deeply happy in their love of God and for each other. Their signal characteristic was gaiety, that *hilaritas* combined with the simplicity of the monks, which Fulbert de Chartres had said produced "a certain angelic quality". St Bernard, too, sang of the bridal of the soul and God. He portrays in burning language this bride whose only vocation is to love and to be loved. Much later St John of the Cross, whom Charles loved so much, wrote, "We have been created only for love, and it is on this love that we shall be judged at the end of our days."

This is how the monks have been described at their work:

"Let us follow the monks at hay-making time. In the farmyard, they come in a long procession and then stand still. Each one carries his tools under his arm; each one takes his rank according to the time he has been in the Order; it is morning, and the sun is radiant. At least he communicates to nature that exquisite charm of the awakening world: the dew, which is the breath of the earth, melts and imparts a freshness to everything. There are dewdrops on the grass, glittering like diamonds.

"And now it is harvest time. They bring back the wheat, and we find the monks in the barn. If they work hard like mercenaries, in heat, in dust, they earn their bread by the sweat of their brows."

It was not only in the Château de la Barre that Charles learned about the Trappists. When he visited his married sister Mimi de Blic at Barbirey near Dijon, he must surely have walked to near-by Cîteaux where the saint had entered as a novice, and also to Fontaines, his birthplace. Before his birth, St Bernard's mother was told in a dream that she was carrying a saint, and Charles's thoughts went back to a similar vision which his own mother had told him she had had about him.

In 1888, for several weeks in August and September, Charles had to don military uniform again, as he was an officer in the reserve. His chief praised him highly and said he had a very lively intelligence, steady judgment, his morals were perfect, his behaviour excellent, his appearance extremely good. His superiors were also most impressed by his great knowledge of map-reading. They concluded that "he was a devoted officer, conscientious and hard-working, able to fulfil all his responsibilities . . . a very good head of a squadron".

How different from the reports of Saumur and Saint-Cyr in the old days! He had now completely redeemed himself in the eyes of his family, and was carrying on the noble military tradition of the de Foucauld family throughout the centuries.

And that military tradition was to prepare him for his special, his unique vocation.

CHAPTER 9

The Holy Land

VERY often great men and women are shown by God, quite clearly, at the beginning of their lives, what their vocation is to be. Charles's vocation was revealed to him very slowly. He went one step at a time. Seeing that he wanted to give himself completely to God, and that he loved the Gospels, the Abbé Huvelin told him to make a pilgrimage to the Holy Land. Charles did it out of obedience, rather than from his own personal desire. He set sail from Marseilles in December 1888. When he arrived in Jerusalem, he found it covered by a mantle of snow. It is of course impossible now to reconstruct the Holy Land as Charles saw it.

When the Crusaders sighted Jerusalem far off on its hill, Jerusalem the Golden, they would quickly dismount and, kneeling on the ground, bow their heads low in adoration. Jerusalem, the symbol of the celestial city of the Blessed. Jerusalem, adorned as a bride for her Spouse.

Charles followed the usual pilgrim itinerary, guided by the Franciscan Fathers, for so long custodians of the Holy places: the Temple area, then in Muslim hands, Mosque of Omar, the Via Dolorosa, through the narrow streets, making the Stations of the Cross, on the short journey to Calvary within the Church of the Holy Sepulchre. With what emotion he saw and touched the place of the entombment of Christ may well be imagined.

Charles travelled as a well-to-do pilgrim, hiring a horse and a servant. He spent Christmas at Bethlehem, where he found that the grotto where the Divine Infant was born had remained unaltered.

And then Charles made an excursion into Galilee, where Nazareth made a lasting impression, with its green hills, its scented breezes. Did he see the well where Our Lady would go and fetch water in an urn, which she carried on her head? The air was sweet, the sky grey, almost violet at times. The water gurgled at the springs and flowed rippling away into the meadows.

Charles fell deeply in love with Nazareth, and it was here that his vocation truly began to dawn. It can be epitomized in one short sentence: in Nazareth he discovered the face of Jesus. He fell in love with His poverty, the intense humility of His life. How strange that He, who was God the Son, should spend the first thirty years of His life in abjection, humiliation and hard work as a lowly village carpenter. As he bent down by the roadside to pick flowers and stones to give to the family on his return, Charles thought of the Divine Feet which had trodden these very paths. Nazareth inspired him with a passionate love for the hidden life. The memory of Nazareth was to shape the whole of his inward existence. On his return, he wrote, "Now I am free no longer in anything at all. I am in a state which I have never experienced before, except perhaps on my return from Jerusalem ... I felt a need to withdraw, to keep silent, to kneel at God's feet and to gaze at Him almost in silence." And indeed, in the Holy Land, he learned to love that silence which was to be his more fully in the Sahara.

On his return, of course, he hastened to the Abbé Huvelin, his spiritual father, who himself had so much longed to become a Trappist monk and who knew about all the religious Orders in France. After hearing all about Charles's travels, he advised him to visit several of these Orders and gave him introductions. At Easter, Charles went to the Benedictine monks of Solesmes. But the sung plain-chant and the glory of the liturgy did not appeal to him. At that time, he was received by Dom Delatte, and the Abbot's parting words to Charles were, "Don't forget: God loves you, and this life doesn't last for ever." Unfortunately, any further record of this interesting visit was lost when the monks were illegally turned out of their monastery and finally sought refuge in England. One wonders if he heard the choir office sung at the near-by Abbey of Sainte Cécile, where Madame Cécile Bruyère was Abbess, and where that other penitent, Huysmans, had described the plain-chant as "delicate pearls dropped into a silver salver".

Charles had decided against entering at Fontgombault where he had fallen in love with the poverty of the ragged lay brother, because it was too near the family. He wanted to give up everything dear to him, and his family was the dearest thing in the world. At Trinity-tide, he went to La Grande Trappe, near Grenoble, then on October 20th, he travelled to Notre-Dame-des-Neiges in the Ardèche for a week; and still he could not make up his mind. In mid-November Marie de Bondy suggested that he should go to Clamart near Paris and spend some time in retreat under the direction of a Jesuit in Manresa House. There he finally decided to become a Trappist, and wrote to his sister to tell her so. The Abbot of Notre-Dame-des-Neiges agreed to receive him, and Charles begged that after several months of probation, he should be sent to the very poor, very obscure Trappist convent of Akbès in Syria, for he felt quite certain that this was God's will for him.

CHAPTER 10

Notre-Dame-des-Neiges

IN early December, Charles went to Dijon to say goodbye to his sister and his brother-in-law, the de Blics. This was the last week in which he would be free. It was painful for him, for he loved their château and their children very dearly. He gazed, as he thought, for the last time at the weeping willows on the brink of the water; he recalled all the beautiful spring flowers that he had loved there and the kingfishers he had seen darting about by the river bank. He looked at the vast courtyard of the château, went for a last walk in the park, and looked up at the poplar trees whose leaves had almost all fallen. And he recalled the happy visits he had made there, when he had been surrounded by so much kindness and affection. He had written to his sister Marie some time before to say, "Life in your home is not only extremely sweet, but it even makes you better, by its atmosphere of affection and quiet." He recalled the days hunting with his brother-in-law, pushing young Maurice in a wheel-barrow, dipping into the library of Monsieur de Blic, and the delightful evenings spent with the whole family around the fire.

Then came the heart-rending parting from Marie de Bondy in Paris. He had already spent August and September with her at the Château de la Barre, and he realized that it would be for the last time. But her great influence on him had already borne fruit, for on the preceding June 6th, he had consecrated himself to the Sacred Heart of Our Lord at the Basilica of Montmartre, already surrounded by its galaxy of obscure, poor adorers. Then he visited for the last time the churches he had loved and haunted before and after his conversion. This conversion was so total, so complete, that he never once afterwards referred to the sins of his youth. He had already begun to practise greater poverty, and one of his friends was very surprised to see him sitting on the top of an omnibus.

It was arranged that he would say goodbye to nobody. The others would hear of his departure only when he had finally left Paris. Indeed, a letter from a cousin in the Vosges, inviting him to come and eat venison with him, arrived at his flat just too late. His Aunt Inez and his learned cousin, the Vicomtesse de Flavigny, looked upon this step as another of his strange eccentricities. They did not understand it in the very least. But Marie de Bondy did. On his last evening in his flat in the Rue de Miromesnil, on January 14th, 1890, the one book which he fingered lovingly was the Bossuet which she had given him when he made his first Communion. He lighted again on a passage which was attuned to the pain of that moment: "To be truly in conformity with the will of God, one must know how to sacrifice to Him that which is most dear, and with a lacerated heart to say to Him, 'Everything is Yours, do what You will.' "

On January 15th, one can follow him step by step throughout the day. At six forty-five in the morning, he went to the Rue de la Borde, to the Abbé Huvelin who was again bed-ridden. At nine o'clock he went to the Church of St Augustin with Marie de Bondy; they heard Mass at the Lady altar and made their Communion together, and afterwards he accompanied her home. At two forty-five, he crossed over again to the Abbé Huvelin. He was there at three o'clock when he received a last blessing from that so greatly loved spiritual father. Then once more he prayed in St Augustin's. He returned to Marie at five o'clock to spend the last two hours with her, for he had decided never to see her again, indeed never to see any of his relations. He wrote to her a year later, "It was five minutes to seven in Paris at that moment: I was sitting near you in your drawing-room, looking first at you and then at the clock. How real it is for me, that day . . ." At ten past seven, the hour of parting had definitely come. Marie blessed him and he went away in floods of tears. One recalls St Teresa of Avila who, when she left her home to become a Carmelite, was in such agony of mind, that she felt as if all her bones were being dislocated. This separation was equally terrible for Charles. He said later, "It was a sacrifice which cost me all my tears, and since that day I never weep, I feel as if I have no more tears left . . . and it is only sometimes, as I think about it . . . that the wound of January 15th still gives me pain. The sacrifice of that day remains an hourly sacrifice."

One can picture him taking the night train and travelling third class. No heating, except perhaps a hot water bottle which very soon grew cold; difficult to sleep because the lamp-man would be walking on the roof of the carriage, tending the oil lamps. Very little space, hard wooden benches, nothing on which to lean your elbows or your head—people with long legs suffered miseries.

But in the middle of that night, Charles was already finding consolation. Eleven years later he was to confide to his friend, Henri de Castries, of "that infinite peace, that radiant light, that changeless happiness which I have enjoyed for the last twelve years".

He had been very much consoled at that last Mass together, for in a letter to Marie he said, "May we find ourselves together at the feet of the Lord, possessing Him as we possessed Him that morning." Before going on his pilgrimage to the Holy Land, the Abbé Huvelin had given him a rosary. Before parting, Marie gave him hers, for he was to write, "Dear little rosary, do you not think it also does me good? And I pray I may always hold it with increasing devotion; thank you for giving it to me; I am truly unworthy. At this very moment, at five o'clock, I was with you once again, and for the last time in this world. I was in Hell and you led me to Heaven. How I remember your clock ticking away my last minutes." The final letter he was to write to the Abbé Huvelin (the last to go unread by his novice master) spoke of his visit to his dear room, and he said he would finish that day at the feet of Our Lord. "There I am still with her and with you." He was to write to her a year later, "Always say everything you think to your child; you know with what tender gratitude he will receive any words you deign to speak, words that give proof of your affection, of which he is so unworthy and which is the most precious thing he has on earth."

At last the strange, wearisome journey came to an end. He was consoled by two things; he could never really be parted from Marie. "There has been so little to keep us apart in the past, how can we be so completely apart in the future? . . . How happy you made those last days, those last hours . . ." Also, he remembered the liturgy of the Feast of the Crown of Thorns, and thought of that day as the Feast of his Espousals with the Beloved, a day of great joy. And so, on that January morning, he at long last arrived at Notre-Dame-des-Neiges in the Ardêche, surely one of the bleakest, most wind-swept, most desolate regions of France.

But there were high mountains and immense distances, and the ravines were of a deep violet colour. He passed one or two isolated farms built to withstand six months of storms and snow. At last he reached the poor monastery surrounded with its barns and stables. He rang the bell and the lay brother brought him silently to the bare white cell of Dom Martin, the Abbot.

Now the Abbot knew very well who Charles was, a nobleman and a soldier; also a distinguished explorer and a man who had given up great riches. But all these things meant nothing to a man whose only ambition was to train men for God. He said to him, "What can you do?"

"Not much."

"Can you read?"

"Just a little."

"Will you take this broom and sweep the room, please."

Charles did it somewhat clumsily. "Hm," said the Abbot, "I see we will have to complete your education."

All this interview may smack of mock humility. Surely it would be known that Charles was a famous scholar and writer? But in those days, superiors treated distinguished postulants like this, another notable example being St Bernadette, when she became a nun at Nevers.

He was given the name of Brother Marie Albéric and led to the common dormitory. All was silent, for the Trappists speak only by signs. Here was his time-table. He rose at two A.M., went to the church, and spent two hours reciting psalms in choir. Then for an hour and a half he was free, and he read or prayed as the priests said their Masses.

The cloister was the place where the monks usually did their spiritual reading. It is always the heart of a monastic house and a blessed refuge. All the monks walked slowly with their eyes downcast, and their hands in their sleeves. Towards five-thirty in the morning, they all returned to choir and recited the office of Prime and heard the community Mass; then they went to the chapter room, where, after a few prayers and some comment on a passage of the Rule by the Abbot, they accused themselves of any faults against the Rule and were given a penance. There followed three quarters of an hour of free time, to read or to pray, and then the office of Terce. Towards seven o'clock, manual work began. The superior distributed the special tasks as the monks came out of Terce. They worked till eleven o'clock, then said the office of Sext. They went to the refectory at half past eleven. Meagre fare indeed, mostly consisting of vegetables. In the Lenten season, the first meal was at four-thirty, and that for men exhausted by heavy agricultural work (Pope Leo XIII discontinued this practice). After the meal, there was a siesta in the dormitory for an hour and a half. At one-thirty, the office of None; an interval of three quarters of an hour after this time for private prayer or spiritual reading. At two-thirty, Vespers. After Vespers, work until a quarter to six. Six o'clock, prayers. At six-fifteen supper, also very sparse; then a little free time. At seven-fifteen, spiritual reading for the whole community in the chapter room followed by Compline and the singing of the *Salve Regina*, after which they went to bed at eight o'clock—unless they had leave to keep vigil.

The other monks soon realized that they had a saint in their midst. He surprised them most by his extreme humility, and when, many years later, René Bazin went there and interviewed one of the old monks who had known Charles, a rough lay brother who was a reaper and looked after the oxen said, "Monsieur, I spoke to him as if he were a peasant." Then he added, "Ay, I saw him every day; he never refused to do a good turn to anyone; he was glorious, like a second Francis of Assisi!"

What a good thing it is to be blessed by good health in a strong and vigorous body from youth. Charles wrote home to assure Marie and the Abbé Huvelin that neither the fasting nor the vigils nor the work nor the cold had any effect upon him. The only thing which he found difficult was obedience. But then it must be remembered that he had an exceptional vocation, which was gradually to unfold before him. There are in the Church some souls who are called to special vocations, like Marthe de Noaillat who, inspired by God to bring the feast of Christ the King into the liturgy, had failed time and again when she had tried her vocation as nun at the Assumption. She fell so seriously ill every time that she had to be brought home almost dying. Charles wrote to Marie, "It is not that I do not love obedience, my dear mother, but I do not wish to put obedience to men before obedience to God."

To start with, he was not given very much arduous field work, but he was told to carry branches and make garlands and wreaths to decorate the church for Perpetual Adoration, to sweep the church and polish the candlesticks. He wrote, "They are excellent to me, with a charity full of tenderness; a great charity reigns supreme in the monastery."

He had said, "I wanted to enter into the religious life to keep Our Lord company as much as possible in His sufferings." But at Easter he said he had not suffered in the very least from the fast and the cold of Lent, in fact he had thought it agreeable and convenient to have only one meal a day. He found manual work a consolation because Our Lord did it, and he meditated continually as he worked.

But in reality, although he loved individual Trappists and found them admirable, he was not a Trappist at heart. He failed to appreciate the Office sung in choir; he preferred long, contemplative prayer and night vigils. He discovered it was irritating always to be changing his tasks, and he thought the Rule too narrow, too meticulous. One extraordinary reason for his dissatisfaction in this very poor Trappist monastery was that he believed they did not follow Christ in His poverty, and thus he himself would risk losing the love of the Beloved. He even wrote, "Poverty is loved so little around me, austerity is not loved ..." Later he wrote even more surprisingly, "I see the spirit of the world holds us all in thrall."

Also, feeling that he had been a great sinner, he wanted to obey Our Lord's behest to Mary Magdalene, that, as she sinned much, she must love much. And it must be remembered that Charles, in the nineteenth century and coming from the aristocracy, looked upon manual labour as a 'come-down'. He transposed this conception into the life of Our Lord; he thought that the life of work at Nazareth was an abjection. He did not know that in Hebraic society in the time of Our Lord, manual labour was not at all considered to be a dishonour. It was, on the contrary, an act of piety. A Dominican has written in *La Vie Spirituelle* that the very fact that Christ did not have nor wish to have access to the schools of Jerusalem and become a Rabbi, makes one think that He wanted to mark his association with the world of "little people". Jesus did not want to become a Jew of the first rank. And that is why in His public life, the "little people" were familiar and simple with Him.

The conception that Charles had of manual work differs

radically from the conception of housework which prevails in the world today, when the upper-class man or woman does not think it a disgrace to do menial tasks, whereas the charwoman, for example, will not scrub nor do black-leading of grates any more!

And then this criticism of poverty. He did not like the monks using outside labourers, nor approve of the difference between lay and choir brethren, nor that there should be any collective property, and any putting aside for the morrow. He thought that he was not given sufficient manual labour: for him manual work was not only a means of purification, but a positive way of union with Christ, who was a workman. And he could not see how the complicated liturgy of St Benedict could appeal to poor people.

He read St Teresa a great deal at that time. There seems to have been a fellow feeling between the two of them. The saint desired that her new monastery should know absolute poverty, and that the nuns should live completely on alms.

He devoured her *Book of the Foundations*. And no wonder! It has that racy touch which belongs particularly to a woman brought up in a large family of adventurous brothers. Could Charles forget that, as a child, she had run away from home with one of those brothers, planning to convert the Moors? He loved the spirited accounts of all those dangerous journeys of hers, journeys undertaken by this aristocratic woman with no health and no money. One day her cart got stuck in the mud, and she said to Our Lord, "Is this how you treat me?" He replied, "That is how I deal with my friends." Quick as lightning came St Teresa's spirited reply, "That's why you have so few." So often she concludes an account of a horrible journey, or an encounter with disagreeable persons, by saying, "I was very much amused." Her style alone is riveting. Can one forget her account of a young girl who wanted to become a Carmelite nun against the wishes of her parents? One day, in church, this gallant child enticed her mother into a confessional, sent her duenna to the sacristy to ask for some Masses, then, taking off her shoes and stuffing them up her sleeves, ran out of the church, and never stopped running until she reached the Carmelites.

Yes indeed, the gallant St Teresa, who said, "God loveth the courageous soul", was very much his kindred spirit during those difficult days when he was beginning to realize that he was a square peg in a round hole.

CHAPTER 11

Syria and Rome

TO everyone's regret, but as had been previously arranged, Charles left Notre-Dame-des-Neiges after six months, and in June went to Akbès in Syria. He was going to the East, to become still poorer, and to be even closer to the Holy Land where Christ had suffered and worked.

At Marseilles, as he boarded the boat which was to take him to Alexandria, he had a momentary pang at the thought that—as he believed—he would never again see the shores of France. The day before the voyage ended he scribbled to Marie on a scrap of paper, "Tomorrow I will be at Alexandria, and I will say good-bye to that sea, my last link with the country where you all live." He arrived on the afternoon of July 10th; he and another monk, who had come from Notre Dame du Sacré Coeur to fetch him, travelled on mules throughout that night and then the whole of the next day, with only five hours' halt.

At long last, he found the poorest monastery imaginable, with twenty monks and fifteen orphans aged from six to twelve. The estate was called Cheiklé and had been improvised a few years before as a refuge in case the Trappists were obliged to leave France. It is encircled by a pine-clad mountain forest with great cascades and torrents. It was easy to see that everything had been built in haste. Stone had been reserved for the chapel, everything else was made of earth and wattle, and the roofs were thatched. In summer the monks slept in a loft above the stables, and the floor-boards were so badly joined that one could hear and smell the beasts underneath. In winter, they moved to another loft, but there things were just as bad because of the makeshift roof—so low, and in winter so heavily covered with snow, that it was difficult to sleep, even when they had blankets or covers stuffed with moss. And then, although like most French monks they grew all manner of good things, and even made a white wine which was delicious, they were so far away from any markets that they could not afford the transport to sell their produce.

Charles was set to gather cotton, carry the stones which were in the fields and pile them into heaps, wash clothes, saw wood; once he spent eight or ten days gathering potatoes, a back-breaking task. He also helped to pick grapes. He realized quite soon that the monastery was surrounded by Turkish brigands, and he began to have missionary aspirations. He wrote to Comte Louis de Foucauld: "It is for us to create a future for these peoples"—that is to say, the Syrians, the Kurds, the Turks and the Armenians. How different it all was from France! In the winter he could hear the howling of wolves, the cries of panthers and growling of bears, and, of course, there were many boars in the neighbourhood. Whereas in France he had been told to pray as he worked, here he was ordered to work with all his strength, even if meditation had to suffer: it was more in conformity with poverty and the example of Our Lord.

Because Akbès was even poorer than Notre-Dame-des-Neiges, there was more manual labour, and he was encouraged to give his mind and strength to it. As he worked barefoot his feet became so swollen and chapped that by autumn he could no longer stand. So the Abbot made him librarian and bell-ringer. There, he learned both to knit and to sew, skills which he found very useful later in the Sahara.

The novice master was Dom Polycarpe, and one can truthfully say that this Trappist, a very spiritual man, influenced Charles quite as much as the Abbé Huvelin. He wanted him to learn to imitate the poverty of Christ on earth. Of Dom Polycarpe, Charles wrote, "He, so learned and who loved study so much, with what delight did he plunge into the humblest of manual tasks. . . . When he no longer had the strength to dig, he washed the linen, then he had to be content with doing the mending. It was always edifying when one came into his cell during work time, to see him, needle in hand, mending stockings." Charles did not get on so well with his confessor, Père Marie Raphael, who complained of his eccentricities, not the least of which was his refusal, even on Easter Day, to take food other than bread and water. It appears that Brother Marie Albéric on this point was "as obstinate as a mule from Auvergne". This confessor also seems to have disapproved of his neglected appearance, his torn and dirty habit. (Certainly, his friend St Teresa would have had caustic comments to make about this, for she had told her nuns, "Dirt is a terrible thing.") And even at Akbès Charles was disappointed from the very beginning by the mediocre poverty. He wrote to the Abbé Huvelin, "You hope that I have found enough poverty. No, we appear poor to rich men, but not poor as Our Lord was, not poor as I myself was in Morocco, not poor like St Francis."

And yet he overlooked the poverty of the miserable lodging of Dom Polycarpe himself. "How many years we saw him live in a hut of several square feet, and you could touch the straw ceiling with your hand, and you only got daylight through a skylight. No glass, but just a cotton curtain. He had really espoused poverty, that inseparable companion of Our Lord Jesus Christ."

One must indeed censure Charles's obstinacy about food, for he eventually became very tired, and a slight trace of tuberculosis was suspected. Since he came from a tubercular family, that was enough to make the wise authorities wish that he were more amenable about eating.

On January 3rd, 1891, he wrote to Mimi to tell her that he made her a final gift of all that was in his Paris flat. It was hers now, for ever; she could do what she liked with it, sell, give away, anything.

He pronounced his first, simple vows on the Feast of Candlemas, February 2nd, 1892. The ceremony was presided over by Dom Martin, who had come over from France to the East to make a regular visitation. Charles wrote, "I am in a state which I have never felt before, unless it is a little like what I experienced on my return from Jerusalem. . . . I feel a need for recollection, for silence, to be at the feet of God and to look at Him almost in silence." Dom Martin wrote, "Our Brother Marie Albéric appears like an angel in the midst of us. He lacks only wings."

The Prior of Cheiklé wrote to Charles's sister on the day after his simple profession, saying that Dom Polycarpe had told him that, never in his long life, had he met anyone so entirely given to God. He then expressed the wish that Frère Marie Albéric should start theological studies. Charles's protestations were ignored, and he was referred to a professor of theology, a very learned Neapolitan. All this while, an inner voice kept saying to him, "Go further into solitude". He continued to find obedience difficult. Dom Louis, the Prior of Cheiklé, had written to Dom Martin that the root of the trouble was an inability to submit to prolonged obedience and discipline under a superior. "He could become a saint," he added, "and I hope he will, but only if he is given a free rein, not under obedience."

Also, there was dawning in Charles a desire to consecrate all his strength to the salvation of the Infidel. Although there was enough in his apparent restlessness to worry the Abbé Huvelin, he, with the especial perspicacity of holiness, at long last wrote to him, "Yes, my child, go to that prodigious unknown of which you are dreaming!" He realized that Charles perhaps had the vocation to be like the Fathers of the Desert, but he should certainly found no Order. He wrote most explicity: "You are not at all made to lead others." Charles kept thinking about the life of Nazareth where he hoped he could become a simple, plain, day labourer or journeyman attached to some convent.

And then came a terrible event which helped finally to decide Charles: the Armenian massacres, permitted or commanded by the Turkish Sultan. Charles described the massacres, the fires, the pillaging; of how many Christians had been really martyrs, and that they died of their own free will, without defending themselves, rather than deny their Faith. A hundred and forty thousand Christians had been slaughtered in several months. He wrote that he himself was unworthy of martyrdom: "Pray that I become converted, and that another time I will not be pushed away, in spite of my wretchedness, from the door of Heaven which was just half open." The sufferings of the refugees in the mountains haunted him, and he wrote to his family in France, asking them to help them by alms.

At last came February 2nd, 1897, when the period of simple vows would come to an end, and he would either have to pronounce his final vows or ask for a dispensation and leave the Order. He was still tormented with the desire to follow more closely in the footsteps of Our Lord, the poor workman in the streets of Nazareth, lost in obscurity and abjection. Again the Abbé Huvelin understood. Though he regretted that his penitent could not remain in the Order, he told him, "You are drawn too strongly towards another ideal." And two months later, "Yes, like you, my dear child, I see the East."

His superiors wanted to test his obedience. They ordered him to go to the Trappist monastery of Staouëli, and when he got there, he was told he was to go to Rome for about two years to study theology.

Although he spent only a short time at Staouëli, just a few weeks, he made an enormous impact on the rest of the community. An eyewitness, the Père Yves who was a novice at the time, speaks of how he impressed the whole house. "In church his eyes were always fixed on the Blessed Sacrament. He did not believe, he saw. He lived on practically nothing, eating just the vegetables which he found in his soup without having the soup itself, and simply nothing else. And that only once a day, at midday. He slept for only two hours. He watched until midnight, in a little chapel of the infirmary from where you could see the Blessed Sacrament. At midnight he would go and take a little rest, and at two o'clock, he was in choir with the community."

At Staouëli, Frère Marie Albéric made a precious spiritual friendship with a Père Jérôme, and it is through his letters to him that we learn some very interesting details. On November 8th, 1896, he writes to Père Jérôme from Rome, "We arrived in Rome on Friday at one-thirty in the afternoon; we did not go to the station of San Paolo, which is near St Peter's, it was not convenient and we blessed God for that: if we had got out there, we would have had to take cab after cab, and that would have been a real grief to me to go in such fashion into this city where St Peter and St Paul both came so poor and so wretched, St Paul in chains. . . . So we went on foot from the station, and on our way we stopped in two churches where we adored the Blessed Sacrament."

Living as he did in the Mother house near St John Lateran, he often passed the Colosseum "where so many martyrs have given, with such joy and such love, their blood for Our Lord! How Our Lord has been loved in that place! What flames of love have risen from there towards Heaven! What are we compared to souls like those?" He seems to have gone to the catacomb where St Cecilia was first buried, for on November 29th he sent Père Jérôme a little flower which he picked for him whilst he was praying for him in her catacomb on her feast day. "May this flower of the martyr remind you, as it did me also, what the saints have suffered and how we should desire to suffer. . . . It is in this way that we are more fortunate than the angels."

Towards Christmas time, his thoughts turned to Bethlehem, and he told Père Jérôme of the happiness which he had felt as he prayed in the grotto in which had been heard the voices of Jesus, Mary and Joseph, "and where I had been so near them."

However, he continued to study theology as his superiors had ordered, and in the end they relented. The perfection of his obedience impressed them and they saw that he was called to be something other than a Trappist. The Father General of the Order arrived in Rome on January 16th, 1897, and summoned all the members of his council. They studied the case of Frère Marie Albéric, and having prayed about it and discussed it, they recognized that he had an exceptional vocation outside the Rule of St Benedict and St Bernard, and that he should follow it immediately with all his heart. A Trappist wrote to Charles's brother-in-law, Monsieur de Blic, "I am used to looking at him, used to thinking of him as a real saint." The Trappists, who were really the most understanding and kindly of men, generously gave him his ticket for the boat which would take him to the Holy Land, to the convent of the Nazareth Franciscans. He said at that time that only once had he regretted not being a priest, and that was during the height of the Armenian persecution. "I would so much have liked to be a priest, to know the language of the poor, persecuted Christians, and to go from village to village, encouraging them to die for their God . . . I was not worthy of it."

Charles de Foucauld was released from his vows. But he made a vow of chastity and the kind of poverty of a poor workman who would need tools. He left Rome in the first days of February to sail from Brindisi. He thought he was going to remain in the Holy Land for good, but he did not realize at the time that this was but another step in the long and strange pilgrimage he would be called to make. The Holy Land was to prepare him to lead his double life, both active and contemplative, and finally to become a priest who would bring the Host to Africa.

CHAPTER 12

Nazareth and Jerusalem

BEFORE Charles left Rome, the Father General of the Cistercian order said something which proved him to have been a man of understanding.

"How fortunate you are to have been given this exceptional vocation."

Charles landed at the port of Jaffa dressed in a most extraordinary outfit, a long shirt with a hood of blue and white stripes, blue cotton trousers, a thick white wool cap round which he had twirled some material to form a turban, and on his feet, sandals which were falling to pieces. An enormous rosary hung from his leather belt. When he landed, he believed he was going to live and die in the Holy Land. He wanted to follow in the footsteps of Our Lord, to haunt the places which He had known, to breathe the air He had breathed. He wanted to be poor, abject and despised like Christ. A lover grows akin to the image of the Beloved, just as Alphonse de Chateaubriant noticed so admirably that a certain moth which had stayed a long time on a tree assumed the colour of the tree itself.

Like his friend St Teresa of Avila, Charles was filled with love for the humanity of Christ. St Teresa said in her autobiography, "I see clearly, and since then have always seen, that if we are to please God, and if He is to give us His great graces, everything must pass through the hands of His most Sacred Humanity." Charles had read her constantly when he was a Trappist, and must have been much struck and indeed blissful when he came to the words, "The very beauty and whiteness of one of Our Lord's hands are altogether beyond our imagining." Or her description of a vision, "Although I see that He looks upon me at times with great tenderness, yet so strong is His gaze, that my soul cannot endure it. . . . I was contemplating His great beauty."*

Though the Holy Land was not to be the last stage in Charles's long journey in his search for God's will for him, it was to be a sweet and happy preparation for his mission to the Sahara. By his spiritual reading and his long night vigils of prayer, he amassed an immense store from which to draw for the rest of his life, and then pass on to others, "to contemplate and to bring others to contemplation", in the words of the Dominican motto. Also, by the discipline of long days and nights of entire solitude, Charles was trained to lead an ordered life without master or Rule, and this was eventually to serve him in great stead in Africa.

He had written to his sister, "He who gives its place to each leaf will know how to put me in my own niche." The well-dressed Vicomte, who had visited the Holy Land some years before accompanied by a servant and riding a horse, this time came on foot, and alone. He reached Nazareth on March 5th, 1897. He wrote to his cousin Louis de Foucauld that letters could be sent to him at the following address: Charles Foucauld, Nazareth, Holy Land, *Poste Restante*. In this letter he sounded utterly happy; for he wrote that he had found poverty, solitude, abjection, very humble work, complete security, and as perfect an imitation as possible of the life of Our Lord in Nazareth. "Love imitates, love wishes to be like the Beloved. . . . Keep my secrets, they are love secrets which I am confiding in you."

At first he went to the Franciscan Fathers, who give hospitality to pilgrims, and asked if he could be a servant to the Friars. After three days, he went to confession to one of these Friars, who by happy chance was the chaplain of the Poor Clares of Nazareth. This priest said to him, "I will tell them about you at St Clare's; perhaps there is something there for you." Unfortunately Charles had been recognized by the guest master, who told this chaplain who he was. The chaplain went to see the Abbess, in the humble little white-walled parlour with the double iron grille.

Now it happened that, in the world, Mother Mary of St

* A love for the Sacred Humanity of Our Lord was one of the chief traits which the Spanish Carmelites inculcated in the Paris Carmel of the seventeenth century. In this land ravaged by the dangers of Quietism, the Spanish nuns complained that their French novices were drawn to a nebulous form of prayer after the manner of pseudo-Dionysius.

Michael had been called Edith de Miomandre; she was an aristocrat descended from François de Miomandre, who had been
wounded at Versailles on the night of October 6th, 1789, when
he had saved Marie Antoinette from the invading mob by crying
out "Save the Queen!" In her youth Mother Mary had entered
the Poor Clares at Périgueux, so the Périgord name of de Foucauld could not have been unknown to her. "*Ma mère,*" said
Father Gabriel to her, "you're not scared of vermin, are you?"

She laughed. "No father, why?"

"I am bringing to you a remarkable hermit, the Vicomte de
Foucauld, but he doesn't want it to be known that he was a
Vicomte. He is dressed in the most extraordinary rags, and
indeed, a girl seeing him in Alexandria cried out, 'I am so scared
of vermin.' But he didn't mind at all. He thinks it an honour to
be taken for a madman and a fool. If he comes to you and asks
for employment, I should give it him, if I were you. He is not an
adventurer or one of those eccentrics you find in the East; I think
there is genuine goodness there."

Several days later, on the Feast of St Colette, the Blessed Sacrament was exposed on the high altar. That was enough to attract
Charles, with his deep love of the Sacred Host. He came in his
strange outfit and knelt before the altar, without moving, for one
hour, two hours, three hours. After a while the Arab lay sister
became anxious and said to one of the other sisters, "I had better
watch that man who hasn't left the chapel for three hours. I fear
he is going to steal something." Three days later he came back,
and asked if he could speak to the Mother Abbess. A brown serge
curtain was drawn across the grille; it was against the Rule to
draw it back, so the Abbess could not see this mysterious man or
admire the delicacy of his features. But she knew by the tone of
his voice and his choice of words that he certainly was not the
poor beggar he made himself out to be.

"Reverend Mother, I wonder if you could give me some
work?"

"Yes, I think I could. In fact, we need a sacristan and somebody who will go to the post for us and do other little jobs. You
must ask what you want for a salary."

"Oh, no salary, Reverend Mother, just a little bread and
water, and time to spend before the Blessed Sacrament in your
chapel."

"The gardener's cottage is empty; I will put you there."

"Oh no, that's far too good for me; I noticed a wooden hut just beyond your courtyard."

"But that's only a toolshed."

"That would do very well for me. I'd like to stay there. I see that it is built against your enclosure wall."

In a short while, the lay sisters brought two trestles, two planks, a palliasse and a kind of woollen envelope stuffed with rags. Charles wanted to carry all these things himself, but his feet were so swollen and bruised by the journey, and he was so exhausted, that he couldn't lift them, so he had to drag his bedding to the hut. It was so tiny that it could hold only him, his wretched bed and some books. But to him it soon became a corner of Paradise.

He begged for work: at first he was asked to sort lentils, or to repair a corner of the enclosure wall which was falling down, or to dig a little in the garden. He was not very successful at all this, so the Abbess asked him to serve the Masses and sweep the chapel, and then she left him to pray for as long as he liked, motionless for hours, and then to go to his hut where he spent very little time in sleep, it is said, but many hours in meditation, reading, and writing out his meditations, so many of which have survived. "*Dieu parle pour ceux qui se taisent.*" (God speaks to those who keep silence.)

Unfortunately, the Eternal Word, who first visited this planet in the silence of the night, has a way of encroaching on necessary mortal activities. The Abbess was to prove this for herself in an amusing incident.

One day the lay sister reported to the Mother Abbess, "That wretched jackal has gone off with one of our best hens again. He slunk in last night, and I saw a trail of feathers and bloodstains this morning. What shall we do, Reverend Mother?"

The Abbess thought for a moment, and remembering that Charles had been in the Army, she called for him and asked him to watch that night, armed with a gun which she would procure for him. Unfortunately, Charles came armed not only with a gun, but also with his rosary, and there he spent some peaceful hours pondering on the Joyful, the Sorrowful and the Glorious mysteries, in the very land of their origin. In the distance he saw the houses which looked very like the ones which Christ knew

Himself. The jackal lurked in the darkness, peered up at Charles, sensed that he was far away, slipped into the poultry yard and killed another hen.

When the lay sisters told Charles about the tragedy, he said, "How extraordinary, I never saw him pass."

This was the last time the Abbess asked him to kill a jackal.

When Raymond and Mimi de Blic asked him for details of his time-table, he replied:

"It is a delicious hermitage, perfectly solitary.... I get up when my guardian angel wakes me, and I pray until the Angelus; at the Angelus I leave for the Franciscan convent, I go down to the Grotto which was a part of the Holy Family's house; I stay there until six o'clock in the morning, saying my rosary and hearing the Masses which are said in this adorably holy place, where God became incarnate, where for thirty years the voices of Jesus, Mary and Joseph were heard; it is profoundly sweet to look at those rocky walls on which the eyes of Jesus rested, and which He touched with His hands.

"At six o'clock I go to the sisters who are so good to me that they are really my mothers. In the sacristy and chapel, I prepare all that is necessary for Mass, and I pray.... At seven o'clock I serve Mass.... After my thanksgiving, I put order in the sacristy and chapel. When sweeping must be done, and that is only on Saturdays, I sweep; on Thursdays and Sundays I go to the post to fetch the letters.... I am the postman of the sisters.... Then I do what they ask, first one little job and then another; very often I draw little pictures, very simple, the sisters need them and ask me to do them.

"... On the whole I spend all my day doing little jobs in my small room near the sacristy: towards five o'clock I prepare what is necessary for Benediction of the Blessed Sacrament, on the days when they have it, which are many, thanks be to God.

"From that moment I stay in the chapel until seven-thirty at night. Then I go back to my hermitage, I read till nine o'clock. At nine, the bell warns me that it is time for evening prayer; I say my prayers and go to bed. I read during my meals; I take them all alone; I am the only servant, and this is very sweet to me; I see nobody in the world, except my confessor, every eight days, to go to confession, and the sisters when they have something to say to me, which is rare, for they are silent. . . . The sisters provide me with all the books I need and are infinitely kind to me."

In passing, one should mention that Charles had put himself under the special care of two saints who attracted him and were very like him—St Alexis, the Roman of the third century who, according to the legend, left his bride at the altar and then spent the rest of his life as a poor unknown beggar under her staircase, which can still be seen on the Aventine Hill; and then St Jean Benoit Labre, also a Roman beggar saint, but of the eighteenth century, to whom God had given the strange vocation of leaving the Trappists in France, and trudging on all the roads of Christendom to make pilgrimages to holy places. His worn clothes and shoes can still be seen in the house where he died. Yet another of Charles's protectors was St Margaret Mary, recently canonized, with her deep devotion to the Sacred Heart of Our Lord and her love for humiliation and suffering. He prayed to all his saints and begged them to crush him and then to place him like a fragrant perfume at the feet of Our Lord.

He wrote, "Prayer consists, as St Teresa has said, not in speaking much, but in loving much."

And then he wanted to console Christ in His agony.

How can we account for the great length of time spent on these night vigils? During those hours, which to outsiders seem unendurable, his mind went beneath the perception of the senses, and he became lost in a state wherein time was meaningless. Time is, after all, an artificial, human invention. God is the eternal Now. So, for Charles, time ceased to exist. It was ever, for him, the eternal Now—a foretaste of heavenly beatitude. The hours passed unnoticed and the dawn came.

Some are refreshed by long contemplation, others find it exhausting; the difference is probably a matter of temperament. Dom Bede Griffiths, O.S.B., in *The Golden String*, describes a similar experience before his conversion in the twenties, after coming down from Oxford. He speaks of his absorption in timeless prayer, lasting four or five hours. Eventually he found his vocation as a Benedictine monk. Just as Charles de Foucauld lost all sense of time, no doubt aided by being constantly in the desert

atmosphere, so when young Griffiths eventually found his vocation, it was in an isolated cottage in the Cotswolds, to which he
had retired in penance and prayer, to find God's holy will.

As Hosea said, the desert is the marriage place of the soul with
God.

But Charles's contemplation was not wholly personal. His
charity, which was to become universal and boundless, made him
think of others more and more. He said that one should see Christ
in every man. "He wishes us to believe that He is united, with
the tenderest love, to every human being." One sees the signs of
this double vocation developing in him in the Holy Land, but it
had begun earlier. He was to write much later, "My retreat before
becoming a deacon showed me that this life of Nazareth . . . one
had to lead it . . . among the souls who were the most sick, the
sheep who were the most neglected."

"When you make a feast, invite the poor, the lame, and the
blind."

He used to read the austere inscriptions on the white parlour
walls: "God alone. For God I have left all, in God I have found
all." He wrote to his relations, "Why did I go so far, you may
well ask me. . . . I never looked for joy, I just sought to follow
Him by the fragrance of His perfumes, and if I have found my
delights in following Him, it is without having sought them. But
these delights in no way prevent me from feeling deeply the grief
of being separated from all those I love."

He loved long night vigils, because Christ himself had so often
spent the night in prayer. Charles was not all a poet, but when he
describes one of those vigils he becomes quite lyrical. "It is night,
everything sleeps. One only hears some far-off cocks crowing."
(The Mohammedans say that cocks only crow to mock St Peter.)
"Thus crowed the cocks on the night that He was betrayed. Oh
how happy we are, my Saviour Jesus, to be so far away from this
sad world whose echoes barely reach us with the wind's gusts. . . .
How good it is to cling close to You in this secure room, between
Your mother, St Mary Magdalene and Your apostles, to look at
You, to contemplate You, to listen to You, and now that night is
deeper, to remain silent at Your feet, amongst these holy souls,
losing oneself with them in contemplating You."

The Poor Clares began to realize that they probably had a
saint in their midst. They remarked that when he was at the

altar, he looked like an angel, and whether the Blessed Sacrament was exposed or not, he spent whole hours without moving, as if he were in ecstasy.

Meditating on Psalm 83, he said, "The sparrow has found her dwelling and the dove a nest—here in this dear nest of Nazareth where You have so providentially, so miraculously prepared a dwelling for me, a house, a nest, this cloister of St Clare, so deliciously sweet . . ."

But his ecstatic vigils did not protect Charles from many a snub from people who had no idea who he was and who took him at his face value. One of the priests who came to preach a retreat to the nuns, when he saw Charles spending so long in the chapel, and thinking it was perhaps through idleness, said to the turn sister, "Tell that poor man to go and work, it's not necessary to stay for Benediction, he mustn't lose his day's work." Once, as he was sitting crouched in the courtyard shelling lentils, two French soldiers passed by, and he went scarlet in the face. And then, another day, a certain confessor of the nuns said jovially to him, "What have you been up to, my good friend? Have you got ringworm?" That was the result of Charles cutting his own hair. And then the little Arabs always threw stones at him in the street. This only increased his joy. It made him feel he was imitating Our Lord, and also it was an occasion to offer something to Him.

"Oh dear, oh dear," said the garden sister. "Look at what our hermit's been doing to my young plants. He's watered them in full sunlight. And that's not all: the other day I saw him putting fresh manure on them."

"Don't scold him," said the other sister. "He will learn in time. Think of how he goes rambling about the hillsides, digging up cyclamen roots for that garden of yours. Also I think it's very humble of him to go picking up manure on the roads. He doesn't know it's got to mature before you can use it."

Much to his disgust, Charles began to be talked about. A Salesian brother, oozing with pious curiosity, said to him, "They say that at home you are a count." Charles laughed and replied, "Oh, I am nothing but an old soldier."

One is glad to hear of the kindnesses which he sometimes received. At Christmas he waited at the table of a visiting priest, who afterwards said to him very kindly, "It's your turn now, sit down and eat heartily." And this he did, surprisingly glad for once to give up his usual fast.

He ate the poor fare of the nuns, but put away the figs and almonds of feast days in a box in the choir, because he wanted to give them to the cruel little Arabs he met in the streets. As there was no heating in his hut, he suffered from the cold, and after a while the nuns noticed his chapped hands and that he limped from rheumatism of the knees. So when he was out, they stuffed some rags into his kneeling pads. Later they added several thicknesses of material. Charles thanked them and said, "I see the pads have been fattening in my absence."

The sisters bought him a large coat to wear in the cold and rain, and added a hood to it.

When he described his daily round to the Abbé Huvelin, he said that he took the discipline every day, but did not wear a hair shirt.

The Abbé became a little alarmed when Charles wrote, "To follow the crucified Christ, I must lead a life of the Cross, and here it is a life of delights, it is peace, rest, enjoyment, it cannot last."

His heart went out to strangers. One very cold night, three beggars appeared in the courtyard and sought him out. "We have nothing to cover ourselves with, look, it's going to be a cold night." Filled with pity, and remembering the example of St Martin of Tours, he cut his cloak in half, then took his spare tunic which was hanging on a nail and told the third beggar to accompany him. They both went to the portress's lodge.

"My sister," said Charles to the turn sister, "please help me to make this tunic fit this poor man; it only needs a little cutting out, and a stitch or two."

"But, Brother Charles, it is Sunday today."

"I will help you; I will cut and you will sew; one is allowed to work a little, because these poor people are in dire need."

His letters home at that time were full of tenderness. Those to Henri de Castries, a fellow soldier, are admirable. His sister, Mimi, had just lost her newly born baby. Charles tried to console the parents. Of the child, he said, "How he is great, compared to us, all of us. . . . None of your children loves you so much, for he quenches his thirst in the torrent of Divine Love. . . . I have already prayed to him, that little saint, my nephew. . . . pray to him always, my dear Marie. And thank God for having made you the mother of a saint. A mother lives in her children: so here is a part of yourself in Heaven! More than ever, from now on, you will have your conversation in Heaven."

The Abbé Huvelin had urged him to write more than four times a year to Marie de Bondy. She needed it. In one of his long written meditations, which reminds one of St Augustine, a meditation in which he thanks God for all the graces that He has given him, he speaks of Marie de Bondy with regard to his conversion. "All that was Your work, my God. Your work alone. . . . There was one who helped You, but by her silence, her sweetness, her kindness, her perfection. . . . She was good, and there was a mysterious perfume in her virtue, but she said nothing. . . . You drew me to virtue by the beauty of a character in whom virtue seemed to me so lovely that it had irrevocably ravished my heart. . . . You drew me to truth by the beauty of that same soul." In one of his famous written meditations, there is a foreshadowing of things to come. Christ, here, is speaking: "He who loves cherishes solitude in the company of the loved one; he who loves God loves solitude at the feet of God. All the saints without exception have loved solitude, for they have all loved Me, and when anyone begins to love Me, he naturally desires to be alone with Me. . . . Also, as soon as My will begins to be heard, you must run, fly, give up all solitude, and plunge yourself among men." Yes, indeed the thought of suffering mankind began more and more to enter that great heart of his. And so he spent at Nazareth the summer, autumn and winter of 1897 and the spring of 1898.

The Mother Abbess of Nazareth had written to her superior at Jerusalem, Mother Elizabeth of Calvary, who now wished to meet Charles to find out if he were an impostor imposing on her nuns. She was the foundress of the two monasteries. And providentially, it was this obscure but valiant Poor Clare who came to have a tremendous influence on Charles and guided his vocation to its destined end.

Towards the late spring of 1898 Mother Elizabeth, wishing to judge for herself whether this Charles of whom everybody was speaking was really a saint, and being a very prudent woman, told her daughter Abbess of Nazareth to send him to Jerusalem on the pretext of personally delivering a very important letter.

The lay sisters told him various things about her before he set out on his journey, and these made him long to meet her.

"I suppose you know that she founded our very poor convent at Paray-le-Monial."

Charles's eyes brightened. "Oh, so she will be able to talk to me about St Margaret Mary and devotion to the Sacred Heart."

"Oh yes, I am sure she will do that. And she'll tell you about the wonderful poverty which our Poor Clares practise there, quite on a level with the Carmelites who, as you know, live in a hut where certain insects have to be swept off the floor at night and where the snow falls through the roof on to the sleeping sisters! And yet they are as joyous as larks, just as we are."

"Yes, I have noticed," said Charles, "that the merriest nuns are always in the severe Orders."

The lay sister continued, "Well now, I must get a food basket ready for your journey; for remember, you have a long walk before you, all the way across Galilee and Samaria."

"Well, sister, that's just why I don't want you to give me any food. I want to live by begging for help from Christians and Turks alike, they surely can't refuse me a little bread and water."

He set off. Lost in thoughts of the Master who had trodden the same paths, Charles disregarded his bleeding feet and his growing exhaustion, indeed on one terribly hot day he had nothing to eat or drink at all for twenty-four hours. He arrived in Jerusalem on the feast of St John the Baptist, June 24th. As it was nearly night time, he had to sleep on the ground in a field near the Poor Clares.

The Abbess did not take long to make up her mind about him, and hearing from the lay sisters that his feet were in a terrible state because of his bad sandals, she begged him to stay on for a while. "There is an empty hut just outside our enclosure, quite near another hut occupied by a negro and his wife; they are the guardians of our little estate."

She had already proposed to house him in the chaplain's lodging, but he completely refused this, just as he had refused the gardener's cottage in Nazareth.

Spiritual affinities resulting in hallowed friendships are rare and precious. Such a relationship was now given to Charles, who had renounced everything for God. He felt himself understood by

Mother Elizabeth, spoke little of himself, and then relapsed into sudden silence.

That evening at recreation, Mother Elizabeth told her daughters, "Nazareth is not mistaken: this is really a man of God, we have a saint in the house."

On his part he wrote, "She is a saint. What beautiful souls God creates, and how good of Him to let me see them. What treasures of moral beauty there are hidden away in cloisters, and what lovely flowers bloom there for God alone."

The next day she summoned him to the parlour and offered to lend him a book called *Abandonment to Divine Providence* by Père de Caussade, a seventeenth-century Jesuit. It was formed largely of a collection of letters to various nuns.

It did not need very much to encourage Charles to live from day to day, thus finding "the Sacrament of the Present Moment" as de Caussade calls it, and to have a great love for God's Providence for His children. But he found one letter in this book which deepened his conviction:

"My dear sister, I have made a discovery here that has given me more satisfaction than anything else could have done. In this town of Albi there is a convent of Poor Clares of the Great Reform, entirely separated from the world, who take no dowry and live on daily alms. The superior is the most saintly person I have ever encountered in my life. It was a joy to have a share in their holy conversation, and nearly all of them had told me that they felt the same about me. I believe that God intends to bestow some great graces on me through their holy prayers. They lead a very prayerful life and practise a profound confidence in God's Providence. You cannot imagine anything more wonderful than their union, candour and simplicity. Impressed by their great austerity, I asked them one day whether such a hard life did not affect their health and shorten their lives. They replied that there were hardly any invalids among them, and that very few died young, most of them living to be over eighty. They added that fasting and mortification contributed to improve their health and to a long life, which good cheer usually tended to shorten. I have never beheld such gaiety and holy joy anywhere else as I found among these good nuns.

"To please them I had to talk continually on spiritual subjects, as they could not tolerate gossip and worldly news, but said, 'Of what use is all that to us?' "

And Charles could not fail to be influenced by de Caussade's spiritual teaching about prayer, written in a letter to a nun in 1731, which quotes his beloved St Teresa:

"Here is a very simple method given by Jesus Christ to St Teresa when He appeared to her. 'Daughter,' He said to her, 'never think of anything but how to please Me, to love Me, and to do My will, and I, on My side, will attend to all your affairs, both temporal and spiritual.' Thoroughly to grasp this lofty precept, look upon yourself as one who has entered the service of the King, like Solomon, for example, the greatest, wisest and best of kings."

Likewise there is the short letter written to a sister in Perpignan in 1741, about the great isolation in which he was living at the time and which she looked upon as a misfortune. He reassured her:

"I am in a veritable desert, alone with God. How delightful it is! A great interior desolation is joined to this exterior solitude.... Once more have I learned by experience that we cannot do better than to follow step by step the course appointed by Divine Providence. That is my main attraction, and more than ever am I resolved to devote myself to it, blindly, without reservation, and in all things, such as places, employment, seasons ..."

Whilst he was meditating on the admirable lesson of this book which was to influence his whole life, Charles was writing home to France:

"My life here is exactly the same as at Nazareth, with this difference that I am even more solitary; that is far better. The convent is two kilometres from Jerusalem, on the road to Bethany, in an admirable situation, just by the Cedron ravine facing the Mount of Olives. From the windows one can see the whole of Jerusalem, Gethsemane, all the Mount of Olives, Bethany, and in the distance, the mountains of Moab and Edom which rise like sombre ramparts on the other bank of the Jordan: it is extremely beautiful . . . from the other side of the convent, you can see the hillocks of Bethlehem in the south and those of St John the Baptist (his birthplace and the deserts where he lived) in the west . . . the Cenacle, the path which Jesus followed with His apostles to go to the Garden of Agony after the Last Supper, that Garden, the palace of the High Priest where He was brought when they had bound Him, the palace of Herod, Calvary, the cupola of the Basilica of the Holy Sepulchre, the place of the Ascension, that dear and blessed Bethany, the only place where Our Lord was always well received, all the path which leads from Jerusalem to Bethany and on which Our Lord had walked so often. . . . If only you could come here! How happy you would be! How you would feel Jesus speaking to your heart, with emotion and happiness."

On October 15th that same year, on the Feast of St Teresa of Avila, he was writing home, "The Abbess, very different in character from the one of Nazareth, whose spiritual mother she is, resembles her in her kindness to me: the first one was a sister to me, but this one is a mother: the first is a very beautiful soul, this one is a saint. She has to a supreme degree the quality you most admire in St Teresa . . . a head of ice and a heart of fire, and that force of character which alone makes it possible to undertake anything and to accomplish anything for God and with God. . . . That is also what we used to admire in my so-dear cousin, no doubt near you in Paris now . . ."

Both the Arabs and the French who met him at this time remembered the kindness of his eyes and his very friendly manner. As René Bazin has said, "They marvelled also at the joy about which they guessed and which filled this man without a house, without parents, without wealth and without a situation." They did not know that he slept on two boards covered with a cloth and that his pillow was a stone. The negro caretaker was not deceived by his appalling appearance and extraordinary clothes. Charles always called him and his wife "my brother, my sister" and treated them with great courtesy. One day the Abbess said to this caretaker, "Go and take this to the workman," and the man replied, "To the gentleman, you mean."

Charles soon declared that he wanted to follow the Trappist Rule in the matter of food: at midday, milk, soup, some figs and honey, in the evening a very small piece of bread. In Advent 1898 and during the Lent of 1899, he simply had a piece of bread at midday and in the evening. All the nuns realized that he had never ceased being influenced by his Trappist training and background, and in fact he very often quoted the Rule.

He did various little tasks to help the extern sisters, but in particular he drew pictures for them to sell. For his saintly Mother Elizabeth of Calvary, he drew two big pictures, one of the life of St Elizabeth of Hungary, in grey and gold, and one of nine medallions depicting her own life from the day she left Périgueux until she came to Jerusalem.

Then one day he had the most important conversation of his whole spiritual life. This is how he reported it to France.

"The day before yesterday, the good Abbess summoned me to the parlour. 'We would like to make you for the winter, and for always, a longer tunic with a hood such as are worn here by the natives, something which is both more contemplative and more religious than your blue canvas trousers and shirt, and which, moreover, would not be the colour of any special religious order.'

"Charles: 'I? As I am French and not Syrian, it would always be for me a worthless disguise, or a religious habit, the clothing of the hermit if you like, but anyhow a religious habit which I cannot wear without the permission of the Ordinary. ... Poverty would not lose by it, but abjection would disappear: I would no longer cry out so well on the roof tops, "Jesus, workman of Nazareth", and I would no longer sing so faithfully that beautiful poem of His divine abjection." '

" 'Well, ask your director what he thinks of my proposal.'

"Charles: 'Very well, I'll ask him.'

"The Abbess: 'And then, why aren't you a priest?'

"Charles: 'First of all because I wanted to leave my Order; and then I wanted to remain in the last place of all; and finally it is impossible, because I have no means of existence.'

"The Abbess: 'You would imitate Jesus just as well as now,

for you could practise His poverty in the same way, you could imitate Him in His public life instead of in His hidden life. Even abjection would not diminish; instead of finding it as He did at Nazareth, in obscurity and the humiliation of a workman's life, you would find Him by preaching the Gospel amid contradictions, difficulties and failures, in calumnies and persecutions, just as He did. . . . As for the question of a means of existence, I am surprised that you speak of it; I invite you to be our chaplain, either in our convent here, or in the one at Nazareth. You can choose, and that for your whole life, and the sooner the better. If it were possible in a year, we would be very happy about it; what I see for you, is not, however, only to be our chaplain: I offer you this as a means; ask to be received into the priesthood to be our chaplain. Stay with us as long as you want; and at the same time you can train some disciples, near us, in the shadow of our cloister, just as you are, and then, when they are numerous enough, when the moment has come, go with them where the Holy Spirit impels. . . Anyhow, if you are to have any disciples, it would be far better for you to be a priest in order to form them.' "

And all this to a man to whom the Abbé Huvelin had said, "You are not meant to make a Rule, you are not meant to have disciples." Really, women were rarely meant to direct monks! When the Abbé saw that something almost beyond his control was pushing his penitent elsewhere, he became very anxious about what he thought was sheer restlessness.

Even in the peace of Nazareth, Charles had written something strange, doubtless thinking of his ancestor in the September massacres: "Think that you ought to die a martyr, stripped of everything, stretched naked on the ground and unrecognizable, covered with wounds and blood, killed violently and painfully—desire that it be today."

But he was not lost in an idle vision of contemplative prayer or martyrdom or of founding an Order: he was still a soldier. An event was to prove it quite soon. One day, he heard a terrific noise coming from the courtyard of the lay sisters, so he went to discover what was happening. He found three Italian beggars screaming and threatening the sisters, asking for dinner which they could not give, for it was against the Rule, and anyhow they had hardly anything to eat themselves. The sisters were frightened to death and did not know what to do. They were much relieved when they saw Brother Charles appear. Without a word, he grappled with the worst of the vagabonds and threw him outside. Then he followed suit with the second one and finally the third. His eyes were on fire. He said when he came back, "I am sorry if I wasn't very edifying."

"Oh no, you delivered us. Thank you."

The Abbess thought and prayed much about the saint living so near her. She recalled that the Poor Clares of Nazareth had told her how every evening Charles would go out and collect the dung on the roads, for the garden. He put it into an old basket, regardless of what anybody might say, and merrily called the pieces his flowers: he would offer them to the lay sister triumphantly. "That's all very well, that kind of *Fioretti*," she said to herself, "and very charming for the lay sister to be able to look after her little garden through his humble care, but I think he is made for greater things, and there are souls all over the world whom he could save and help if he became a priest."

So she summoned him again to the parlour and said, "Brother Charles, if you become a priest, there would be one more Mass in the world, and an infinitude of graces for men. It is in your power either to bring a new blessing on the world, or to withhold it. God has given you a long training, you've done a great deal of study, you have prayed much. Was all this intended for you to serve God alone in solitude? Haven't you thought of your suffering brothers and sisters?"

He excused himself on the grounds that he had been called to a hidden life.

The Abbess was perspicacious. She had a strong will and had been used to directing others. She was quite determined to give a holy priest to the Church, so she spoke to her daughters at recreation and asked them all to pray about it, which they did. She then called Charles to the parlour again, and told him, "Write to your director about this." He obediently complied.

At that moment, a disagreeable dispute had arisen with the Poor Clares of Nazareth about the little piece of land on which Charles's hut was built. They wrote to him begging him to come back and take possession of it again, and thus settle the whole matter. He returned to Nazareth at the beginning of 1899. And it was there in that little hut that he finally decided to become a priest. But he was still puzzled about his vocation; how could one combine an enormous love of the mystical life of solitude with the priestly life, when one was at the mercy of everybody? Where would he go?

CHAPTER 13

The Priesthood

THE Abbé Huvelin was again extremely ill. He was harassed by continual notes from Charles about various schemes he had taken up and then been obliged to abandon. Both priest and penitent were held up by the slowness of the post. So, although the Abbé Huvelin had telegraphed to him not to come, Charles, with his usual impetuosity, defied his instructions and there and then set out for France in order to speak to the Abbé in person. He left the Holy Land at the beginning of August 1900, taking with him only an old basket with some food in it and his breviary, on the first page of which he had written, "Live as though you should die today a martyr", followed by the names of his saintly ancestors. He travelled steerage in the greatest discomfort. Spiritually, as he lived from day to day, he became more and more convinced that his vocation was to carry the Sacred Host into distant lands among the Infidels, and to live in adoration of the Host, without preaching, but just bestowing heroic charity on everyone and serving all and sundry.

Charles arrived in Paris without telling any of his relations, very poorly dressed and looking worn out. He did not find the Abbé Huvelin in the Rue de la Borde, so he went straight to the Carmelite convent of Fontainebleau where he discovered his saintly director tormented by gout. The Abbé started by giving him a little scolding for disobedience, and then, remembering that it is almost impossible to direct a chosen soul at a distance of four thousand kilometres, he listened to him. They returned to Paris, where they spent twenty-four hours together, mostly talking, and when he saw Charles go the Abbé Huvelin wrote, "He dined, slept in the house and then he lunched with me and went on to Notre-Dame-des-Neiges and then to Rome. . . . He is very holy. He wants to be a priest. I showed him how this could be arranged. He had very little money; I gave him a little. He knew very well what I thought; I told him so in a telegram; but something stronger is drawing him, and it is only left for me to admire and love him."

And so, without seeing anybody else, Brother Charles entered his third-class compartment and travelled back to Notre-Dame-des-Neiges, his first monastery in the Ardèche. One can picture him occasionally glancing out of the window at the fresh scenery, so different from what he had been used to for many years now. His fellow travellers must have been a little puzzled by this worn-out man in his white cotton robe, with a huge rosary around his waist. His face was deeply lined and his eyes were very often lowered in prayer. He seemed barely to notice his surroundings. When he got off the train, he had to make the long journey to the monastery on foot, and in the sunset he saw the high rocks he had known as a novice. Quite soon, to his amazement, a lot of other vagabonds joined him. He arrived at the door of the Abbey completely tired out, grey with dust. The porter who opened the door did not remember him from ten years ago, and Charles did not remind him that he had once been a novice there. At the hour named by the Rule, the porter counted his guests, and then said, "Come in, my friends, we'll give you some soup and afterwards a good corner for a night's sleep." Brother Charles did as the others. He only made himself known the next morning. When the old lay brother was told who this beggar was, he laughed heartily. He told René Bazin, "Oh, he looked so seedy, the Père de Foucauld. He was covered in dust, even his shoulders, and dust all over his head; and around his waist, monsieur, he had a rosary so long, so large, so heavy, that it was quite strong enough to tether a calf." And he went on chuckling.

Don Martin received Charles with joy, and obtained permission from Monseigneur de Viviers that, after a short stay in Rome, he should be accepted as a cleric of his diocese.

In September 1900 Charles again found himself in Rome. He went there principally because he wanted to speak about his foundation of the Little Brothers of the Sacred Heart, of which he had dreamed for the last seven years. He had even written out a Rule to show the Abbé Huvelin, who did not approve of it at all, because it was entirely lacking in prudence. His abode in Rome was in what he called a little nest which God seemed to have prepared especially for him, just facing the Fathers of the

Blessed Sacrament, in whose church was kept the Host Exposed day and night. The fathers had found him a tiny room where he could be quiet and solitary, in the home of the devout Signora Maria Bassetti at 105 Via Pozetto, and there he lived the life of a hermit, hardly leaving the church, where day and night he prayed or studied theology. He used to read mostly on his knees, from the great books he had brought with him. If he ever took an airing, perhaps in the Borghese gardens, one can picture him gazing up at the large and moving statue of the Prodigal Son being embraced by a most tender father—one of Rome's little-known but admirable groups. How much that Gospel story meant to him! He, too, had begun by feeding the swine and squandering his inheritance on harlots. And now, the Father had prepared a banquet for him.

God had rescued him, and now Charles wanted to rescue the most forsaken of His children, and to be able to prepare a banquet for them.

In one of his great meditations, composed in the Holy Land, Charles showed how much the story of the Prodigal Son had meant to him. He says that God had inspired his relations, after his conversion, to receive him "like the Prodigal child", and they never let him feel that he had ever left the Father's House.

Towards the end of September, he went back to France. But this time he had received permission from the Abbé Huvelin to stop at Barbirey and see his sister and brother-in-law and their children. They had not met for ten years. It is easy to imagine his joy at being reunited with the ones he loved so much, and at being in a traditional French household again. They were amazed at the change in his appearance, particularly his face.

The time was all too short; there were long talks about their childhood, and there was so much that Marie wanted to hear from him. But he had to follow that urgent vocation. Burgundy must be left quite soon. "On the day I am ordained, you must come and hear my first Mass," he told his sister.

He went back to Notre-Dame-des-Neiges and went into retreat on September 29th, the Feast of St Michael and All Angels, 1900.

Here is the testimony of one who was ordered by the Father Abbot to teach him how to say Mass.

"He was ordained sub-deacon at Viviers, and a short time

afterwards, Reverend Father Abbot asked me to explain to him the ceremonies of the Mass, and, every morning, in the sacristy, put him through the necessary rehearsal; he added, however, with his subtle smile, 'Arm yourself with patience, my dear friend, for the good Brother is very absent-minded.' Certainly Father Abbot, who was the director of the solitary's conscience, knew very well what he was saying when he warned me affectionately, because I saw for myself my pupil in his distractions, which certainly were not ordinary. At the very first rehearsal, I soon understood that the Brother was performing all the gestures quite mechanically, as if his soul were deep in prayer. How many sessions were necessary, simply for the preliminary prayers at the foot of the altar. The *Introibo ad altare Dei* was enough to plunge the Brother into distractions in the manner of St Ignatius, who at once always began praying as he pronounced these words. Contemplation seized hold of the Brother, and would have lasted a long time had I not put a stop to it. He was completely absorbed in the Unitive Life:* and on the slightest pretext, he would enter into it, in spite of himself."

Charles prepared for the priesthood in a tiny little room in the attics which had a door looking on to a tribune, and from which he could see the high altar, day and night. In that little garret cell, he made his own meals of a dish of beans or a cabbage cooked in water, and one wonders, therefore, how he kept alive at all. Many years later, somebody told how, passing the cell by chance, he had caught a glimpse through the half-open door of the most terrible instruments of penance, enough to make an ordinary man shudder. Charles was to write much later that these retreats showed him quite clearly that this life he had known at Nazareth had to be led amongst the souls who were most sick, most neglected. "This divine banquet of which I was to become a minister, it has to be presented, not to parents and rich neighbours, but to the lame, the blind and the poor, that is to say to souls who have no priest. In my youth I had travelled in Algeria and Morocco. In Morocco, as big as France, with ten million inhabitants, not a single priest in the interior; in the Sahara, seven

* This is a mystical term referring to the last and greatest stage of the contemplative life.

or eight times bigger than France and with many more people than one would have thought in the old days, a dozen missionaries! No people seem to me more bereft than those."

In the course of time he received minor orders, and on June 8th, 1901, which was the eve of his ordination as priest at Viviers, the Abbot, Dom Martin, told him, "I will come with you; bring the necessary provisions for both of us." And they set out together. When it was lunch time, Charles pulled out of his pocket a little parcel and put it on his Abbot's knees: three figs each, two nuts and a bottle of water! After his ordination, he set out that very evening for Notre-Dame-des-Neiges. His sister Mimi had been lodging in a little house just outside the monastery, and when she arrived they gave her a letter from her brother.

"*Ma bonne chérie*,

"Thank you for coming, your arrival touches me to the bottom of my heart. I will return in the night of Sunday to Monday, towards midnight or one o'clock in the morning. Please don't wait up for me, on the contrary go to bed very early, like the Trappists who retire at eight o'clock. When I arrive, I will go straight to the church, to the Blessed Sacrament to whom I owe my first visit. And I will stay in silence and adoration until the next day after my first Mass. You will not be able to speak to me before my first Mass, but afterwards we'll make up for it, *ma chérie*; a community Mass is sung at six o'clock in front of the Blessed Sacrament Exposed; I will be the deacon there. . . . As soon as the High Mass is finished, I will go to the sacristy, put on a chasuble and I will re-appear at the same altar where they will celebrate a High Mass, to say my first Mass; at this one I will give you Holy Communion, through one of the grilles of the little chapel where you will be. . . . After the thanksgiving of my first Mass—three quarters of an hour—an hour afterwards I will go and spend a long time with you. . . . Wait for me in your room at that moment; take care to have a good breakfast after having received Holy Communion. Be assured that your arrival here is a real joy for the whole community which, full of illusions about me, loves me a thousand times more than I deserve, and in particular the good Father Abbot, who is going to Viviers in spite of all he has to do, but he wants to accompany me.

"You are very welcome, *ma chérie*, and I thank you for coming. I kiss you and I love you: with all my heart in the Heart of Jesus.

Brother Albéric."

Charles said his first Mass in a chasuble made for him by Marie de Bondy.

At Viviers, his bishop's hands had been laid upon his head, and he, who had always considered himself too unworthy to be raised to the dignity of a priest, received the power which Christ had bestowed on the twelve Apostles, and which had been handed down, throughout the ages, by His bishops. As Philo remarks: "A fire can light thousands of torches without being in any way impaired." What a fire was lit that June morning! After the ceremonial of the laying on of hands, the bishop made Charles touch a chalice containing wine and a paten with a Host on it, and said to him: "Receive power to offer sacrifice to God and to celebrate Masses for the living and the dead, in the name of the Lord, Amen." Charles rose from his knees, able, as St Peter has said in his first Epistle, "To proclaim the exploits of God, who has called [him] out of darkness into his marvellous light." Now he shared in the Lord's royal power. As St Ambrose has said, "Those are Kings, who have received the grace to utter the word . . . and to charm the souls of the saints."

Pius XI, in his admirable Encyclical on the priesthood, says of the newly ordained priest: "We have been at the feet of a man who represented Jesus Christ . . . we have been there to gain the characteristics of free men and of God's children."

The following morning, Père de Foucauld gave Holy Communion to his sister.

It was an unforgettable moment in the lives of both of them. Charles had always been a most loving brother—*un coeur d'or*—since his childhood. Now he could give his loved Mimi the Perfect Gift, and One which would unite them even more closely through all the vicissitudes of long separation.

CHAPTER 14

Beni Abbès: I

MIMI went home to Barbirey, and Charles, with the aid of his Abbot, made his final preparations for settling in North Africa.

When Charles had been asked to bake some Hosts, he became so greatly lost in contemplation that all the Hosts got burned. But when it came to making practical arrangements for being a priest, missionary and hermit in North Africa, surprisingly he suddenly became intensely practical, and all his training as a soldier and an explorer seemed to come to his aid. The brothers helped him to fill large packing cases, to label them and tie them up with cord. Inside was everything necessary for a chapel, a few books, fifty metres of cord and a pail to get water from desert wells, solid cloth to make a tent and sacks to serve as rugs. The Trappists were broken-hearted to see him go again, for he had grown in holiness in Palestine since they had seen him last, and he had endeared himself to them all, even more.

The Abbé Huvelin wrote to Monseigneur Bazin in North Africa, to tell him about Charles and his heroic devotion, his limitless endurance and his vocation for the Moslem world. Dom Martin, his Abbot, also wrote to say that never in his life had he seen a man who had realized such a high ideal of holiness. "Only in books have I seen such prodigies of penance, humility, poverty and love of God." Charles himself wrote to Monseigneur Bazin asking for permission to make a small public oratory near one of the French garrisons established between Ain-Sefra and Tuat. But not only was he thinking of helping the French soldiers of those regions, but more particularly the Infidels, by bringing into their midst Jesus present in the most Holy Sacrament. In such a way did Mary sanctify the house of John the Baptist when she came into it, carrying Jesus in her womb. Later the Abbé Huvelin wrote to Monseigneur Livinhac, to say that Charles was "hard material, fit for hard labour". His Abbot wrote later to

Monseigneur Bazin, "His is the most beautiful soul I have ever known; of an incredible generosity, he advances with giant strides in the way of sacrifice, and has an insatiable desire to devote himself to the work of the redemption of the Infidel. He is capable of all things . . . he has in him the stuff of several saints. His presence alone will be an eloquent testimony."

The cases were lifted on to a cart, and at length, very much moved, Père de Foucauld said goodbye to his Abbot and his brethren and drove away. As he crossed the sea, he watched the coastline of France getting fainter and fainter, and at length vanishing.

At last he sighted Africa. He was about to realize his life's mission, that for which God had called him from a life of sin to one of penance and prayer. He was returning to Africa to obey God's strange call, to fulfil that destiny for which he had been prepared by his life as a soldier, an explorer, a Trappist and a hermit. He was received for a time at the Maison Carré, the headquarters of the White Fathers, as he had to wait for the necessary permission to establish himself in the south of the province of Oran, near Morocco. Later he met Monseigneur Guérin, who wrote of him, "A true saint like Charles de Jésus will, of course, do good. He cannot help but radiate around him something of the gentleness and goodness of Jesus, who, from henceforth, is all his life."

As we follow Père de Foucauld to North Africa, we see that his vocation was entirely individual, absolutely new in the Church, almost, as it were, conceived especially for him. When God creates a man for a special destiny, He is not afraid to reverse the normal laws of nature. This had been recognized when Charles had ceased to be a Trappist. Dom Sebastian Lyart, Abbot General of the Cistercians, who had personally studied his vocation and recognized its special character, had said to him, "It is no small favour, this permission to follow Our Lord so near, so closely: thank Him very much, very much, very much . . ." Charles was a man thirsting for brotherhood, but whom, on the other hand, God drew unceasingly to solitude.

No life in common, no companion in the desert; in the end death, alone, betrayed.

Charles's entry into the Sahara was dramatic. He was accompanied by several officers, some of whom he had known during his army service. They lent him a horse and together they took the long road from Ain-Safra to Beni Abbès. As they neared Taghit, they were met by Capitaine de Susbielle at the head of a native squadron. He had already told his men, "You are about to see a French *marabout*, a holy man; he comes out of friendship for you: receive him with due honour." De Foucauld galloped towards them, his white robes billowing in the wind, and when he halted by Capitaine de Susbielle, all the natives leaped off their horses and surrounded him, several of them bending low to kiss the hem of his robe.

Beni Abbès, where Charles first settled, was an oasis of seven to eight thousand palm-trees on the left bank of the river Saoura. There was plenty of water, for in the Sahara rivers often go underground for a certain time, and thus avoid evaporation by the sun. They cross the desert as if it were a tunnel, and reappear only at the entrance to an oasis. Charles chose this oasis because he thought it was the right spot for a community of Poor Solitaries, living in adoration of the Blessed Sacrament and doing manual labour; it is so solitary and yet so central, between Algeria, Morocco and the Sahara.

The native population was about twelve to fifteen hundred souls. Père de Foucauld had always called Christ "the Master of the impossible", and indeed it looked to everyone as if he were attempting an impossible task, even bearing in mind the words about missions of the great Pope St Gregory, who had sent St Augustine to Christianize England: "One cannot take away from obstinate spirits all their habits at one go, one cannot reach the summit of a steep mountain in leaps and bounds, but by dragging oneself up step by step."

In those days it was the fashion to say that it was impossible to convert Moslems to Christianity; even the White Fathers, founded by Cardinal Lavigerie, had given up hope and gone further afield, with resounding success. Until the end of his life, one might almost call Charles de Foucauld a sublime failure; but others were to reap where he had sown. He himself realized that he would probably see no results in his own lifetime; he was merely going to prepare the way.

At Beni Abbès there was a garrison encamped on the top of a cliff. It comprised three companies of African sharp-shooters and a company of French light infantry. At once Charles bought a piece of land, unfortunately paying a very high price for it. The territory had several springs and some old wells. He began by clearing the wells and growing fruit and vegetables, enough to help the poor, and particularly the French soldiers and slaves.

For the first few days he lodged in the buildings of the Arab Bureau. He was delighted when some French soldiers came to him and said, "Father, we'll help you to build a house, whenever you want." They looked such good French lads and so honestly pleased to see another Frenchman in their midst, particularly one who was himself a soldier and who so well understood the ways of soldiers. They felt far away from home and had attacks of depression and homesickness.

So they all went out together and picked up stones and started to build with bricks they shaped out of dried earth. The trunks of palm trees served as beams, while reeds and great palm leaves covered a flat roof. Charles described to Marie de Bondy the humble little chapel they made between them. The inside was plastered in dark pearl grey, and there was the wooden altar which Notre-Dame-des-Neiges had given him after he had explained to them exactly what he wanted. He had an oil lamp for his night vigils, and, on the altar, the wooden candlesticks, again given by the generosity of his Abbey. From Marie's chasuble he had made himself, "all alone" he emphasized, a lining for the tabernacle. It only rained about once a year, but the rain, of course, penetrated everything, so he had protected the altar with a canopy of dark green canvas. Above the altar he put up a large picture which he had painted himself of a life-size figure of Christ opening His arms to embrace all men. The floor was desert sand, warm and red. It was an utterly silent place, a solitude, as it were, within the vastness of the desert. He painted fourteen Stations of the Cross to hang on the walls of the nave: they were not done on paper, but on the planks of his wooden packing cases which he had sawn up. He loved this place, and said that it suited him perfectly. On the Epistle side he had put an alarm clock.

To start with, Père de Foucauld slept at the foot of the altar, but after a little while he went into the so-called sacristy which was so short that he could not lie comfortably on the sand. The adjutant of the sharp-shooters told him, "Father, you can't stretch out there", and Père de Foucauld replied, "Jesus on the

Cross did not stretch out." The soldiers, who were much younger than himself, and very clever at making the best out of poor material, worked with a will for this man who was as poor as they were. They had heard all sorts of rumours about his being a great explorer, a Vicomte and a rich man who had renounced everything, but here he worked with them, just as if he were one of themselves. They could not help being impressed by his great kindness, his other-worldliness. A soldier who met him later described his face on his return from a long journey. "On his face, most emaciated, lit by a piercing glance, was reflected an expression which, so to speak, was indefinable, the look of a man who wasn't there at all, whose thoughts were floating elsewhere."

The Moslems, too, were full of admiration. The Moslems, who pray to Allah five times a day, have a great respect for holiness. If a missionary were to live a life of a St Anthony in the desert, they would say he was a saint. Men in the East are puzzled by Christians. Some Indian mystics once said to some Christians, "Where are those who live in silence, content to contemplate God? . . . . But where are those wholly consecrated to silence, who beget silence?"

Not only was Charles bringing France to Africa, that Africa which Gladstone had contemptuously dismissed as a "heap of sand and stones", adding that the French were welcome to keep the Sahara; not only was he bringing French civilization, but above all things he brought the charity of that country which has always been called the elder daughter of the Church. This charity was symbolized in the chasuble which Marie de Bondy had made for him for his ordination and which he had brought to Africa in one of the packing cases. He had asked for it to be white, except for the red heart surmounted by a little brown Cross and yellow flames above the Cross, leaping out of the Heart. The Cross was to be outlined in gold, and the chasuble's lining was old gold also: "It will remind me to be all charity inside, to be lined with charity."

CHAPTER 15

Beni Abbès: 2

WHEN Laperrine saw Charles soon after his arrival at Beni Abbès, he said half laughingly, half ruefully, "That wretched Huvelin, in five seconds he turned my friend Charles inside out and made a monk of him." He would follow the soldiers in single file when they were carrying stones, and help them build the chapel. Soon, they began to love him. And later it was said that both soldiers and officers simply idolized him. In fact, someone said that Père de Foucauld never ceased being a soldier. The long training had penetrated into his whole being.

One day, a young soldier saw him writing in script a text which he was going to hang up in his sacristy. "Live as though you should die today a martyr."

Thinking to distract him from what he thought a sad meditation, the soldier said, "*Mon père*, would you like to come and see how they are digging a well? It might be useful to you in the future."

Charles came at once.

The soldier said enthusiastically, "Oh! the thrilling moment after you have been marching all day, and you are tired out and dying of thirst. You start to dig feverishly; the sand becomes damp, then a little muddy, then a sort of yellow mixture appears, and later, it clears. Salvation—there's water! Do you know the Arab saying about the secret of growing a good date palm?"

"No, tell me."

" 'Feet in the water, face in the sun.' Ah, here we are. I'm glad I caught you early, the divers only work in the morning, for one franc a day, and each man goes down about five times."

Charles and the young soldier watched them at work. The process has been most interestingly described by Anne Fremantle:

Sitting round a fire on dried palm fronds (it was 90° in the shade) were five shivering men, naked except for their ragged breeches, their heads shaved. A sixth was standing over the well which fed a small lake, leaning on a wooden bar from which hung some taut rope; presently the surface of the well was broken and out of the water a shaven head appeared. The watcher seized it and dragged out the owner, panting, teeth chattering.

"He has been to the bottom; with a tiny pick he frees the spring from the sand which stifles it," the guide explained to Charles.

"Is it deep?" asked Charles.

"About ninety feet," replied the guide.

Then up the rope followed a sieve filled with sand, with one pebble in it. Another man prepared to go down; sticking grease into his ears, he was let down on the rope to the surface of the water, and then dived. Charles looked at his watch. One minute, two, three minutes . . . never had time dragged so heavily. Three minutes, ten seconds; the man was up again and his sieve was hauled up after him.

One of the soldiers has told how, very often, Charles would come to their camp at sunset. He was always courteous to the ordinary soldiers, and of course they felt that very keenly. They used to go for walks together and have long talks. Charles wrote home that at Beni Abbès the sunsets were admirable. "Almost every evening the western sky was on fire, and for an hour there were tints of a great beauty, of an ideal gentleness." He said to the young man who accompanied him: "How peaceful and calm it makes you feel! Don't you love this solitude and silence? I love it especially at night, when everything is so serene and the great sky and the vast horizons are lit by the stars; silently they sing in so affecting a manner of the Eternal, the Infinite, the Beyond. I could spend my whole life contemplating them."

"Well, why don't you sleep out of doors, Father, if you love the night sky so much?"

Charles smiled and was silent. He was not going to say that, if he occasionally slipped out for a moment and glanced up at the immense African sky, he would quickly return to his chapel and kneel before the tabernacle in a long night vigil. Nature is nothing compared with the Beloved. The Abbé Huvelin, far ahead of his times, had advised him, long ago, to read St John of the Cross, and Charles himself had given the same counsel to a friend, saying that even a few lines a day would refresh him. That evening, he thought of his two favourite stanzas from "A spiritual canticle", composed when the saint was locked up in his foetid prison cell of Toledo:

> My Belovèd is the Mountains,
> The solitary wooded valleys,
> The strange islands,
> The roaring torrents,
> The whisper of the amorous gales.

> The tranquil night
> At the approaches of the dawn,
> The silent music,
> The murmuring solitude,
> The supper which revives and enkindles love.

The dark came suddenly, Charles lit his lantern and they walked until they reached the neighbourhood of what he called his "Fraternity". Père de Foucauld bent down, felt the ground, and when he found the stones which formed his enclosure, he said: "I can't ask you in any further. Here's the enclosure, I'll see you again quite soon."

One can imagine how touched a soldier was to receive the following letter.

"Dear Friend, you told me that you are sad in the evenings, that your evenings are oppressive. If you are allowed to leave the camp, which I don't know, would you care to come habitually and spend the evenings with me: we will prolong them as long as it is agreeable to you, talking in brotherly fashion about the future, of your children, of your projects . . . of what you desire and hope, for yourself and for those whom you love more than yourself. . . . To make up for anything else, you will find here a brother's heart.

"You said you wanted a little history of St Paul . . . I would very much like to have written this for you, but I can't, I have other urgent things to write at this moment . . . but I could tell it to you, interspersing my wretched words with passages from his letters, which I have got and which are admirable . . .

"The poor man offers you what he has. What he offers you above all is his very tender, very brotherly affection and his profound devotion in the heart of Jesus.

"Brother Charles of Jesus."

That little enclosure of his, even the natives respected it, although so many of them were thieves. If a merchant left his caravan and put his merchandise within the enclosure for the night, the next morning he would find it intact, which, of course, was a miracle. After a time, the line of stones was replaced by wooden stakes. But even so, Charles was interrupted so often that he had to say his Mass at crack of dawn in order to be able to make his thanksgiving in comparative peace; and even then, he had to go out several times in the middle of it. He wanted to be the universal brother of all men, whatever their nationality and class. He wanted to be like the Host which he adored, consumed by the poor.

His hope of founding a small community engaged his attention at first. He hired two natives to be gardeners. They knew how to protect the vegetable seeds from the torrid heat. As these men had to come from quite a long way, Charles asked them to share his meal, but when the *marabout* offered them a piece of barley bread dipped in a kind of desert tea brewed from a Sahara plant, they declared that his régime would kill them off and politely declined to return.

Charles planted young palms, fig trees and even olives and vines. From Vilmorin, the celebrated Parisian seed merchants (who still have their fascinating shop on the *quais* of the Seine) he ordered seeds, and when later he went to the southern Sahara, he listed those which did well there—the Egyptian beetroot, the red carrot of Nantes, the Parisian cucumber, the Brazilian gourd, the Madeira onion, the Cayenne pimento, the Cuban bean. He was very observant, and later was able to help the Touaregs to care for their camels. He wrote in his notes: "In summer, the camel almost always has worms in his nose. Rub the interior of the nostrils with butter and salt." He even told them how to prevent camels from eating poisonous oleanders. One day as he was staring up at a dromedary, a native told him, "Allah has a thousand names, but the last and most mysterious of all, no one knows it except the dromedary. And that's why he looks at us with such a haughty air, us mortals."

Sometimes he accepted invitations to dine in the mess with the officers. But only very rarely; and if he were questioned about his Moroccan exploits, he was so anxious to remain in the background that he would suddenly become silent. There were occasional lapses from this seclusion, for he was a soldier at heart, and always interested in stories of military exploits. One day when he heard about some brigands who had stolen the women of a tribe, and the cattle, and murdered or mutilated the men, he suddenly exclaimed: "We've got to catch up with them and be very tough!" And yet he was the most tender of men, and when he saw a mouse caught by a dog, he whispered: "Poor little beast, what a pity."

In 1902, he wrote his timetable for the Apostolic Prefect of the Sahara:

"I rise at four, that is if I hear the alarm clock, which isn't always! I say the Angelus, the *Veni Creator*, Prime and Terce, and then Mass followed by thanksgiving.

"At six o'clock I take some dates or figs, and give myself the discipline; immediately afterwards an hour of adoration before the Blessed Sacrament. Then manual work or its equivalent, that is to say, correspondence, copying various things, extracts of authors which must be kept, reading aloud or explanations of the catechism to someone or other until eleven o'clock. At eleven, I say Sext and Nones, I have a short time for prayer, examine my conscience until half past eleven.

"At half past eleven a meal.

"Midday. The Angelus and the *Veni Creator*, this last is sung. You would laugh if you heard me sing! Without meaning to, I have certainly invented a new tune.

"The afternoon is wholly for God, before the Blessed Sacrament, except for an hour devoted to necessary conversations, answers given here and there, the kitchen, the sacristy, etc., household needs and alms-giving . . .

"From noon till half past twelve, Adoration; from half past twelve to one-thirty, the Way of the Cross and several vocal prayers. I read a chapter of the Old and a chapter of the New Testament, and a portion of the Imitation and several pages of some spiritual author; St Teresa or St John Chrysostom, St John of the Cross succeed each other perpetually.

"From one-thirty to two, a written meditation on the Gospel.

"From two to two-thirty, moral or dogmatic theology.

"From two-thirty to three-thirty, an hour kept for the catechumens.

"From three-thirty to five-thirty, Adoration; it is the best moment of the day, after Mass and the night vigils; work is finished, I say to myself that there is nothing more to do than to look at Jesus . . . it is an hour full of sweetness.

"At five-thirty, Vespers, at six o'clock collation.

"At seven o'clock, explanation of the Gospel to some soldiers, prayer and Benediction of the Blessed Sacrament . . . followed by the Angelus and the *Veni Creator*. Then the soldiers go, after we've had a little conversation out of doors; I recite the Rosary and I say Compline, if I have not been able to say it before the little explanation of the Gospel. And then I go to sleep towards half past eight.

"At midnight I get up, that is when I hear the alarm clock, I sing the *Veni Creator* and I recite Matins and Lauds; that also is a very precious moment: alone with the Belovèd in the deep silence in that Sahara, under the vast sky, that hour alone with Him is supreme joy. I go back to bed at one o'clock."

> Come Holy Ghost, our souls inspire
> And lighten with celestial fire,
> Thou the anointing Spirit art,
> Who dost thy sevenfold gifts impart.

One of the greatest trials for Charles, whose contemplative soul was always yearning for solitude, was to be interrupted all the time because he adhered to his rule of charity. Of course he was imposed upon, particularly by the slaves employed by the Arabs. The nomad, the Arab from the desert, found work degrading and left it to his women and his slaves whom he treated very badly. The black slaves came to show Charles their branded cheeks, their raw and bleeding backs, their wounded ankles. Charles wrote to his relations, "They are subjected to daily beatings, gross overwork, and if they attempt to escape, they are shot in both legs. And when their work is done, they are expected to roam around and pick up what food they can find. There is no remedy but enfranchisement. The natives know we do not allow slavery at home and that we forbid it in Algeria; therefore they say we are frightened and daren't abolish it, and they both fear and despise us."

These slaves were the worst wastrels. They were liars and thieves, profligate, and extremely idle, but Charles became their servant. He reserved a room for them in the house of the brotherhood, himself washed their filthy rags, provided them with whatever food he could possibly scratch up, and tried to comfort them. He even cleaned their room, and it was then that he found lice. We have his written resolution about vermin. When he was examining his conscience at Beni Abbès, he accused himself of fearing dirt and vermin. And he resolved not to fear the slaves' lice, not to seek out lice, but not to be frightened of them, to behave as if they did not exist. "When I catch them, I rid myself of them as best I can, but without excessive speed, so that I don't let them get into the church vestments, and I must not fear to catch more in future."

And all that from a fastidious man who in his young days had had a daily bath, who had frequented the best barbers, shoemakers and tailors of Saumur, and in Paris always dressed in the height of fashion.

On October 29th, 1901, he was able to write triumphantly: "Celebrated for the first time Mass at Beni Abbès. Ex-voto of Our Lady of Africa." At Christmas-tide he wrote: "First time that the Blessed Sacrament was exposed for ten hours."

He was simply delighted with the good will and the completely unhoped-for piety of these poor soldiers who had helped him build.

He always said the Sunday Mass at a time which would suit the soldiers. This was remembered a long time afterwards, and one of them said, "If we had asked him to say it at four in the morning or at midday, he would always have said 'yes'. And what a Mass! The man who has not assisted at that Mass does not know what a Mass is. When he pronounced the *Domine non sum dignus*, it was with such an expressive voice that one wanted to weep with him."

Then, in January 1902, he started to buy slaves. The first one was called Joseph du Sacré-Coeur, and directly news of his emancipation became known, other slaves would beg Charles to do the same for them, and Charles sent pitiful demands for money to his French relations. Of course, the Arab Bureau would have nothing to do with all that, because it was against all the customs of the country. Up to date, the French occupying forces had tolerated slavery; this passion of Charles's was quite a new thing in colonial administration and caused a great deal of annoyance. Unfortunately, in the long run, Charles found his slaves very disappointing, particularly the second one he bought called Paul Embarek, who was about fifteen years of age and who caused him nothing but trouble. Financially, the White Fathers would occasionally help Charles, and so would the officers of Beni Abbès.

He himself lived on bread and water, which cost him seven francs a month. He would not accept any offerings for Masses, although he had been urged to do so by the Abbot of Notre-Dame-des-Neiges. He believed it would be much more perfect not to.

He said, "I want all the inhabitants, whether Christians, Moslems, Greeks, Jews or idolaters, to look upon me as their brother, the universal brother. They begin to call the house the fraternity, the *Khaoua* in Arabic. I find that very consoling." He also said once, that it is in loving men that one learns to love God. And, like St Irenaeus, he believed that one could find in every soul the trace of the divine fingers. He preached his Gospel both to his relatives in France and to the French officers and soldiers around Beni Abbès.

One day, one of the officers called on him: "Come and see something very odd that is happening near us." And he took him to watch a big lizard fighting a rattlesnake in a soap box. "You see, Father, this is a favourite Saharan sport."

Charles looked horrified.

"I interrupted you when I came to fetch you; what were you doing?"

"I was taking my little recreation. I believe very much in working with my hands, so I was carving some wooden dishes." He took him back to his narrow little sacristy where his writing desk was a wooden packing case. "I like to feel that I am using the same kind of tools as Jesus and Joseph."

The soldier sat down by him and watched him at work. His appearance was not very prepossessing, for his white tunic was too short, full of holes and not too clean, but on the breast was a red heart surmounted by a Cross. His hands were very worn.

The officer said, "I am told that you have dismissed the orderly who helped you with the housework."

Charles replied simply, "The Master had no orderly."

"Well," said the officer, "you're certainly not like the Arabs, who just let things slide. Everything is beautifully neat and tidy here, and I do congratulate you on the way you've filed your papers."

Charles said smilingly, "And yet I rather admire the extraordinary detachment of the Arabs. They don't even mend their tents when they're falling to pieces. They simply enjoy existing, basking in the sun. In my young days, I thought I enjoyed life intensely, but certainly never as much as those Arabs."

The officer said, "Well, I suppose their whole philosophy is a total acceptance of everything that happens, because it is ordained by Allah; that's why they surrender everything to him."

Charles said, "They despise us completely."

The officer said, "Yes, I know. I heard them talking about you the other day, and somebody said, 'How terrible it is to think of a man so good, so charitable, going to Hell because he's not a Moslem.'"

Charles said, "All our African missionary problems are much hindered by the paganism of the French people who come out here. Some of them are atheists, and indeed I've heard North Africans say how strange it is that these French, who are supposed to be Christians, despise the natives, get drunk and go to brothels. Above all, they don't pray." A draught blew a paper on to the sand and the officer picked it up. "Oh," said Charles, "thank you. I must put it into the box file marked 'Illnesses and Remedies'." Charles's handwriting had completely altered since his conversion. When he was a young man of the world in Paris, writing on expensive writing paper with a coronet at the top, a graphologist said that his handwriting showed all the signs of snobbery and elegance. It had been slanting, now it was upright, small, neat and disciplined. He glanced at the paper. "Yes, I am trying to pick up all the information I can. This one is how to look after the dromedary when he's wounded in the mountain paths. You have to wash the wounds with permanganate, and then you sprinkle them with powdered charcoal. You mustn't forget a double ration of date stones, which he loves."

The officer said, his eyes gleaming with admiration, "You are several men rolled into one. I really don't know how you get through your day's work. What's that odd bundle hanging down from your waist, Father?"

Charles laughed. "Well, you see, I can't really afford good writing paper, so I use all the envelopes which come to me from France or elsewhere. I cut them out neatly and slip a piece of string through them, and I tie it round my waist. I always carry a pencil out of doors. I take notes in ink when I get home."

"I see you use purple ink."

"Yes," said Charles, "It's cheaper than black."

"If you don't mind my saying so, Father," said the officer, "I think you waste your time on the slaves. They have all the vices imaginable, and they just impose on you, as they think you're gullible."

Charles said, "Yes, but just think of their lot. They have no hope, no friends. You must remember that the first Christian communities of Rome were formed mostly of slaves. It was so often the slaves who converted their masters and mistresses, as in the story of St Perpetua and St Felicitas, martyred at Carthage. And both mistress and slave girl finished up together on the same day in the arena, to offer their lives to God." Charles lifted his splendid eyes and they shone with enthusiasm. "Think how wonderful to give your life to God in that way!"

"Oh, don't talk of dying yet," laughed the officer, "you've got so much to do."

Charles replied, "That is true. One of the principal things I want to do is to found the Little Brothers of the Sacred Heart of Jesus. I was already thinking about this religious family in the Holy Land. They won't be exactly missionaries, but they will form a cloistered family, vowed to adore the Sacred Host Exposed day and night. They will have no financial security, but will live in poverty and work. They won't preach except by their silence, which is always more eloquent than words. They will be adoring souls bringing the Master to the Infidel. If just the very touch of the hem of Christ's garment could heal a sick woman, think how much His very presence in the Sahara could do! I can't tell you what it meant to me to say Mass here for the first time. I couldn't believe it; here I was holding Our Lord in my wretched hands. He put Himself into my hands. Shall I tell you why I love Rome so much?"

"Please do," said the officer.

"It is because there are more tabernacles in Rome than anywhere else in the world. The Body of Jesus is in all those tabernacles. One of my dreams has been to build in the Sahara a little chapel like the Roman one called *Domine quo vadis?* in the Via Appia. It's on the spot where tradition says that St Peter, fleeing from Rome and martyrdom under Nero, met the Lord and asked Him where He was going, and Christ replied, 'I am going to Rome to be martyred in your place.' Think of the thousands and thousands of Christians in Rome who have loved God. I love Rome so much that I say my breviary according to the Roman rite. It is a way of being united to all those souls in the past and in the present in the Eternal City. And then, after thinking about the tabernacles of Rome, my mind wanders to the immense wastes where the Saviour has never been in the Blessed Sacrament. I hunger to give Him to all these men. Just think, *mon capitaine*, they are dying every day, and many of them will go to Hell, these souls bought at so great a price, with the blood of the Saviour. In a vision the Poor Clare St Colette saw souls falling into Hell like huge drifts of snowflakes in a winter storm. If only God would send me a companion or two to help me in my work!"

The officer said nothing, but thought much. He realized that Charles would make a bad founder of a religious Order, just as the Abbé Huvelin had said a long time ago. He was inimitable, his austerities were too great. A man of tremendous strength of will and iron health, he perhaps did not realize that others could not follow him, and he expected too much of them. The dreadful food, for example, and the very early rising and the entire lack of recreation. He would forget that his companions were mortal men, and not yet disembodied spirits.

There is every likelihood that at this period God was sending Charles extraordinary and exceptional graces in Communion and prayer. Of course he never spoke of this, but he once, so to speak, 'let the cat out of the bag'. Somebody came to make a short call; when he left, he apologized for leaving him alone; Charles replied quickly, without thinking, "Oh, but I'm never alone." It

is like the flashing reply of the saintly Curé d'Ars who once acci-
dentally revealed that he was not always "sleeping on straw", in
other words, in the middle of his trials and austerities, God sometimes came to console him.

But even the hardest will and the strongest health have their
limits. Charles began to suffer from high temperatures, and the
soldiers immediately became anxious. The military doctor called
and gave him the right medicines, and all the officers saw to it
that their goats' milk should go to him, also jam, coffee, tea and
other things which he had not seen for a long time. Charles was
very surprised that they took so much care of him. He felt so
useless, so worthless. He little knew how much the Army loved
him. Men came back to the Faith of their childhood through him.
Four men of the garrison who died during a period of great heat
all received the Last Sacraments from him.

In the Christmas of 1902, Charles got a delightful surprise. A
porter came to the door of his hut with a carefully wrapped
parcel, which had been brought to the local bureau by the don-
keys. "A Christmas present for you, Father," he said.

Charles said, "Who can it be from? From the East? People
remember me there?" Indeed, it was from the Poor Clares of
the Holy Land, who remembered this beggar who had been their
servant and whom they had always looked upon as a saint. The
parcel was poor and very moving. It contained relics of the saints,
little stones from the Holy Sepulchre at Jerusalem or from the
Rock of the Nativity at Bethlehem, and then there were those
gifts which only nuns' delicate fingers knew how to make so
beautifully. There were all the flowers of the Holy Land deftly
arranged in the form of posies and stuck on to parchment leaves.
There were also some more mundane presents, a wooden spoon,
a mousetrap and a length of white cotton material. Charles was
delighted. The porter took one glance at his miserable tunic, and
on his way home he called on his regimental tailor and said, "I
advise you to go to the hermitage, you'll find some work there."
But, alas, he got there too late. Charles had given the piece of
material away, and the tailor saw a small black boy running out
of the hermitage wrapped up in the spotless white stuff, jumping
up and down with glee.

Another present caused Charles a great deal of amusement. An
officer who looked after the rations of the oases had noticed, on

the platform of the station of Oran, a small barrel addressed to the Reverend Père de Foucauld at Beni Abbès, and immediately concluded, "Oh, it must be some Mass wine. I am sure it will turn sour in the heat, and the journey won't do it any good. It will reach the poor Father in a terrible state." So quickly he put the barrel in the shade in a store room. A kindly official agreed to souse it several times a day with buckets of cold water. And then, when it was put on the train from Oran to Beni Ounif, and at length placed on the camel going to Beni Abbès, never had a barrel been so well looked after. It was even wrapped in wool. At last, when the caravan halted at the Fraternity, the precious barrel was carefully unloaded.

"Here is your Mass wine, *mon père*."

"But I never ordered any."

"Well, they're sending you some. Look at the address."

Charles opened the barrel, and what was the astonishment of everyone to see that it was not Mass wine at all. It was a big bell whose clapper had been wrapped in rags! Charles was delighted, and hung it up at once on the little rectangular tower of the chapel.

And so he rang the hours, ten o'clock, midnight, four o'clock in the morning. The desert air is very clear, and sounds carry far. Sometimes the soldiers began to regret that the bell had ever come to Beni Abbès. On the other hand, if they did happen to hear it ringing in the middle of the night, it reminded them of many goodly things, and some lonely French soldier, far away from his native village, would recall the sound of bells wafted across the French fields, summoning him to Mass on Sunday morning. Or he would think of this man of the world who had left everything, beloved family, devoted friends, fame and riches, who was now keeping his night vigil before the Blessed Sacrament, burning with love for the Beloved, and consumed with a vast love for the whole of mankind.

In March 1903, Charles's old friend, Henri Laperrine, came to Beni Abbès. Five years previously he had been made head of all the oases in the Sahara. There has been much speculation as to whether Laperrine used Charles or whether Charles used Laperrine. It would be more fitting to say that these two great men combined in the service of North Africa and of the Sahara. These two were meant to understand one another, although

Laperrine with his spotless and immaculate appearance always remained a man of the world, even in the desert. Laperrine had, too, a great gift of sympathy and a very kind heart; he was also very ascetic, for even after he had ridden eighty kilometres he would, after quickly drinking a cup of tea, immediately sit down at the table in his tent and answer his voluminous correspondence at once. He was the only man in his entourage who was never asleep during the hour of siesta. Henri Laperrine soon realized that Charles was not only a contemplative monk, but also able to give him accurate information about any desert subject. Laperrine for his part took Charles to remote parts of Africa where he could never have penetrated alone. He vowed that he would establish his friend as the first curé of the Hoggar, which is in the southern Sahara on the road to Timbuktu.

These two Frenchmen, who were friends for forty years, understood one another very well. They shared a common understanding of the civilizing role of France. And though Laperrine sometimes did not practise his religion, his early training by the Dominicans of Sorèze influenced the rest of his life. He always spoke of anything to do with religion with profound respect. Laperrine understood perfectly that the roots of French civilization lay in her Catholicism. And at that moment Catholicism was being ruthlessly suppressed in France by the Combes Government. Religious orders had to leave the country and seek refuge elsewhere. The teaching of religion was not allowed in state schools. The Moslems of North Africa were essentially religious, and very soon came to despise the type of French colonial sent out to them. All this republicanism and talk of liberty and the rights of the citizen were no good to the Arab, with his spirit of insubordination. All that he would learn from republican France could only encourage his natural vices, his temptations to rebellion, which were rooted in his very nature, his race and his religion. And then this unwise idea, in liberty's name, of allowing the Moslems to build more mosques, when the experience of fourteen centuries has shown that hatred of the Christian grows as the Arabs learn the Koran. Laperrine saw that Christian charity was glowing in the eyes of his ragged little hermit. So they both planned a campaign of helping the Moslems, by first making friends with them.

Charles hesitated some time before he accepted Laperrine's

invitation to go on his first expedition with him. But by now he had almost given up hope of having companions at Beni Abbès. Latterly, he had had some great disappointments. Two Fathers and two Brothers of the Trappist monastery of Staouëli, having spoken rather vaguely of imitating and following Charles and making him their Superior in Africa, must have been rather discouraged when, at the end of a long letter, Charles asked them if they were ready to have their heads chopped off or to die of hunger. Hardly a question calculated to attract new recruits.

He would have been more dismayed had he known of the correspondence between his African superior Monseigneur Guérin, and the Abbot of Notre-Dame-des-Neiges. The Abbot wrote: "I must confess that I have some doubts about his prudence and his discretion. The austerities which he practises, and which he thinks he can impose on his companions, are of such a nature that I feel obliged to believe that the beginner would succumb quite quickly. Moreover, the intense application of mind which he imposes on himself, and which he wants to impose on his disciples, seems to be so superhuman that I fear he would make his disciples go mad by this excessive intensity, before killing them off by excess of austerities."

The Abbot of Staouëli himself had said that his life was more admirable than imitable.

No companion! And above all, no converts except an old, blind native woman called Marie, whom he received into the Catholic Church on what he thought was her deathbed. He wrote asking for prayers "for this poor old negro woman whose soul is so white, and who, this evening, would be in Paradise if she died now".

Paul Embarek, whom he had baptized, turned out to be most unreliable, and Joseph, another slave whom he had bought back, had fled. Pondering sadly on these examples of base and disheartening ingratitude, Charles recalled the behaviour of Our Lord towards Judas Iscariot.

After Laperrine's temporary departure, Charles had the great joy of at last meeting his ecclesiastical superior, Monseigneur Guérin, who arrived towards the end of May, and who received a warm welcome from Charles at the Fraternity. Charles laughingly asked him to bring his chef, otherwise he would kill him off with his own attempts at cooking. During the five days that he was there they had long talks, which Charles recorded in his diary. He noted how Monseigneur Guérin had said, "All souls are made for the light, for Jesus, all are His heritage, and not one man, if he is a man of good will, is incapable of knowing Him and loving Him." He told Charles that he must allow himself to be seen quite often by the Moslems, and that if only Christians were holy, it would be a silent form of preaching.

Charles himself, in his young days, had experienced this by the silent presence of his cousin Marie de Bondy.

On June 24th, he wrote to Monseigneur Guérin asking for permission to install himself amid the Touaregs, where he would pray and study the language and translate the Gospels. Above all he would get in touch with the Touareg people and live without an enclosure. Every year he would go north to make his confession.

On June 29th, he wrote to Laperrine telling him of this project, and asking for his permission, and this he received on July 22nd. On the previous July 13th, he had already got leave from the Abbé Huvelin. On August 1st, he received a letter from Monseigneur Guérin, asking for time to think it all over.

Providentially, it was a good thing that there was a pause. At three in the morning of July 16th, two hundred Berbers, mounted on camels, had attacked a detachment of fifty Algerian sharpshooters and killed twenty-two of them. Reprisals were swift and successful. And then more terrifying rumours spread throughout the desert, all of which, of course, reached Charles. He realized that Taghit was in greater danger than other places, and begged to be allowed to go there. He even removed the Blessed Sacrament from the tabernacle of his chapel, and held himself in readiness for swift action. For six days, no news came to Beni Abbès. But the great storm cloud was drawing nearer. Nine thousand Berbers were on the march, commanded by one of France's most dangerous enemies. Most of them were armed with guns. The French could oppose only 470 men and two cannon. During the last days of August, the garrison of Taghit fought furiously and emerged victorious. Charles was to write to the Marquise de Foucauld, "It is the finest feat of arms in Algeria for the last forty years."

He regretted bitterly that he was not allowed to go and fight. There were twenty-one wounded at Taghit. Another battle followed, and forty-nine wounded men were moved to Taghit. Three days later, at seven in the morning, the news of this encounter reached Beni Abbés, and Charles went to the Bureau of

Native Affairs, renewed his demand as military chaplain of the Sahara, and this time he was allowed to set off to minister to the wounded men. The Arab Bureau lent him a horse, an Arab hooded cloak and some spurs. When somebody suggested that he ought to be under escort, as it was very dangerous and there might be men lurking behind the sand dunes prepared for revenge, the Captain of the Arab Bureau replied that no one would attack him, for the *marabout* was sacred. He travelled the whole day and the whole night in order to cross the 120 kilometres which separated Beni Abbès from Taghit. He got there at nine o'clock in the morning.

There occurred a disagreeable incident which would have discouraged any other man. A German called Hans Held, seeing this rather unprepossessing hermit who had come to them, led a burst of ribald song, and then started to grumble about "that dog of a priest, that pig of a priest!" Charles was nothing daunted. He said, "No, I am not a pig, I am just a poor little mole who works underground." And lo and behold! When Sunday came, each one of the forty-nine men received Holy Communion at Charles's hands. He was particularly kind to the German, because he thought he was the most seriously wounded and the least pleasant of the lot. After a while, he even managed to conciliate him by his gentleness. In the end, Hans Held was always calling out for him, sometimes to tell him rather ribald stories.

When Charles returned to Beni Abbès, he again took up the subject of going to the Hoggar. He wrote to the Abbé Huvelin to say that in that region the French soldiers never heard Mass and the Moslems never saw a minister of Jesus. And then to his amazement, he expressed almost a repugnance for further travel. Although he was ashamed of it, he admitted that he shivered at the thought of leaving Beni Abbès, of abandoning the calm at the foot of his altar. He now had developed an excessive horror of journeys. Restlessness had vanished.

On January 13th, the convoy had to leave for Touat and the Tidikelt. He had been accustomed to say that fear was a sign of duty to be done, so he went.

CHAPTER 16

Journey to the Hoggar

AND so he left on January 13th, 1904. He took with him Paul, a she-ass carrying the chapel and the provisions, a little donkey which carried nothing, some new sandals and two pairs of *espadrilles*. Capitaine Regnault, afraid that he might get tired out, had ordered a horse for him, but Charles persevered in his idea that he should walk behind the she-ass. The sand was so scorching that his feet felt as if they were on fire.

Capitaine Dinaux described Charles on the march: "Charles walked fast, bent almost double, pulling along one of his baggage camels, while Paul led the other. His emaciated face, with a straggly beard which he trimmed himself with a pair of scissors, was illuminated by his deep-set eyes with their penetrating glance and his wide smile. He wore sandals made of camel skin, of his own making, which he fastened as did the Saharan shepherds, with a thong between his toes."

In the carefully packed baggage were some medicines, a few presents for the Touareg women, writing materials and the Saharan ink which is a mixture of camel urine and charcoal. With his usual thoroughness, Charles had learned about Touareg illnesses—venereal disease, dysentery, eye trouble—and he had brought the appropriate remedies; even opium pills to relieve pain. After marching for eighteen days, the convoy reached Adrar on February 1st, and there Laperrine advised him to go to Akabli for three weeks to learn the Touareg language, and to wait until he fetched him to continue his journey. He stayed there for the appointed three weeks, working with all his might.

Monseigneur Guérin had given him an unusual permission for celebrating his Mass on these long journeys. If he wished, he could say it one hour after midnight. Once he wrote in his diary that he could not say Mass because of a wind storm. This is how such a storm has been described by Père Pichon:

"On the sixth day Foucauld looks at the barometer, and he finds that it is very low. It is hotter than usual, and instead of grilling, you suffocate. The dromedaries look as if they've been seized with madness: they go at full speed straight in front of them, or else they turn in circles and brusquely go backwards, dropping their rider over their twisted mouths. . . .

"A little breeze comes, which fills one with delight, for it allays the sufferings of the caravan. Laperrine takes advantage of it to give his orders very quickly. The tents are solidly pitched, and behind their cloth walls the camels are housed; they are snug in this shelter against the wind. A kind of anguish keeps all the men silent. Then the tents are closed as carefully as possible, and the men lie down in them, covering their faces, and they wait motionless and speechless. . . . They are only just in time. The breeze suddenly falls, and from the far horizon springs a great fiery-coloured cloud, brandishing its thongs, and which soon darts up in the sky and fills the firmament with livid reflections. . . . At once the wind rises again—not the breeze of a short time back, but a furious blast, formidable, incessant, which projects horizontally millions of grains of sand . . . and millions of stones, like bullets. Under this scourging, the eyes burn, the whole body is wounded, the sand gets into your teeth, and your lungs are choking. Beasts and men remain always motionless, deadly silent: to open one's eyelids or one's lips would be to die, and the only voice which can be heard is the great clamour, the inhuman howling of the wind, rising ceaselessly from Hades into the sky. . . .

[After it is over] ". . . Men rinse their mouths carefully. Outside, the tents, the harnesses, the cases appear all covered with a thick coat of dust, yellow green, almost white, the only trace of the cataclysm.

". . . The men are very weary. They go on foot so as not to exhaust their mounts; the camels walk with short steps, their humps collapsing, their ribs sticking out, with difficulty following the camel driver who pulls them by a ring in the right nostril. Sometimes a beast lies down. The caravan continues. And then the men themselves stumble. Some of them drop down, and Laperinne straps them on to one of the dromedaries who is not sick. All the men have dry throats, the inside of the mouth is like parchment and all swollen. The glands give only very little saliva; the men feel their arteries beating madly. They imagine they see in the torrid distance lakes of a very pale blue, and their thirst becomes a conflagration ... their mind conceives only one idea: to drink ... to drink ... Already a man goes to one of the dromedaries which has dropped down, his dagger in his hand, to open a vein and quench his thirst with its blood: but the dromedary is no more, and the man will suck his own blood and then his urine, and then he'll die.... Carrion birds fly quietly around, circling lower and lower...."

Such an atrocious thirst is indeed an assassin. It even drew a cry of agony from Christ on the Cross. It made Charles's austerity in this respect seem absolutely heroic. He had insisted on going on foot, until Laperrine said he really must ride, because the convoy could not proceed at his pace and he was holding everything up. One day, after a terrible sirocco, an officer, guessing that Père de Foucauld had had no water for several hours, brought him some in a leather bottle, full to the brim. "Father," he said, "here is some good fresh water," and he poured him out a goblet full. Père de Foucauld was about to bring the cup to his parched mouth when, just as he was dipping his lips into it, brusquely he pulled himself up and pushed it away. "No," he said. "You want me to fall back into my old sin of gluttony. Take back this water, I don't want it." And as he said this, he threw the water to the ground, and they had to take away the goat skin.

At Beni Abbès, when Capitaine de Susbielle reproached him for his fasting, Père de Foucauld replied, "When you want to write on a blackboard, you have first to wipe out all that has been written on it before. I have plenty to wipe out on my blackboard, I can tell you."

The nights in the Sahara can be icily cold, in fact one can hear the cracking of the rocks when their crevices are split by ice, and can see small fragments of rock being shot on to the sand because of the sudden change of temperature. Charles's superior, Monseigneur Guérin, had provided him with a warm woollen vest for these nights. Charles accepted it, but the next day, gave it back: he said that he was providing for the old Adam.

On these preliminary journeys, when he wanted to become familiar with his surroundings and its inhabitants, Charles wrote in his meditations: "Why should I establish myself in this

country, and how?" Reply. "Silently, secretly, like Jesus of Nazareth, obscurely, like He did, poorly, laboriously, humbly, gently,
disarmed and dumb before injustice as He was, allowing myself to
be mown down and immolated, just as He was, without resisting
or speaking."

On all his journeys, in spite of being almost always absorbed in
contemplation, he noted and scribbled down on his little torn
envelopes many things which might be useful to future missionaries. His charity of course was inspired by the Cistercian tradition of agriculture, of which the monks of the Middle Ages were
the pioneers in Christendom, in the way they went through
swamps and thick forests, breaking up the soil for tillage. And so
he wrote a little booklet which reviewed his five months of travel,
his conversations with the natives and the officers. It was called
Notes on the Journeys of Missionaries in the Sahara. Incidentally,
one sees that he envisaged a convoy of Little Brothers, unaccom-
panied by the Army or by a Laperrine who insisted on him
riding a horse or a camel, for he said in his Rule that "the missionaries would make the greater part of their journeys on foot,
to imitate Our Lord, and for love of penance, abjection and
poverty, and to spare their animals and economize on the purse
of Jesus and that of the poor". In conversations with the natives,
he insisted that one should never preach to them or enter into
theological discussions, as yet. One should stay in the domain of
natural theology, and on the whole not explain Christian dogmas:
one should not throw one's pearls to swine.

His pity went out particularly to those who seemed most unworthy—the slaves without families, who had neither chastity
nor probity nor truth nor kindness, and the young negro slave
women who were used by the Touaregs for their sexual pleasures.
That is why he was so anxious, gently but progressively, to help
the slaves and finally to suppress slavery.

That first reconnaissance journey completely exhausted him.
His eyes sank deep into their sockets, he became very thin and
wrinkled, in fact his whole body looked as if it had shrivelled.
And yet, when he once admitted to one of his French friends that
he was tired, he added, "Yes, I need rest, but not in the sense
that you imagine; it is not the material solitude which weighs
heavily on me, but the spiritual solitude: several days of silence at
the foot of the tabernacle, that is what I need!" He took six

weeks' rest at the end of 1904 at Ghardaïa, surrounded by the silent friendship of Monseigneur Guérin and his missionaries. They got quite a shock when they saw him, for he looked like some dervish mendicant. But for his eyes, which were full of joy, and his glorious smile, he was almost unrecognizable.

He gave his superior his translation of the Four Gospels into the Touareg language, at which he had worked during the long marches and even at night in his tent.

During his stay at Ghardaïa, he avoided walking in the narrow alleyways and the streets, for his reputation had gone before him, and some of the notables of the region came to beg for the favour of being received by "him who has sold this world for the next". Some of them used to peep through his window to see him at work or at prayer; when eventually one of them called on him, he was extremely impressed. He reported: "When I came in, he said to me: 'May the Lord be with thee!' and that moved my heart." Sometimes the little Arab children used to climb on to each other's backs in order to boast that they had caught a glimpse of him through his window. In early January of 1905, he was back at Beni Abbès. And there he had to break his law of silence to receive Maréchal Lyautey—who had become even more distinguished-looking with the passing of the years, with his hooked nose, bright eyes, and white moustache. Much later, he told René Bazin about this famous meeting:

"We dined together with the officers on the Saturday in the reception room. After dinner they turned on a gramophone and put on some of the songs of Montmartre. I was looking at Foucauld, saying to myself, 'He'll go out now'. He didn't go out, he was even laughing. The next day, Sunday, at seven o'clock, the officers and I assisted at Mass in the hermitage. A hovel, that hermitage! His chapel, a miserable corridor with columns, covered with reeds! For altar, a plank! For decoration a calico panel painted with a picture of Christ, the candlesticks of tin plate! Our feet were on sand. Well! I've never heard a Mass said in the way that the Père de Foucauld said his. I thought I was in the Egyptian desert of the early days. It remains one of the great experiences of my life."

CHAPTER 17

Tamanrasset

THE invitation to return to the Touareg country came again from Laperrine in April 1905, when he asked Père de Foucauld to spend the summer in the Hoggar with Capitaine Dinaux. As a letter to the Abbé Huvelin reveals, Charles hesitated a little. He still had a lingering hope of bringing at least one Little Brother of the Sacred Heart to the Fraternity of Beni Abbès. But when, at the end of April, Père Guérin sent him a telegram urging him to accept the invitation, and when the Abbé Huvelin also wired his approval, Charles left his cherished Beni Abbès and started on another of those long and arduous journeys which he had begun to dread more and more.

On June 8th, he found Capitaine Dinaux waiting for him near a well in the region of the Touat. He was accompanied by four French civilians: an explorer-geographer, a geologist, a writer, Pierre Mille, and an inspector of posts and telegraphs. This post office official, Monsieur Etiennot, took an instant dislike to Charles, and on every possible occasion tried to make him appear ridiculous. Sometimes he sang bawdy songs within earshot. Charles of course took no notice, but one day when the heat was scorching after a sandstorm, Charles offered him some water. Etiennot grabbed it and then said, "Pooh, it stinks."

Charles used to follow the convoy on foot, his head down, wrapped in his customary silence. The Jesuit poet Gerard Manley Hopkins sang:

> Elected Silence, sing to me
> And beat upon my whorlèd ear,
> Pipe me to pastures still and be
> The music that I care to hear.
>
> Shape nothing, lips, be lovely-dumb:
> It is the shut, the curfew sent
> From there where all surrenders come
> Which only makes you eloquent.

Be shellèd, eyes, with double dark
And find the uncreated light:
This ruck and reel which you remark
Coils, keeps, and teases simple sight.

Palate, the hutch of tasty lust,
Desire not to be rinsed with wine:
The can must be so sweet, the crust
So fresh that come in fasts Divine.

O feel-of-primrose hands, O feet
That want the yield of plushy sward,
But you shall walk the golden street
And you unhouse and house the Lord.

And, Poverty, be thou the bride
And now the marriage feast begun,
And lily-coloured clothes provide
Your spouse not laboured at nor spun.

The Sahara matched that silence in his soul which was so precious
to him. That is why he always walked at the end of the convoy.
He loved his few hours alone at night, in his tent. This got on the
nerves of the post office official, who had the impertinence to put
his head through his tent one night and say, "Well, Brother
Charles, silent as usual." And then came the soft reply, "I have a
horror of wind-bags."

Charles has written, "It is in solitude, in this life alone with
God, in this deep withdrawal of the soul, which forgets all created
things, that God gives Himself wholly to the one who thus offers
himself entirely to Him. One must cross the desert and live there
to receive God's grace. It is there that one can drive away from
oneself all that is not God. The senses have a horror of pain, Faith
blesses pain as the bridal crown which unites it to the Beloved."

The Rule of Africa is silence. Just as the monk in the cloister
keeps silence, so the desert in its white cowl is hushed. This secret
of the desert was closed to Monsieur Etiennot. Charles simply
irritated him, and at night he must have wanted to curse when he
caught him star-gazing.

"The heavens declare the glory of the Lord." O those stars of
Africa, how they pull you into the eternal regions. Gerard Manley
Hopkins expressed this so movingly:

Look at the stars! Look, look up at the skies!
O look at all the fire-folk sitting in the air!
The bright boroughs, the circle-citadels there!
Down in dim woods the diamond delves! the elves' eyes!
The grey lawns cold where gold, where quickgold lies!
Wind-beat whitebeam! Airy abeles set on a flare!
Flake-doves sent floating forth at a farmyard scare!
Ah well! it is all a purchase, all is a prize.

Buy then! bid then!—What?—Prayer, patience, alms, vows.
Look, look: A May-mess, like on orchard boughs!
Look! March bloom, like a mealed-with-yellow sallows!
These are indeed the barn; withindoors house,
The shocks—This piece-bright paling shuts the spouse,
Christ home, Christ and his mother and all his hallows.

But they were not all as unsympathetic to Charles as that dim little official. The author, Pierre Mille, wrote, "Poor, dear Père de Foucauld. I believe that all of us had realized his worth; he was an admirable man and a saint, tinged, if you like, with an Oriental passion; we loved him. Sometimes we used to smile at his extraordinary passion for the desert. With the carelessness of youth we used to nickname him amongst ourselves 'the Man who thinks that tramways are too near together'."

Towards the end of June, a letter arrived from the Amenokal or head of the Hoggar Touaregs, called Moussa ag Amastane. Two days later he arrived in the camp, and Charles set eyes on the man of whom he was to see a great deal for the rest of his life. This first time he was with them for a fortnight, and Charles said of him, "*Il est très bien*, he is very intelligent, very open, very pious, a Moslem, desiring the good in the way a Moslem does, but at the same time ambitious, loving money, pleasure, honour, like Mohammed, who in his eyes is the most perfect teacher."

Having shed the other four Frenchmen, Capitaine Dinaux and Charles arrived at Tamanrasset, in which place Charles decided to settle. It was a village of twenty nomad families, surrounded by mountains, in the very heart of the Hoggar. He started at once, as he had done at Beni Abbès, by building a very poor hut, and he said his first Mass on September 7th, 1905. Immediately he became attached to this country of red- and rose-coloured sandstone, of mountains and high plateaux, cut by valleys and ravines where sometimes you saw trees, very tall ethels or gum-trees. With delight he breathed in the sharp air and enjoyed the respite of this mountain freshness, after the torrid marches in the sand-dunes. . . .

But still more this great bastion of the desert, peopled with shepherds, pleased him by its human aspect. This Hoggar resurrected the France and the hierarchies of the tenth century, with its dukes, its great and little noblemen, its men at arms, its bourgeois and its peasants. In dim, faraway centuries, the Hoggar peoples, coming from the sea, had mingled with Roman legions riding from Cyrenaica on their way to the river Niger. They drove their splendid chariots down the trade and military routes. Indeed, to the thoughtful archaeologist, the very ground under his feet is a fascinating interpolated palimpsest, with layer upon layer of bygone civilizations. The very faces of the people are living history books.

However, in spite of all their picturesque appearance, Charles wrote: "The morals of the Touaregs are about the same as those of the Paris *apaches*, or hooligans; the men exist by pillaging, the women applaud them and live quite freely. . . ."

Here was an example of the prayer they made to Allah. "O great God, I lift my hands toward thee. I say a hundred thousand prayers. . . . O great God, I ask from thee three favours: the love of young girls, courage in combat, and forgiveness on the day of resurrection. . . ."

Charles was very much interested in the origins of these people, and had written:

"When the type was pure, their face resembled the ancient Egyptians and was very white. They were slim, their arms and legs quite long, rather spindle-shaped: in fact they are like the Egyptians of ancient sculptures. When the thin, tall devils leaning on their lances approach a stranger, they hold their head even higher, and they affect a gait more solemn than if they were all princes of some olden times. The women are not veiled and are heavily made up in red and ochre, their eyes are underlined with black, their hands are tinted blue and their nails reddened with henna. It is the men, strangely enough, who are veiled, with a blue cloth called the *litham*."

Comte Lafon has written:

"When a group of Touaregs advances towards one, their faces veiled by the *litham*, draped in ample robes, a long cane in their hands, one recalls the ancient classic quotation, but this time it refers to men and not to women, 'By his walk ye will know him. Ye will know a god.' They have a great air about them. Whatever certain travellers have said about them, you do not cancel your obligation towards them by some small gift; you feel that there must be something more to gain their confidence and friendship. One notices that the Targuia lady has delicate features under her paint, and she receives guests with extreme charm: she knows how to accompany this welcome with a gracious smile, enhanced by magnificent teeth and by the glow of very fine eyes, which are made up with kohl."

One completely unexpected penance now assailed Charles, who had once been very fastidious, and that was the terrible aroma of these Hoggar women, for they never washed. They said that washing made them ill. One of the first things that Charles wrote down in his rules for his Brotherhood was that Frenchwomen should teach the native women the use of soap and face flannels, and how to perform their ablutions screened off from the wind, so that they would not catch cold.

These people were mostly nomads and lived in tents which they just put up for the night.

After Charles had lived among them for some time, more durable living quarters began to replace the transitory tents. He had begun to inspire them with his stabilizing influence to renounce their nomadic tendencies.*

The Amenokal Moussa ag Amastane imitated Charles de Foucauld, and chose Tamanrasset as his capital, as it was the central point among the most important tribes. Charles was never to forget that first historic meeting with Moussa at a well. He was very fat and large, and his enormous girth was amplified by

---

* Sir Kenneth Clark writes in "The Skin of our Teeth", the first chapter of his book *Civilization*, of the nomadic Vikings slaughtering and stealing and, as yet, creating no art of any importance—save the sinister prows of their ships—until they settled more quietly in their own Nordic lands.

the multiple yards of stuff enveloping him. His heavy face was of course covered with the dark blue *litham*, so that you could see only his very bright eyes, the expression of which varied between avidity and contempt. Like all those of his race, his obstinate pride was prodigious: he thought that all Europeans were destined for Hell, whereas all Moslems would go straight to a wonderful Paradise. He had taken care to make a great impression and had himself surrounded by horsemen, sharp-shooters and camel-drivers, all riding in impeccable array; gleaming trumpets snarled and drums were beaten. It was easy to see that Moussa was treated like a king. The French explorers had shown him all their tools, their agricultural implements, their instruments, their drills to bore wells; he wanted to touch every-thing, he was in transports of joy, and if he could have done so unseen, he would have slipped all sorts of things away into his capacious pockets. Not to be outdone by the Frenchmen, he then recounted his own exploits in the hope of dazzling them. He told them of the long list of his thefts and murders. It was owing to his misdeeds that he had gained such a reputation for courage and audacity. He laughed about simply everything. This taught Charles something most important, that when dealing with these people, one must also laugh. He told Dr Hérisson who later came to the Hoggar, that "one must always smile, it mustn't be an artificial smile but a loving one".

Moussa entered into negotiations with the French and sought their favour. After the battle of Tit, Moussa had already made peaceful gestures to the French, offering to keep the country for them if they would agree to install him as Amenokal. Eventually, Moussa developed a very great affection for de Foucauld, though at the end of his life he rather disappeared into a dim back-ground, because he started taking Islam more seriously. But when eventually Moussa visited Charles at Barbirey, on his famous official visit to France, Captain Nieger, who went with him, wrote: "To those who did not know him, this man's affection for de Foucauld was evident in every gesture, every word, even to the gentle, unassuming tone in which he said '*Meryem*', the Arabic for Marie, which was the Christian name of de Foucauld's sister."

And so Charles settled among a barbaric people, far from any fellow European. Moussa called on him, and no doubt in his

Oriental way wondered how he could live without women. And then, finding de Foucauld so sympathetic and so hospitable, he opened his heart to him about the great sorrow of his life. "I have been in love for many years and am still in love with Dassine. I have written many poems about her, but she will have none of me. We remain great friends."

Charles said, smiling: "Recite me one of your poems."

"Well, I will declaim the one which I call 'Dassine of the beautiful rings'." And taking up a becoming stance, Moussa recited:

"Dassine is the moon—her neck is more beautiful than that of a young pony, tethered in a wheat field in April—God has created her with perfect proportion in all her person. He has bestowed on her universal consideration and the love of all. . . . She paints her face with indigo and yellow ochre, she has a beautiful complexion. God has given her enough to boast about—she walks with her head high, proud among men.— Whoever has gone to visit Dassine, limps and walks away with his head down, he has no more blood in his veins, not even enough blood for one blood-letting, and then he spends his night dreaming of her, if he were not far from her. But she never turns her head towards him, she pays no attention to him."

"Very fine, very fine," said de Foucauld. "When will I have the privilege of meeting this paragon among women?"

The introduction was effected. Dassine very soon became a blessing to Charles. She knew her power over Moussa, and she tried to encourage him to help the friendly French priest. De Foucauld wrote: "The real person to take decisions is Dassine. She commands without appearing to do so. She is very intelligent and knows all that is going on."

In the Hoggar Dassine was admired by everybody, and listened to by all. Each week she invited several of her women friends, who belonged, like her, to the Touareg aristocracy, to tea parties, which were also eventually organized by the *marabout* Charles, where discussions on all the questions of the day took place. Charles would be the principal guest, sitting cross-legged in Oriental fashion, his pencil in his hand; in the middle of the tent were the old ladies, also seated on the floor, chatting as they sipped their tea and smoked their pipes.

And at the end of the session, Charles would distribute his little gifts, black hair dye, sugar, or needles, which they were delighted to get, for so far they had had to manage with thorns. Marie de Bondy must have been much amused when she was asked to send Charles hair dye. One day, joy of joys, came a gift of dolls. He wrote to Marie: "They are so much admired, that before giving them away, I am keeping them for a while to show visitors. There is no one, big or small, who does not ask to see them, I have become a sort of exhibitor of dolls." He might have been less enthusiastic had he known that some of these dolls were used for fertility rites, or carried in procession to bless the fields and invoke rain. He also gave them knitting needles ordered from France, and taught them how to knit, for he had learned as a Trappist. It seems he got very muddled himself when learning to do so.

He began to feel even more convinced that these people, before they had been conquered by Islam, had once been Christian. The Cross was honoured among them, and they were not polygamous. Moreover, though they believed in God, they did not practise as ordinary Moslems, and they certainly never kept the fast of Ramadan.

Charles returned the hospitality of the Touaregs in his own way. It is diverting to think that this man, who could have become the attraction of Parisian society when his book on Morocco came out, this hermit had the gift of entertaining what Europeans would call savages. At one party, he read aloud some of the fables of La Fontaine, notably the fable of the lion and the rat, and they were immensely amused. Here it is:

> One must as far as possible be obliging to everybody;
> One often needs a smaller one than oneself.
> Of this truth two fables will prove it,
> For here proofs abound.
> Between the paws of a lion
> A rat came out of a hole in the earth in a scatter-brained
> fashion.
> The king of animals, on this occasion,
> Showed what he was, and granted him his life.
> This kind deed was not forgotten.

Would anyone ever have thought
That a lion should need a rat?
However it happened, one day, coming out of the forests,
This lion was caught in some nets,
And his roaring could not extricate him from them.
So rat rushed forward, and nibbled so hard with his teeth
That a mesh which he chewed saved the situation.
Patience and the passing of time
Do more than force and rage.

Charles looked round and smiled his rather engaging, wide tooth-less smile, and was gratified to hear the loud applause and mur-murs of pleasure. "May we have some more, if you please?" they called out. They tried to peep over his shoulder at the illustrations in the book. "Oh, this one, this one, it's about a little frog."

"Yes," said Charles. "It's about a frog who wanted to be as large as an ox."

A frog saw an ox,
Who seemed to her of good stature.
She herself was no bigger than an egg.
Full of envy, she lay down, puffed herself out and did all
    she could
To equal the animal in size,
Saying "Look well, my sister;
Is it enough, do tell me, have I got there yet?
Nenni, I've got there?" "Not at all." "I'm there?"
"You're nowhere near it." The puny creature
Swelled up to such an extent that she died.
The world is full of people who are no wiser:
Every bourgeois wants to build like the great lords,
Every little princeling has his ambassadors,
Every marquis wants to have his pages.

Charles's junketings kept his Touaregs from going too often to their own rather sinister orgies, called *Ahals*. They had been terri-fied lest Laperrine, as a condition of their allegiance to France, would suppress these famous traditional *Ahals*, but he was too wise a colonizer to do so, and left them alone. Needless to say, Charles never went to them, but heard about them with dismay. This is how Père Pichon describes them:

"... The men have their shoulders covered with a fine *dokhali* of a dark blue tint which is almost black. From the neck to the feet they are wrapped in the long *tékemest*, blue, embroidered, newly dyed, and there is a barbaric contrast, not without its own peculiar beauty, in all these sombre materials, those austere silhouettes, the look of the whites of their immense eyes, which the *litham* intensifies with a savage glow, and with the glistening indigo of the robe, on which the setting sun paints rosy lacquer tints. Quite soon, a male choir sings in unison, their mouths shut, the song of sadness, of desire, of love, which is breathed forth from the *amzad* [a Touareg violin with one string]. This is a song which each of the young men dedicates to her whose name alone makes his blood tingle—Hekkoiu, Eberkaou, Kenoua, Geggé—whilst under the oblique rays, the red and black *Haguerane* is on fire.... Conversations have begun again, but no longer the flowery tittle-tattle, the quips and the *bons mots* of the day's end, but nocturnal dialogues, equivocal; couples start to disappear."

Many a child was conceived on those nights of the *Ahals*, destined, alas, to be strangled at birth.

Remembering St Vincent de Paul, and how he had established the anonymous convent turnstiles where the thousands of unwanted babies of seventeenth-century Paris could be placed, and then looked after by nuns, Charles longed for the same thing in his Hoggar country. He knew the people's faults and sins, their duplicity, their terrible covetousness, ignorance and violence, but he said, "I work so that the Hoggar may become Christian in several centuries." And knowing full well that hungry mouths never praised God, when there was a famine he would distribute food from his own small reserve. He was a born colonizer. He wanted to bring to the Hoggar a nursery gardener, a man who could dig wells, a doctor, and several women who knew how to weave wool, because the Touaregs just wasted it, allowing the Sahara wind to blow away the stray hairs from their camels and the wool from their sheep. Apart from these Frenchwomen who could teach the natives how to weave, he wanted several cotton merchants, hardware merchants and men who sold sugar and salt; good, worthy French people who would make the native bless the French instead of cursing them. At first these material benefits did not impress the Touaregs, for the Moslem always says to the Christian, "You have the earth, but we have Heaven."

In his usual methodical way, Charles noticed the prevalent illnesses rampant among the Touaregs, and made notes of them. Then he wrote to France, to his relations, asking them to send the appropriate medicines. The Touaregs had inflammation of the eyes, rheumatism, liver complaints and venereal diseases. Charles advised that any missionary travelling for about three months should take with him at least two litres of tincture of iodine, four thousand opium pills, a kilo of quinine and then remedies against worms, especially against *le ver solitaire* or tapeworm, which is as prevalent in these regions as it is in Abyssinia, where they say most wittily that "the depths of shame for any man is not to have enough to keep *un ver solitaire*". (How amusing these people could be with their witticisms, their definition of a miser being that he was a man who begrudged even his piss to the earth.) Then Charles found out that they had fevers and skin diseases and chest complaints, untended wounds and neglected insect bites. Strangely enough, there were no fleas in that part. To his list, he soon added sulphate of zinc, boric acid, calomel, quinine, ipecacuanha, sulphate of soda, mercury pills, laudanum and serum against snake bites, with the appropriate needles for injections. Also some black tea to wash sore eyes.

Besides remedies, he would give them vegetable and fruit seeds, and when French soldiers came to the neighbourhood, they introduced the Touaregs to all kinds of French delicacies, including vines, peach, apricot and fig trees, and all manner of good vegetables such as marrows, tomatoes, carrots and onions. All this reminds one of a remarkable book about seventeenth-century Quebec called *Shadows on the Rock* by Willa Cather. The French family installed in Canada were able to create a little corner of their native France, for which they were so homesick, by planting all the vegetables that they had enjoyed in their own country and knew so well how to cook.

On November 29th, 1906, Charles went back to the headquarters of the White Fathers, the Maison Carrée, and there, to his immense joy, for the first time he was given a companion, Frère Michel, a Breton who was enthusiastic and wanted to follow him to the Hoggar. So on December 10th they left together for Beni Abbès, where they spent a short time and celebrated the feast of Christmas, and then two days later, on December 27th, they left together for the Hoggar.

Unfortunately, the venture barely lasted three months. On March 6th, 1907, Frère Michel, who had been very ill with dysentery, left that terrible novice master of his and returned to El Golea. Charles's standards were too exacting. One recalls his criticisms of Mardochée on his expedition in Morocco, of how the fellow whined continually and was such a coward. Of Michel, Charles complained that he was weak in mind, in body and in virtue, and with an odd temper. How difficult it is for a tough man, with a constitution of iron, to understand the moral deterioration following on months of dysentery. But one must read several extracts of Michel's own account of the whole unhappy venture. He tells us that Charles's first care was to hire a servant who, when they crossed the Sahara, would be able to look after the camels and lead them. The camels, one hastens to add, which carried the luggage and the provisions, not the brethren. Michel tells us the servant was a great child of thirty, a negro who had once been a slave in Timbuktu, whose name was Oubargua; a drunkard, obstinate, vain, a liar, idle and greedy, of repulsive filthiness and without any religion. Eagerly, he had promised to serve the Father, because he thought he was very rich. Also he hoped to have abundant and delicate food and very little work. After several days, his disappointment was great when he saw that instead of good food, he had just sufficient to keep body and soul alive. And so he was quite resolved to leave his job the moment he could find somebody else who would feed him better.

Michel described the convent, so called, at Beni Abbès, as very modest indeed, and the cells destined for the future monks so low, that a man of ordinary height could touch the ceiling with his hand, and so narrow, that if you stretched your arms out, you could touch the walls. You had to sleep fully clothed on a mat of plaited palm leaves, on the sand. The sacristy served the Father as a library, a storehouse, a bedchamber and a workroom. Michel tells us of his time-table: Charles came to wake him at break of day, and as they had slept completely dressed, they did not take long over their *toilette*; so several moments later, having said the Angelus in his cell, Charles rang a little bell and they went to the tiny church. He exposed the Blessed Sacrament and they sang the *Tantum Ergo*. (Michel does not mention that Charles had laughingly spoken of his unmelodious voice.) Then there was Holy Mass, after which they stayed in silence and adoration for more than two hours. Charles then said his breviary, whilst Michel recited the *Pater* and the *Ave*. There was Benediction at nine o'clock. Charles then locked himself up in his sacristy and either answered his immense correspondence or worked at his dictionary of the Touareg language. As he had no desk he wrote on a packing case; hence perhaps the slight stoop which he developed.

Michel would retire to his cell, which was the only room which had a fireplace, and which was at the same time a workshop, a kitchen and a refectory. There he did a little spiritual reading, and then he ground wheat between two stones, just like the natives, or prepared some dates in a mortar, or cooked pancakes on the hot ashes. At eleven they had a meal, followed by reading a chapter of the New Testament, then they examined their consciences. Before Grace "*Le Père, mon vénéré Père*", as he calls him, would read aloud, standing up, two or three passages of a chapter of the Imitation.

"And then we would all sit down on our mats, around the saucepan, placed on the ground just as it came off the fire, the Father, our negro servant and I, and we ate in the strictest silence, fishing out the food with a spoon, and drinking water from the same goblet. There was no variety in the menu: sometimes it was a dish of rice boiled in water, and exceptionally there was a little condensed milk mixed with those carrots and turnips which grew in the sands of the desert, or else a sort of mixture of quite an agreeable taste, made with wheatmeal, crushed dates and water. No table napkins, no glasses, no tablecloth, no plates, no knives, no forks to take this light collation."

(What a contrast incidentally to the strict regulations of two great aristocratic founders, St Ignatius Loyola and St Teresa of Avila, who were most particular that the table linen should be clean and everything properly served.) "At six o'clock, the same kind of meal and eaten with the same rapidity." Then long prayers, and bed time at twilight, though Michel adds that it was often quite dark when he fell on to his mat for the night.

At length, they left Beni Abbès and started on their journey towards Tamanrasset. But this time, crossing the desert in winter

time, it was freezing at night, and often they snoozed in the open—
very fitfully. In the morning they would find that the water had
frozen in their water butts and the ground was covered with a
light touch of frost. Michel seems particularly to have suffered
from the flail of the wind, the dust clouds which blew into his
eyes, and the little stones which lashed his face. If they passed a
village and were offered hospitality, they slept in a house, but
more often than not it was in the open, without a fire, in a hole
just big enough for the body of a man, which they had to dig themselves with their own hands. Shivering with cold, they turned and
turned all night long, without being able to sleep.

One day the Father invited some French officers to his table,
but they appeared very uncomfortable throughout the meal and
ate with an air of repugnance. They never accepted a second
invitation. In spite of all this, Michel was edified by Charles's
ardent zeal for souls, his charity towards his neighbour and his
complete detachment from the things of this world; particularly
he was overcome by his frightening austerity. If he had one little
fault, it was that, when things didn't go smoothly, *le Père* betrayed, very occasionally, a movement of impatience, quickly
repressed. Michel observed that prayer was Charles's delight; it
was really his entire life and the very breath of his being. When,
at Christmas, he had spent the whole night in the little church
at Beni Abbès, Michel had asked him on the morrow how he
could stay awake so long in such pitch darkness and Charles had
replied, "You don't need to see clearly, to speak to Him who is
the sun of justice and the light of the world."

Michel also mentioned Charles's intense desire for martyrdom.
"If I could be killed one day by the pagans, what a fine death!
My very dear brother, what an honour and what a joy if God
would only listen to my prayer."

Michel praises his great humility, and the way he welcomed
humiliations. He describes his appearance as very unprepossos-
sing. His tunic of brown holland was always too short, very often
unmended and not too clean. He trimmed his own beard, without
using a looking-glass. Michel was impressed when Charles
covered him with his own burnous during those bitter nights. He
said that he never saw him taste wine or liqueurs, and he never
allowed Michel to accept them when the officers offered some to
him. On that point of his Rule, he was inexorable, and he declared

that he would never dispense Michel from it. Charles never had breakfast, but he made Michel interrupt his thanksgiving in the morning towards seven o'clock, for ten minutes, to drink a cup of coffee and eat a piece of girdle cake. In the desert, Charles never took the noonday siesta like others, but instead, exhausted as he was by a long march in the torrid sun, he would work at his dictionary. He never took any recreation. The only repose he allowed himself from prayer and work was to make little wooden crosses to decorate the cells, or he painted pictures of the Sacred Heart or of the Blessed Virgin Mary for the chapel. Also he would write out in beautiful script the sayings of some of the Desert Fathers, the maxims of the saints and of the Doctors of the Church.

Alas, Michel was conquered by his dysentery. Charles made him see a doctor, who stupidly diagnosed indigestion, then Charles gave him a good round sum of money and dismissed him. Perhaps in his heart of hearts, Charles was rather relieved to be alone again, restored to his *"beata solitudo"* in which he was never really alone.

Michel eventually became a Carthusian monk. It must have been Heaven, materially speaking, when he contrasted his little Carthusian house with its fire in winter, with those wretched nights in the desert. And yet, the Carthusian Order was most austere.

Charles returned to Tamanrasset, and there, of course, Paul Embarek had let him down again, and disappeared, and very soon Charles had no one to serve his Mass. Paul was an ungrateful creature; he could not understand noble sentiments or the beauty of devotion. He was quite insensible to any kindness, and never looked one straight in the face. Someone asked Charles if he would ever allow Paul to make his first Communion, and Charles replied: "Never; he will always remain a catechumen, as he is unable to understand the mystery of the Eucharist." It is pathetic to see Charles's diary. Again and again—for example on December 25th—"Christmas, no Mass, for I am alone."

Charles had always despaired of getting the Touaregs to be vaccinated. When a Protestant doctor, Hérrison, came for a short time, and later wrote some notes, he tells us how he himself achieved it. He had brought his 'cello with him to the Sahara. Charles told him, "It's a waste of time to play the 'cello."

A week later Dr Hérrison said to him, "I've just vaccinated a dozen noble Touareg women, Dassine being the first."

"How did you do that?"

"I took my 'cello out of its case. At once all the women around my tent cried out: 'How big it is! It is the father of all *imzads*.' I played two or three notes. I offered to play the songs of my country."

" 'Please do. Please do,' cried all the women, clapping their hands.

" 'On one condition: be vaccinated first.'

"So Dassine put out her arm. 'Vaccinate me.' "

"Dassine of the beautiful rings", loved by Moussa, was very helpful to Charles in another way. Without being asked, she would arrive, her face uncovered like all the Touareg women, and for days at a time, from nine until twelve in the morning and frequently from two till six, she would work with Charles on his famous dictionary. He would ask her questions and take notes on the backs of his used envelopes. She never appeared to be tired, and crouched tailor-like at his feet, answering every question. She was really very intelligent and almost guessed the information he wanted to elicit from her. The grammar he was writing was beginning to take shape, and then he began a collection of proverbs, giving a small sum to each person who came to him with one. They loved riddles; for example:

"What is a round stone with seven holes able to crack nuts?"

The answer is, "The human head". Sometimes he would invite the natives to look at views of France seen through a stereoscope. Then he would give them rosaries which he made himself from dried olive stones. He taught them to say on the small stones, "My God I love you", and on the large ones, "My God I love you above all things". (Mohammedans, like Catholics, have their own rosaries, but theirs have a hundred beads on which they recite the hundred names of Allah, such as "the avenger", "the compassionate", "the merciful".

The author Joergensen describes how the Amenokal Moussa ag Amastane, the prince of the desert, magnificent in appearance and in courage, and now a sincere friend of France, on the last day of August 1909, decided to make a public gesture of affection and respect for France. Général Laperrine was to be the chief witness of a military display in his honour.

"The hour of the *fantasia* has arrived. The valley is deserted. On a small hillock, a sort of pavilion made of Berber carpets has been set up. It is here that Laperrine is standing, tightly buttoned up in his sky-blue tunic with its black brandenburgs and gold laurel-leaves; his beard is well cut; he always looks neat and correct as if he were doing a season at Vichy. Brother Charles is on his right.

"As a sign of homage, Moussa has placed in front of Laperrine the *tobol* which usually marks the site of his own tent as Amenokal. At a gesture from the colonel, Ali starts beating on a large tambourine, and the quick, lugubrious strokes almost make your heart beat, as if it were an alarm signal, and it carries very far across the limpid air, telling of the muffled clamour of war and death.

"Immediately at this call to arms, the far valley comes to life. In a neighbouring encampment where Moussa has kept his men waiting, a first squadron passes by in the *oued*, and now among the tamarisk trees can be seen lively touches of moving frescoes—the great indigo veils, the yellow or the white of the embroideries: the steel and copper of the lances glinting in the sun. And the *tobol* continues to hammer out its alarm call. A second group appears, then a third and then another, and another, and then still another. All the horizons of the valley are now filled with a veritable army in battle array, which Laperrine, with his field glasses in his hand, starts to inspect calmly, examining the groups of the various tribes, their appearance and their respective arms.

'*Ya Allah!*' At the piercing cry of Moussa, the squadron of the first tribe, which is that of Tamanrasset, with the Amenokal leading, emerges from the groups of gum trees and charges, brandishing lances. The fine dromedaries advance at a speedy trot, in lengthy throngs, and they touch the ground so lightly that they appear hardly to lift a stone.

"The warriors begin by acrobatic turns: they stand upright on the saddle, then they leap from one mount to another, or else throw themselves to the ground and then remount at one bound. They seem to play at hide-and-seek, with their great robes, called *mezouadas*, green or red, and their *sabre taches* or long satchels, dancing on the flanks of the dromedaries.... With their big toes, they pinch their dromedaries' necks the whole time, and then whip them frantically with iron thongs, or ceaselessly strike them with large leather bucklers. The over-excited beasts then scatter the stones, as they fly like the wind.

". . . They are nothing more than five hundred and twenty demons, their features convulsed, who raise a cloud of dust and do not hesitate to level their lances towards this handful of Frenchmen, giving vent to a clamour which makes the very heavens quake.

"Laperrine stands still as if he were made of stone, his arms crossed. The Father waits also, his hands hidden in his sleeves. . . . And then there is crackling of thunder, of all the stones being scraped, and with one single movement, the mad charge suddenly stops short, the five hundred and twenty men are changed into statues. They only begin to move at the end of a minute, to file at a trotting pace, smiling before the great chieftain, wave upon wave, holding their lances."

The heart of Charles, which had always remained that of a Saint-Cyrien, beat in his breast as he watched these splendid warriors. Then he went back to his little hermitage and to his life of solitude and suffering, longing to found an Order which would convert these Moslems, but still unable to say Mass, for want of a server.

But in far-distant Rome, Pius X, who was later to become St Pius X, was approached by somebody who knew of Charles's dilemma. One can imagine this Pope, who succeeded Leo XIII, seated at his desk in his white library in the Vatican, his head a little to one side, dressed in white, with his silvery hair, and that diaphanous face and those glowing eyes. Someone has said so truly that he seemed to be a living replica of the Curé d'Ars, recently canonized, whose statuette he kept on his desk.

"Most Holy Father, there is hidden in the depths of the southern Sahara a Frenchman of noble birth who has had a distinguished career as an explorer. He left everything, the Army, family and riches, to give himself to the conversion of the Moslems, and he now has nobody to serve his Mass. Will you give him an extraordinary permission to say his Mass alone?"

The permission was gladly granted, together with a special Papal blessing.

Charles received the joyous news on January 21st, St Agnes'

Day, 1908, and wrote in his diary, "*Deo gratias, Deo gratias, Deo gratias!* My God, how good you are! Tomorrow, I will be able to say Mass. Noël! Noël! Thank you, my God."

Unhappily, this permission had come to him when his health had really broken down. He had had several fainting attacks, and now he was completely overcome by a terrible general fatigue and loss of appetite. He confided in Monseigneur Guérin that he was always out of breath when he made the smallest movement, and he thought his end was near, as he also had pains in the chest. He was obliged to keep completely still. His Touareg friends went to milk their goats and brought gifts to the hut. He eventually recovered, and then had the consolation of hearing that Moussa's efforts to reorganize the Moslem kingdom in the Hoggar had failed, because his agent, whom he had entrusted with large sums to build a mosque, and to collect taxes for it from the Hoggar people, had in three months made himself hated by all, and moreover had dissipated all the sums of money which had been confided to his care. Charles had always been anxious when he heard that the French government was so tolerant of the building of another mosque. He realized that when a man became a fervent Moslem, there was every likelihood that he would come to detest Christians.

Among the Touareg proverbs which he had collected through Dassine and others, Charles had found this one: "He who loves you, even if he is only a dog, you will also love him." He sincerely and truly loved his Touaregs, and though he had not as yet made a single convert, they trusted and loved him in return. And the French soldiers behaved so well and taught the natives so much about agriculture, that soon France was looked upon with less mistrust. Of course, the common soldier always found a friend and ally in Charles, for example the one who came to find Charles when he was alone and told him his great problem. "I've been living with a native woman who had been so ill-treated by her Arab masters that she fled from them. And now she dreads the day when I, who really love her, must return to France, never to come back to Africa. I respect her and have taught her the principles of the Christian religion. But knowing what she had suffered at the hands of the Arabs, I am dreadfully anxious about her, and that is why I am opening my heart to you, *mon Père.*"

Charles at once wrote to Monseigneur Guérin, and asked him to take the woman into his workshop of Ghardaïa.

The Protestant doctor, Robert Hérisson, also came under his spell.

"Beneath his great affability, simplicity, humility of heart, one could see the courtesy, the *finesse*, the refinement of a man of the world. Although he was badly dressed ... the keenness of his glance, its depth, the height of his brow, his expression of intelligence, made him quite a personality. He was below medium height; at first sight he appeared of not much importance, but I soon got the impression that Père de Foucauld was a man of singular intelligence, with a very kind, compassionate heart. I felt a strong liking for him. I felt drawn towards him. I saw that he was idolized by all the Frenchmen who already knew him."

During their long talks, Charles used to tell the doctor, "You must be simple, affable and kind towards the Touaregs. You have to love them and make them feel that they are loved, in order to be loved in return." Also he advised him to be light-hearted always; it was easier to establish a good relationship if you laughed a lot.

But in spite of his many activities, there were two underlying themes in Charles's mind and soul: first of all, a life of prayer with the Only Beloved, and secondly his plan for the foundation of the Little Brothers and Sisters of the Sacred Heart.

He had refused to see his sister in Rome, and again he wrote to her begging her to renounce any idea of his coming to France to visit her and her many children. He said, "Let us offer this sacrifice to the Beloved." But in the end, it was thought wise for him to make a journey to France, to further the interests of the little Brotherhood he wanted.

Perhaps Mimi would get her wish at last.

CHAPTER 18

France and Asekrem

FROM December 25th, 1908, until March 28th, 1909, Charles was in France for the first time for seven years, for the first time, indeed, since his ordination at Viviers. Between February 18th and 22nd, 1909, he had some important talks about his Brotherhood with the Abbé Huvelin. Father and spiritual son rejoiced to see one another again. As an officer was to say later of Charles, he was radiant, and his gentle face was illuminated as though by the interior joy he felt.

As for the saintly Abbé Huvelin, his physical torments had increased tenfold. Like Pope St Gregory, he was twisted by gout, afflicted by perpetual headaches. But just as his pains never prevented St Gregory from being one of the most saintly and active Popes of all times, his miseries never stopped the Abbé Huvelin from going out in all weathers to visit anybody who needed his help. Whenever he was about to meet a great sinner who badly needed his advice, the same strange thing happened to him as occurred to the Curé d'Ars: he felt more unwell than ever. Charles felt a pang when he saw again the Abbé's dear, familiar, untidy room, which he had begun frequenting in the autumn of 1886, twenty-two years ago, after that momentous first confession in St Augustin. There was still the same crucifix of Dom Eugène, his holy ancestor, and the reproduction of *The Last Supper* by Leonardo da Vinci, of which the Abbé was so fond because of the face of the Saviour, already overshadowed by the agony of Gethsemane. He was lowering His tender gaze on St John who was resting on His Sacred Heart.

Yes, it was indeed in that room, and in Marie de Bondy's drawing-room, that he had learned to love this devotion which was surging up more and more in the France of those days.

"Ah," said the Abbé, after he had tenderly embraced his unkempt spiritual child, "I am glad to see that red heart on your habit."

They spoke of many things, first of the beatification of Joan of Arc, who had been born so near Charles's own native countryside. Also they rejoiced in the great event of the pontificate of the late Leo XIII, who in 1899 had consecrated the whole world to the Sacred Heart of Jesus. This had been achieved by the influence of an aristocratic and beautiful German nun, Soeur Marie du Divin Coeur. The Abbé Huvelin must have told Charles how this had happened. Soeur Marie had written to Leo XIII, "It seems that last summer, when your Holiness was suffering from an ailment which, in view of your advanced age, filled the hearts of your children with anxiety, Our Lord gave me the sweet consolation that He would prolong the days of Your Holiness in order to achieve the consecration of the whole world to His Divine Heart."

The Abbé Huvelin continued:

"I was told about her death; the sight of it must have been a great consolation to her fellow nuns. Apparently, her hands were groping to find her little crucifix, and when it was given to her, she looked sublimely happy. Her gaze was often fixed on the same place in the distance. All of a sudden, she said, 'Ah . . .', as if she were seeing something extraordinary, and then she fell back dead. Towards midnight, the sisters kneeling around her bed, reciting the Office of the Dead, all of a sudden saw something quite miraculous. A celestial smile stole on to the dead nun's lips: her companions cried out in surprise. After a few moments, the smile vanished, but a remarkable expression of bliss persisted, as if even her mortal flesh were trembling with joy at this consecration of the human race to the Sacred Heart."

"What a lovely death," said Charles. "Alas that such a death is not for a sinner like myself."

"Ah," said the Abbé Huvelin, smiling, "are you still praying to die a martyr?"

"More than ever," replied Charles. "I want to die for my children of the Sahara, like my great-uncle in the September massacres."

"Well, my dear child, I don't begrudge you a martyr's end, especially since I heard the other day of the horrible

death of Marguerite Gautier, the actress who died of tuberculosis."

"You mean 'La Dame aux Camélias'," said Charles. "She was
such a romantic figure, wasn't she? So many young men became
the despair of their families because they squandered large for-
tunes on her. She was very beautiful, I seem to remember. And I
recall someone at Saint-Cyr telling me how the bailiffs waited in
her hall, as she lay dying. And then, that dreadful auction afterwards. All her beautiful possessions, the dressing table sets of gold
and tortoiseshell given to her by her lovers, peered at and fingered
by crowds of inquisitive society women."

"Ah, but just hear what happened at her death. I can't understand it, for the Curé of the Madeleine had brought her the Last
Sacraments. Apparently, towards the end, she suddenly sat up in
bed, looked with terror at something at the foot of her bed, her
eyes widened in horror, and then, with a piercing cry of dread,
she fell back dead."

There was a pause. The Abbé continued his ponderings. "But
I cannot help feeling glad that this great devotion to the Sacred
Heart—which would have saved this poor sinful woman—has
really gripped our country. St Margaret Mary had said that the
Sacred Heart wished to enter with pomp and magnificence into
the house of princes and kings, to be honoured there, as much as
it had been outraged, despised and humiliated in His passion. She
sent this message to Louis XIV, but alas, he was at that time
entangled in his sins. However, it became the great family devotion of his descendants. During the Revolution, Louis XVI had
promised that if he were freed from his captors, he would consecrate his family and his kingdom to the Sacred Heart. The
saintly Madame Elizabeth, his sister, who was guillotined, most
fervently believed that all graces came from the Sacred Heart of
Our Lord. During the torments of her imprisonment, she was
more and more drawn towards It. So, my dear child, I am glad
that you are bringing this grand devotion to Africa. Great
geniuses like St Thomas Aquinas and Pascal knew that truth can
only finally be reached by love. We mortals can only penetrate
into truth by charity. The Jews themselves used to talk about
'the eyes of the heart'. That holy nun in Portugal said she could
never separate devotion towards the Blessed Sacrament from the
Sacred Heart."

"Yes," said Charles, "that's why I want my little brothers to become like the divine Host Itself, continually consumed by those they serve."

The two of them had a long talk about the Statutes of his Society, and then made plans for approaching the bishops. When Charles said goodbye to the Abbé Huvelin in February, he did not realize that he was seeing him for the last time, for he was to die the following year. On March 6th, the Statutes of the Union of Brothers and Sisters of the Sacred Heart of Jesus were approved by Monseigneur Bonnet. And on March 19th, they won the same approval from Monseigneur Livinhac, Superior of the White Fathers.

These two events consoled Charles for two rather disagreeable snubs he received in Paris. On February 18th, he had gone to call on his young cousin, François de Bondy, Marie's son, but the valet who opened the door soon returned from the drawing-room and said: "Would Monsieur l'Abbé please come back to-morrow?" He did not enlarge on the fact that Monsieur de Bondy was revelling in and engrossed by the visit of a young lady from the Folies Bergères. Charles guessed as much by various feminine fripperies in the entrance hall, and the pervasive scent, and he left heavy-hearted. The whole incident troubled him, for it brought back the memories of his own wild youth. It filled his heart with pity for François's mother, who had had nothing but trouble with her three sons and, indeed, in order to protect their finances from their heedless squanderings, she had put all of them under the control of a judiciary council.

However, very humbly Charles came at the appointed hour on the morrow, and the first thing he said was, "Dear François, I would never have recognized you," and he stretched out his hands towards him. François could easily have said the same about his cousin, but was no doubt too polite, for Charles looked disgraceful, with a ragged and not too clean curé's hat which he twisted in his hands; his neck was red with sunburn and his face brown and wrinkled. His beard, which he had trimmed himself, from being raven black, was now pepper-and-salt.

During that visit to Paris, Charles saw a Monsieur Massignon who had serious thoughts of joining him and returning with him to the desert, but in the end he did not. This Monsieur Massignon accompanied him to his audience with the Cardinal of Paris.

They all three sat together in his study, and there was a deathly, uncomfortable silence. The Cardinal was most unfriendly. He looked down, and tapped a maddening tattoo on his desk. He was awaiting the first word from this strange-looking hermit, while Charles also was hoping that His Eminence would begin the conversation. Finally, when the silence had become quite unbearable, the Cardinal said to Charles, "It appears that you left the Trappists."

"Yes, Your Eminence," replied Charles.

"Well," said the Cardinal, rising from his chair, "the best thing you could do would be to return to them," and he pulled the bell cord for them to be ushered out by his footman.

So it must have been a great consolation when Monseigneur Bonnet at Viviers was really enthusiastic. "Yes, I approve your project and wish it all success. I will help you with my poor prayers."

After this, Charles, a true solitary, only at home in the desert, was glad to return to Tamanrasset by way of Beni Abbès where he made a short stay. In the following year, on July 10th, the Abbé Huvelin died. His last words were, *"Nunquam satis amabo—*I shall never love enough". Charles did not hear of this event until a long time afterwards, because of the long delays in the post. This blow, coming after the death in the preceding May of Monseigneur Guérin at quite an early age, worn out by his labours, filled Charles with an increasing sense of isolation, the same sadness he felt when he heard that his dear, wild friend of Saumur days, the Duc de Vallombrosa, "Vallom", going unprotected on an expedition, had been assassinated by rapacious Arabs in his caravan. On September 1st, 1910, he wrote to Marie de Bondy:

"This solitude is increasing. One feels more and more alone in the world. Some have gone to the fatherland, others live more and more apart; one feels like the olive which is left alone at the end of a branch, forgotten after the harvest. . . . But Jesus remains: Jesus the Immortal Spouse who loves us as no human heart knows how to love; He is here now, and He will always be with us. He has always loved us, He loves us at this very moment, and will love us till we draw our last breath; and if we do not refuse to accept His love, He will love us eter-

nally. . . . My very dear mother, we are not to be pitied, we
are not alone, we are not forgotten; we have the tenderest, the
most loving, the most perfect Spouse, who loves us and will
love us always as no human being has ever loved."

But the death of the Abbé Huvelin must have remained an
ever open wound. He said, "I used to cling to him, just as a child
clings to his mother's gown."

After a second visit to France in 1911 to try again to arouse
enthusiasm about his Brotherhood, Charles decided to go even
further than Tamanrasset in the two-fold search both for souls
and for solitude. The Abbé Huvelin had given him a wooden
altar to say Mass on a very high peak, and in 1911 he left
Tamanrasset and journeyed upwards for three days until he
reached what he called his "hermitage" at Asekrem. It was really
a hovel, just a kind of narrow passage, blown about by a wind
which howled perpetually. The cold was bitter and the assistant
whom Charles took with him to work with him for nine hours a
day on the dictionary, shivered and grumbled. At last, the man
decided to stay there as short a time as possible. Charles wrote to
Marie de Bondy,

"During the day the thermometer never rises above twenty-
five degrees; and with this chill for most of the time, there is a
wind which reminds one of the great winds of Loüye; I love so
much to hear it whistling in the country, and God here treats
me in a way that suits my tastes. Whenever I open the window
or the door, I am lost in admiration at the sight of those mountain peaks which surround me and which I dominate; it is a
marvellous view and a really fine solitude. How good it is to
be in this great calm, surrounded by the beauties of nature, so
tormented and so strange, and then to lift one's heart towards
the Creator and Jesus the Saviour."

And indeed the landscape is quite fantastic, with its needle-
point peaks and giant plateaux. The rocks are sculptured by the
blizzards and hurricanes into fantastic and weird shapes. It is
very high. In prehistoric times, great Saharan rivers had come
foaming down the flanks of these mountains, but now they had
all dried up. Charles had to walk for an hour before he could get

any water, and if an antelope had drunk at the spring before him, he had to wait another hour before he could get water for himself. But he did not seem to notice these discomforts, he merely said:

"It's a beautiful spot in which to adore the Creator. May His kingdom come here! I have the advantage of having many souls around me, and yet of being very solitary on my peak . . . This sweetness of solitude, I have felt it all my life, since the age of twenty. Always revelled in it; even before I was a Christian, I loved solitude surrounded by the beauties of nature, with some books; how much more when the invisible, melodious life of the Spirit makes me feel that in solitude I am never alone. The soul is not made for noise, but for pondering, and life must be a preparation for Heaven, not only in doing good, but by peace and recollection in God."

There was something really Franciscan about Charles's treatment of his antelope, for when she got to the spring first, instead of driving her away, he would hide carefully so as not to frighten her. He believed that water coming from Heaven belonged to the first creature to occupy the spot. After all, he said to himself, she discovered the spring before me, and therefore she has priority over me, and I will never contest it. But then, there was a real resemblance between Charles and St Francis, quite apart from their love of the Lady Poverty.

The good works he did took the form of the best hospitality he could offer. More than once a week, he received a visit from Touareg families, from all the numberless surrounding valleys. They even came from great distances, so of course Charles realized that they must have supper and spend the night with him. He never grumbled at what other men would call a waste of his time, but received them gaily and gave them little presents. Charles wrote, "One or two meals taken together, a day or half a day spent together, strengthen my relationship with them much more than a great number of half-hourly or hourly visits, as at Tamanrasset. . . . And then my presence here gives the officers a chance of coming into the heart of this country."

His renown for kindly welcomes soon spread, and Père Pichon in his book *Le Frère Charles*, describes a delightful incident:

"A Targui man, the victim of an accident, was complaining of very sharp suffering; around him the women and the natives groaned as if they had gone mad, without attempting to do anything to help him. They spoke of going to fetch one of the witch doctors of the mountain, when all of a sudden one of the children, a little girl of thirteen, slipped out without a word. She had thought of the *marabout*, the holy man of Taman-rasset. As soon as Charles heard somebody banging on his door, he got up, took his box of medicines and bandages and followed her. His care soon calmed the patient. But the return at dawn was not as easy as all that; whilst the little girl clambered up the rocks, bounding like a she-goat, the *marabout* was less nimble. What a delicious scene, that little wild girl, so deftly leading the saint in that mountainous dawn solitude. The little girl held Foucauld by the hand to guide him among the masses of fallen rocks, and with the aid of a stick showed him where to place his feet, to avoid falling."

He returned to his fastness. In the old days, he had read of the temptations of the Desert Fathers, the worst of which was the noonday Devil spoken of in the Psalm, and called *accidie*. The fourth-century Cassien de Marseilles describes it thus: "It is akin to dejection and especially felt by wandering monks and solitaries, it is a persistent and obnoxious enemy to those dwelling in the desert, disturbing the monk especially about midday, like a fever rising at a regular time, and bringing its highest peak of inflammation to the sick soul at definite and accustomed hours." Charles certainly had his periods of spiritual dryness, and he was almost in despair during the long months before he had received permission to say Mass alone. As he was unable to go to confession for long periods at a time, he sometimes used to write to the Abbé Huvelin about his thoughts, temptations and faults. He once accused himself of sensuality. Perhaps he underwent some of those terrible demon-like temptations experienced by the early hermits of Egypt. But his memories of the lives of those Desert Fathers must have encouraged him to continue the austerities which tamed any upsurgings of his flesh.

One must remember that the *gourmet* has very sensitive nostrils, they always accompany a keen and delicate palate. The one good thing about Asekrem was that he was far away from the

terrible stench of the unwashed women of the Hoggar, so distaste-
ful to this aristocrat who, in the old days, had soused his hair with
Cuir-de-Russie. He had been surrounded by Parisian society
women who used the choicest scents and toilet waters, so perhaps
at Asekrem Charles recalled the Abbot who would never change
the water in which he steeped his palm leaves, and it stank; he
said to his followers, "For the incense and the fragrance of the
perfumes I used in the world, needs must I now bear this
stench."

But all joys come to an end, sooner or later. Charles had made
a provision of food for about sixteen months. He wrote: "As for
food I am like Noah in the ark, or like somebody who is going for
a sixteen-month sea voyage without touching at a port. I brought
with me for that period a supply of flour, *couscous* [Arab semo-
lina], sugar, salt, pepper, dates and coffee." But the helper from
the Hoggar, not used to a nine-hour day's work and unable any
longer to bear the cold and the solitude, in December said he
was going back. So, very unwillingly, Charles returned to Tamanrasset.

Fifteen years before, in one of his meditations on the Book of
Genesis, Charles had written: "It is at the moment when Jacob
is on the road, poor and alone, when he sleeps on the bare ground
in the desert, to take his rest after a long journey on foot, it is at
the moment when he is in the painful situation of the isolated
traveller in the middle of a long journey in a strange and wild
country, with nowhere to sleep, it is at that moment when he finds
himself in so sad a condition, that God overwhelms him with
incomparable favours."

On January 8th, 1913, he at last finished his Lexicon. Moussa
had gone on an official visit to France, and after seeing all
Charles's grand relations at Barbirey, he wrote to him that he
could not understand how he, who could have so much, should
live like a beggar. Charles felt that Moussa had been shown all
the wrong things: what was needed was for somebody from the
Hoggar to go and live a family life in France, in the French
countryside, to be treated in an affectionate and friendly fashion.
So when he planned his third journey to France, from April 27th
to September 27th, 1913, he took with him a young Touareg,
Ouksem, from a bourgeois family. He would combine showing
France to Ouksem with seeing the French clergy again about the

founding and Rule for his Fraternity. Already, he had prepared his sister and his French cousins to receive this newly married young man, arrayed in his loin cloth and flowing robes, with braided hair, and the lower part of his face covered with a blue veil. And he, who had always travelled steerage, in the greatest discomfort, with a small basket of meagre provisions, this time went first class so that Ouksem should enjoy every European comfort.

He had promised his old friend, the Duc de Fitz-James, to let him know when the boat reached Marseilles, and the Duc gives this account of his arrival:

"When the boat drew alongside the quay, I was there. I saw an ascetic coming down, and I only recognized my de Foucauld by his eyes, which were always so alive and so full of laughter. The young, unconverted Touareg called Ouksem, accompanied him. He had the face of a savage, but with delicate and expressive features. They stayed with the White Fathers in the Rue des Chartreux, but took their meals at my place. . . . The saint charmed us. He was very merry.

"He was a good guest, although he poured a lot of water into his wine, telling us that for the time being he wasn't leading a mortified life, in spite of his principal vow which was of poverty, deprivation and abjection. And I had known him before he had made these perfect vows. Ouksem disdained vegetables and appreciated roast leg of mutton."

The Commandant de St Didier, who met him on this journey, wrote, "On his emaciated face, lit up with a piercing glance, one could see reflected a look, so to speak, which was difficult to define, the look of a man who was absent and whose thoughts travelled elsewhere. In his measured and reserved language, one sensed the turn of mind of one who had once been a man of the world."

They both called on Monseigneur Bonnet, Bishop of Viviers, and there, from his high-perched house, Ouksem was able to see for the first time in his life an immense, swirling French river, flowing very fast with a booming sound, the glorious Rhône, so splendidly different from the little sandy streams of his own land which sometimes hid underground. The Rhône is a grand river, swift and foaming, and in some parts dangerous to people in canoes because of the sudden rapids. But what struck Ouksem most were the river banks, so beautifully cultivated, with all manner of green vegetation round about.

The two travellers went on to Lyons where they were the guests of Laperrine. These two great men of the Sahara were able to indulge in long talks about their main passion, Africa. Charles was scandalized at the changes in France since he had lived there. He had never known such a love of luxury; he began to long to go back to the Sahara, to the desert, to which each brings only what he is. Then they left Laperrine for the moment and went to Barbirey in Burgundy, to stay with the de Blics and their children. And for the first time in history, a young Touareg received hospitality from a French Christian family living on their country estate. When he got to the courtyard, Ouksem stopped short. Charles asked him why he looked so surprised. "But you've got flowers in front of your dwelling!" he exclaimed.

"Well, you'll see more on the terrace on the other side; and look at this lovely field sloping down to the stream, and those green hills beyond."

"And the trees," cried Ouksem, "the trees in your park. I never imagined that our date palm could be superseded by such beautiful trees. What are they all called?"

Charles pointed out one after another. "Here are some white plane trees from Holland, some sycamores, some pines, and over there, some elms."

They stayed a short time at Barbirey, but promised to come back for a week at least. Then they went to visit all the other de Foucauld relations. First it was the Marquis de Foucauld in the Château de Bridoire in the Périgord. Of course the Périgord outdoes every other region of France by the grandiose splendour of its scenery, its medieval châteaux perched on high rocks, its mountains covered in fine trees, its deep forests, and, everywhere at a turn, that queen of rivers, the Dordogne, wide and fast-flowing. They were received very hospitably, and the first thing that Charles and Ouksem did was to go on all fours on the floor of the smoking-room, to cut out a pair of trousers which Ouksem was to sew to occupy his leisure time. There was a chapel where the family assembled every evening, and the Touareg used to stand on the steps just outside the chapel, not daring to go in, out of respect: it seems that his big eyes were full of tears, whilst the French family prayed in common.

Then Charles and Ouksem went to Comte Louis de Foucauld, in the Château de la Renaudie, also in the Périgord, and then to Marie de Bondy who was spending her holidays at St Jean de Luz. We know little about this first meeting between Charles and Marie, after so many years. Finally, after crossing Paris, where they had been invited to an officers' mess in the Place de l'Opéra, and where Charles appeared on the balcony beside Ouksem in his Hoggar clothes, they returned to Barbirey, via Autun, on about July 20th. There is nothing more delightful than a happy French family, with plenty of cousins, aunts and uncles, all very united. The first thing they did was to teach Ouksem to knit, so that he could later give knitting lessons to the women of his tribe. He became most skilful, whereas Charles as usual got very muddled and kept dropping stitches.

"What's that?" asked Ouksem one day, near the stables.

"Oh, it's a bicycle," replied Charles. "Would you like to learn to ride it?"

One of the cousins said, "He can't in those flowing garments. Let me fetch some large safety pins, and turn his robes into trousers."

And so the people on the estate enjoyed the amusing spectacle of Ouksem in his strange costume, wobbling his way towards Autun. It is strange that he returned intact, and full of enthusiasm. But then, roads were nearly empty in those days.

Charles said to his nephew, Edouard, "Teach him French, please, and in return for your lessons, when you come to see me in Africa, he'll teach you how to ride a camel, for he's a past master in that art."

The evenings were delightful. The nieces sang, accompanied by their mamma at the pianoforte, and then they played a parlour game called *furet*, or hunt the ferret, like our hunt the thimble. They all sat in a circle on the drawing-room floor, and a ring was put on a piece of string which they hid under their legs. The great thing was to catch the ring as it passed from one person to another. Charles abandoned all the eccentricities which had so much irritated his cousins in the early days of his conversion. He ate whatever was put before him. His long prayers were said at night, after he had seen to it that Ouksem, his charge, was in bed and asleep.

But no one suspected this, of course; in fact, they were a little surprised one Sunday when Charles demurred about going to Vespers.

"It's not necessary," he said.

"But the village people will be surprised not to see you there."

"All right then, I'll come."

After visiting other parts of France they saw Laperrine again, who said to him, "Your Touareg knows only his mountains of the Hoggar; we ought to go to Switzerland and show him the Alps. I will be of the party."

They were well rewarded, for Ouksem was speechless with delight as he clambered up some rocky peaks near Mont Blanc. Then, after a third and last visit to Barbirey, which lasted a fortnight, they went back to Paris, where a friend of Père de Foucauld gave Ouksem a present which filled him with delight, a gun to go shooting; so, of course, shooting became the order of the day. Ouksem wrote to Edouard de Blic, "It's me, here I am, Ouksem, who says: I salute Edouard very profoundly; I love you very much; I find time goes too slowly after being with you. I have killed a partridge, a hare and a squirrel. I embrace you." Then, alas, it was really goodbye, and none of them realized that it was their last farewell in this world. Charles wrote merrily to Laperrine that Ouksem was learning the disadvantages of civilization: he had just had his finger pinched in a train door. When Charles wrote to his sister and brother-in-law at Barbirey, to thank them for all their kindness to Ouksem, he said, "The apostolate of kindness is the best of all."

Ouksem seemed glad to be returning to his own tent and his nomadic life. He kept fingering his gun and taking out of his boxes the many gifts he had bought for his young wife.

There is a Touareg proverb: "The man who does not question a traveller on his return is a fool." One would love to have overheard Ouksem's account of his adventures to his family. But the first thing he did was to teach them all to knit, for he had brought a large provision of wool and knitting needles, and very soon all the women became very skilful and Charles was always having to write to Marie de Bondy for more materials. In 1917, alas, Ouksem used the gun against France.

On November 22nd, 1913, Charles returned to Tamanrasset and continued to work on his dictionary.

His life was drawing to a close. It would appear as if Divine Providence were waiting for him to finish his dictionary, at which he had worked so hard to help future missionaries, before giving him his heart's desire.

CHAPTER 19

Heart's Desire

THERE came the dread year, 1914. Benedict XV was Pope, and in August, the First World War was declared. Although he was longing to go out and fight, and indeed had asked permission to do so, in the end Charles decided to stay at Tamanrasset to keep the people calm. In December he fell very ill again with scurvy, and in June 1915 he finished his dictionary, after eleven years of unremitting work, most of it done with failing eyesight in great heat, on a packing case, and sometimes by the light of one candle. He kept Laperrine informed of all sorts of rumours going about. On November 19th of that year, he reported that a post in Tunisia had been attacked by the Senoussis.

In his vast book, *The Graces of Interior Prayer*, the Jesuit Père Poulain has spoken of this Moslem confraternity. Writing before the First World War, he said: "The Islamic countries are filled with a multitude of religious associations, many of which are also political and give rise to considerable uneasiness for the future ... One of the more recent and rapidly growing associations, that of the Senussiya, was founded by an Algerian who died in 1859. He instilled into all his followers a common hatred of Christians. It keeps aloof from them and prepares for the revolt which, on the day the Lord has appointed, will drive them away from the land of Islam. ... Its motto is, 'Both Turks and Christians I will break with a single blow.' "

On April 11th, 1916, Charles again wrote to Laperrine and said that the Senoussis would now be able to find their way here freely, and by "here", he meant not Tamanrasset but Fort Motylinski, the capital of the country, which was fifty kilometres away from Tamanrasset, and he advised Laperrine to fortify it properly.

In the meantime the Germans, through their secret agents, seeing that the people of the Hoggar were faithful to France through the influence of Charles, sent the Senoussis as near as they dared, in the hope of capturing Charles as a hostage. And then they would influence the tribes to fight on their side.

In September and October of that year, sensing danger drawing stealthily nearer and nearer, through that strange bush telegraph whereby news travels so fast in the Sahara, Charles decided to build a fort in Tamanrasset itself. In his comings and goings in those days, he used to visit a rogue called El Madani, a negro who spent his time robbing the tents of his neighbours when they were away. Charles would exclude no one from his love, and would say to himself, "Jesus loved Judas". Did he sense that this man was to be his Judas?

Charles moved from his little hut to the fort on June 23rd. He had stocked it with ammunition and provisions, so that in case of an attack, all the inhabitants of the village could take refuge with him there, and defend themselves. In the middle of the courtyard was a deep well. He knew that the French government had forbidden all curés in Algeria, Tunisia or Morocco, and all military chaplains, to make any anti-Moslem propaganda. But Charles went his own way, which was very different. It was quietly, gently and silently to bring the Moslems closer to Christianity by becoming their friends. "And when intimacy is established, I speak ... of God, briefly giving to each one what he can take: flight from sin, an act of perfect love, an act of perfect contrition, the two great commandments, Love of God and of your neighbour, examining your conscience, meditation on the last things, the duty of the creature to think of God, etc."

In the meantime, the war which had begun in earnest in Flanders in 1915, dragged on in the trenches. Then there was the failure of the Dardanelles. Afterwards, between February and July 1916, came the battles of Verdun and the Somme. On November 28th of that year, Charles finished copying out all his Touareg poetry which he had collected with such great and dogged perseverance, helped by Dassine. He had now successfully completed all his arduous work of scholarship, which was to pave the way for those who were to come after him. Like the weavers of great tapestries, he was not to see the unfolding of the creation as he toiled. The weaver's labour is among the warp and woof of the arrases, but the splendid pictures of the tapestries are on the other side, and he must wait to see them.

The Army had constantly asked Charles to take refuge in a safer place, but he as constantly refused to leave his poor Touaregs whom he had loved for ten years. He wanted them to find refuge in the fort with him, if danger threatened. The walls were six feet thick, and the only door was secured by a strong bar. This door was quite low and small, and no one could slip in, except by stooping. In addition, there had been a further precaution; a wall three feet away masked this tiny entrance. Secretly, Charles was quite certain that he would be attacked. In fact, in September of that year, he had heard of a plot to assassinate him. But he never said anything to anybody. The proof of this was found in papers discovered after his death.

And yet a letter written in September of the following year by Capitaine Depommier affirms that at the time of his assassination, "all hearts in the Hoggar had been won over to the cause of our enemies, and their dearest wish was that we should disappear very soon and definitely from the region". Even Ouksem knew about some plot against his benefactor, for only two months after his murder, he took a very effective part in the rebellion in the Hoggar.

The Germans had done their work well. They had influenced the Turks so that they should excite, first of all the Touaregs against the French and her allies, and afterwards, all the desert tribes. This was proved to Laperrine in the following year, when he spoke of a letter which was found in the papers of a certain man, either Turk or German, in which he was advised to rouse the native population and to kill or to take hostage well-known Europeans who had an influence on the natives and the chieftains who were devoted to the French.

For this purpose the Senoussis were most useful. It must be emphasized that the Senoussis were a religious sect whose members might belong to any tribe. The Touaregs called them Fellagas. They occupied Tripolitania, which had been abandoned by the Italians.

There is a Touareg proverb that the viper takes on the colour of his surroundings. Not all the men of the village had remained with Père de Foucauld in the fort. Three of them had slipped out into the camp of the women and committed thefts and acts of violence. The leader of these rogues was that El Madani who had been particularly well cared for by Père de Foucauld. This negro had a diabolical, degenerate appearance, for his skull and face looked as if they had been crushed, and he had hardly any nose. In this black snout or mug, one could distinguish only the heavy garnet-red lips and the protruding eyes glazed like pieces of china, and yet feverish and shifty.

Charles had developed a detestation for snakes since the day in the Hoggar when he had been bitten by an adder, and if his Touaregs had not treated him vigorously with white-hot irons, he would have died. After that he had put a little step outside his hermitage, so that no adder could slip in any more. Adders, both human and animal, might fill him with horror, but his desire for martyrdom persisted. In one of his written meditations addressed to Christ, he said, "The greatest love consists in giving one's life for those one loves, You said to me yesterday night, O my Beloved. . . . Grant me the favour of giving my life for Thee, I beg Thee with all my heart; Thou knowest that I am too cowardly to do it, and unworthy of such an honour. . . . I ask Thee, O my well Beloved, the grace of giving my blood for Thee, lovingly and courageously, in a manner calculated to glorify Thee as much as possible, O my Spouse."

When St Thérèse of Lisieux first saw stains of blood on her kerchief, on Good Friday night in bed, after an attack of coughing, she whispered with joy: "This is the murmur of the Bridegroom, drawing nigh from afar."

Likewise, Charles had written, "Illness, danger, the prospect of death, it is the call. 'Here is the Spouse: go forth to meet Him.' "

And so dawned December 1st, 1916, which was the first day of the month, a day especially dedicated to devotion to the Sacred Heart. As Charles himself had written, "To be united to the Sacred Heart of Jesus, one must share His tastes", we wonder what his prayer was on that last day, alone as far as human beings were concerned, but surrounded in spirit by all his favourite saints and angels, known and unknown. He had a particular love for all guardian angels, for he wrote, "You have tender and very powerful friends, because you have your guardian angel continually with you." And on November 21st, 1903, he had made a vow to Our Lord, uniting his spirit with the nine choirs of angels. "I have decided to maintain in myself the will to be united in all my spiritual life, and in my apostolate, with the nine choirs of angels, and all they do in Heaven, in their relationship with the Father, the Son and the Holy Spirit, with the Blessed Virgin their Queen, and with all they do on earth in their relationships with men."

We know that he wrote some letters that last day, and these he sealed and stamped. One of them was to Marie de Bondy, his last letter to the one he had loved for so long. In it he said, "Our annihilation is the most powerful means that we have of uniting ourselves to Jesus. One finds one doesn't love enough, that is true"—how well that echoes the last words of the Abbé Huvelin, "*nunquam satis amabo*"!—"but Almighty God, who knows with what He has moulded us, and who loves us much more than a mother can love her child, has said that He will not cast out those who come to Him."

He must have been suffering from spiritual dryness, for on that last day he also wrote, "I feel that I am suffering, but I do not always feel that I love, and that is a great additional suffering." As he sealed up this last letter to Marie, no doubt his thoughts turned for the last time to Paris, to the Parisians then suffering in their third winter of a cruel war. He thought of the Boulevard Malesherbes, its chestnut trees now stripped bare by winter's flail. A whole generation of young men had been wiped out, and the streets were full of widows and sorrowing mothers in their long, black veils. The memory of his youthful Parisian follies must have faded away. The Desert Fathers were very often tempted by desire, but Charles had followed their example, and with his iron will had at last conquered the flesh. He had said that he wanted, quite forgetful of himself, "to breathe his life out for Almighty God, like incense or like a gentle luminous lamp". He wanted to offer himself to God, "as a libation, with a melodious sound".

And yet he had not always been able to give himself entirely to his passionate love for contemplation. The solitude of the desert had called him, and then he had found that he could not long ignore the agony of his fellow men, so for them too he had embraced terrible mortifications. Someone has said, "Spirit must brand the flesh that it may live." He remembered that he had infuriated his Trappist novice master by his obstinacy about fasting on bread and water on Easter Day, but he knew that he must imitate those early Desert Fathers who, by the very exaggeration of their lives, "stamped Infinity on the imagination of the West".

John Donne had written

> . . . Thou'rt covetous
> To them whom Thou lovest . . .

In this respect, did Charles's thoughts ever stray back to the beautiful betrothed, rejected so many years ago in Algiers—that young girl whom he had hurt so much, whom he had blighted, like frost in May? Although it had all finally ensued in a greater good for his fellow men, that engagement had been broken because Charles was unable to love a woman, in the highest spiritual sense. His spiritual perceptions had been blunted, in that respect, by associations with sensual and unloving women. And his love for Marie de Bondy had been mostly filial. However, like St Augustine, his heart had been released and then enlarged to embrace all suffering mankind.

It is said that at our end, or when we sense that the end is near, our whole life flashes by in the imagination. Perhaps he thought of the places he had loved: Rome,

> Red with the ruby and rose of the Martyrs,
> White with the lilies and light of the Virgins.

Rome—his first sight of the Colosseum and his thoughts that day of the martyrs. But above all he remembered the first day he ever saw the desert, the Sahara which had eventually drawn him to God, the desert with its solitude, its silence, its immense star-lit nights and its men who prayed continually to Allah. Then he thought of his travels to the Holy Land and his first sight of the tomb of the Lord, the Garden of Gethsemane and dearly loved Nazareth. His early years as a Trappist, surrounded by mountains; his long night vigils. . . .

He had just written a letter to the Prioress of the Poor Clares of Nazareth, who had now taken refuge in Malta. He had said that the saints of France pray always for France. "In choosing France as the cradle of the devotion of the Sacred Heart and for the apparitions of Lourdes, Our Lord has shown clearly that He keeps France in her rank of first-born."

He looked around his little chapel which the Poor Clares had also helped to fill with treasures. He had placed in a reliquary the fragments of the True Cross which they had given him, also shoots of the olive trees of the Agony of Gethsemane, marble chips from the pillar of the Scourging, together with a tiny splinter from the Crown of Thorns, and another from the rock of Calvary. All these were dear to him from the memories and prayers they evoked. Particularly did he love this tiny relic of the True Cross, for he had written, "The more we embrace the Cross, the more closely do we clasp our Spouse Jesus Who is nailed to it." It could almost be said that he had taken the motto of his patroness, St Teresa of Avila: "Either to suffer or to die."

From her, his thoughts perhaps wandered for a moment to St John of the Cross whose spiritual writings he had read again and again. He had advised his intimate friends to read them too. And he recalled how the saint had once attended the death-bed of one of his friars. Suddenly the friar sat up in bed and looked fixedly at something at the end of the cell, invisible to all but him, and he cried out, "I've seen, I've seen!" And before he slipped away, St John of the Cross whispered to him urgently, "Tell me what you have seen." The friar gasped, "I have seen Love." Then he died.

It is a certainty for the Christian, that his invisible friends in the next world, whether known or unknown, aid him at the hour of death, and in some special cases, particular saints and martyrs surround his death-bed. For example, Margaret, the adopted daughter of St Thomas More, who had fed the Carthusian martyrs slowly starving to death, said to her husband on her death-bed, "They have come to fetch me, the blessed martyrs whom I have aided."

Charles was only fifty-eight, but he must have appeared very much older. In his last years, his face was deeply engraved by wind and sand. And his soul had been engraved by God for a long time, and used by Him.

And yet outwardly there was nothing of the terrifying asceticism that we find in the pictures of El Greco, Zurbarán and Ribera. His standard of holiness was derived from imitating Our Lord who had said, "I am meek and lowly of heart." He had longed to reproduce His humility, His gentleness, His heart-breaking courtesy. Charles, starved and sick and obscure as he was, had become a living embodiment of the beatitude of meekness, and

Our Lord had said, "Blessed are the meek, for they shall inherit the Earth." Charles himself had imitated this gentleness, even in his thoughts. He had written: "Gentleness in thoughts, in words, in actions. . . . Nothing bitter, nothing violent, nothing hard. . . . To be honey, a light and fragrant breeze, velvet, something tender and refreshing and consoling and sweet for all men; that is one of the duties imposed by charity towards all men."

How different from the vindictive little boy who had trampled on his fort in a rage!

Dark had fallen over the Sahara. Charles loved the time of evening prayer. "My Beloved, when all sleeps, how sweet it is to say to You that I love, that I adore You, that I can only live for You alone: You alone: my Beloved, You alone . . ."

Outside it was very quiet, a deathly, almost sinister, stillness, full of impending doom. At that very moment twenty Fellagas were stealthily drawing nearer and nearer to Tamanrasset. On the way they recruited several Touareg nomads, also slaves, some of whom had been looked after by Père de Foucauld as if they were his brothers. The Fellagas spotted the negro, El Madani, and said, "You come and help us." They were all armed with Italian guns, some were on foot, others riding camels. Unheard, unseen, creeping in the dusk, they were within two hundred metres of the fort near the deserted garden. Without clacking their tongues, but simply by pressing their knees against the camels, or caressing their long necks, the murderers halted their mounts behind the wall. No camel grunted or growled or snarled. The forty men dismounted. The sand was their accomplice, as it deadened the sound of their murderous footsteps. They crept, they crawled, nearer and nearer; they spread out and entirely encircled the fort. Everything was then pitch dark, there was no light; they were invisible.

They surrounded the house of silence, which now was already a tomb. Not even a whisper of command. All had been cunningly planned beforehand. As we know, somebody had pressed El Madani into service, and he too slithered to the fort, prepared to join the ranks of Judas. He had told them previously, when they had plotted all this, "Oh, yes, I know his habits and I know the password." So he went to the tiny door and knocked. A moment of tense waiting. Charles came to the closed door, and asked as he usually did, "Who is there?"

In an assumed voice, El Madani answered, "The post office employee from Motylinski." Indeed, this was the day when the post came.

Charles opened the door and put out his hand to receive the letters. His hand was seized and violently clutched. The shadows came to life and the Fellagas who had hidden now threw themselves at the door and pulled Charles out with victorious yells and yelps. They tied his hands behind his back and left him on the small patch of ground between the door and the little masking wall. They set a man to watch him, armed with a gun. His name was Sermi Ag Thora, a wretched treacherous creature, if one can judge by his photograph. Charles knelt down and stayed motionless. Like Christ before Pilate he was silent. He was praying. He even seemed unaware of the presence of his servant, the negro Paul Embarek, who had been forced to come.

This is Paul's account of what happened, collated by René Bazin from various military reports, letters and documents.

"On December 1st, after having served the dinner of the *marabout*, I went to my hut, which was situated at about 450 metres from there. It was towards seven o'clock, and it was night.

"A short time afterwards, just as I was finishing my meal, two armed Touaregs loomed up suddenly in the hut and said to me, 'Are you Paul, the servant of the *marabout*? Why are you hiding? Come and see with your own eyes what is happening, follow us!' I answered that I was not hiding, and what was happening was God's will.

"As I drew near to the house of the *marabout*, I noticed that he was sitting down, leaning against the wall, at the right of the door, his hands tied behind his back, looking straight in front of him. We did not exchange a word. I crouched down as I was ordered, to the left of the door. Innumerable Touaregs surrounded the *marabout*; they spoke and gesticulated, congratulating and blessing the slave El Madani who had lured the *marabout* into his trap, prophesying that, as a reward for his work, he would enjoy a life of delights in the next world. Other Touaregs were in the house, rushing in and out, bringing with them various things they had found inside, guns, munitions, food and cloth etc. Those who surrounded the *marabout* were pressing him with the following questions, 'When is the convoy coming? Where is it? What will it bring? Are there soldiers in the fort? Where are they? Have they left? Where are the soldiers of Motylinski?' The *marabout* remained impassive, he did not say a word. The same questions were put to me, also to another slave passing near by and who was seized upon at once.

"The whole thing lasted less than half an hour.

"The house was surrounded by sentinels. At that moment one of the sentinels gave the alarm, crying, 'Here are the Arabs, here are the Arabs!' [The soldiers of Motylinski.] Hearing these cries, the Touaregs, with the exception of three, of whom two stayed in front of me and another stood up to guard the *marabout*, all went towards the place where they heard those cries. Almost immediately they burst out with lively rifle fire. The Touareg who was near the *marabout* had put his gun near his head and fired. The *marabout* neither moved nor cried out. I did not think he was wounded: it was only after several minutes that I saw the blood flow, and the body of the *marabout* gently slip down, falling on his side. He was dead."

When he had seen the camel riders approaching, Charles had realized that they were two soldiers coming to call on him, and he made an instinctive warning movement, foreseeing the fate that was in store for them. That must have made Sermi Ag Thora lose his head and shoot.

Then the Fellagas stripped Charles entirely and threw him into the ditch which surrounded the house.

"What shall we do with his body? Shall we kill Paul Embarek, because he is an Infidel like his master?"

Just then, some camel drivers of the village rushed up, because they had heard gunfire. They begged the men to spare Paul and he was freed.

The discussion about the disposal of Charles's corpse continued.

"I think we should take it away and hide it."

"Oh that's far too good a fate for him. Tie him to a tree quite near the house, and then all the dogs of the Touaregs will eat their fill. The dogs of his friend Chikkat. He's a personal friend of the *marabout*."

"Come along, let's stop wrangling about such a trifling question. Now, each of us must divide the booty equally. And everybody must guard his own share; there's something to eat in here and some drink. Let's have a feast."

And so they spent the night revelling, having rifled the place from top to bottom.

They left Tamanrasset towards noon on the following day, taking their booty with them. The camel drivers then buried the *marabout* and the two soldiers. In the evening, Paul Embarek went to Fort Motylinski where he arrived on December 3rd at midday.

On further testimony, there seems to be a difference of opinion as to whether the murderers asked Charles to pronounce the *chehada*, which involved a denial of his Faith, or as to whether he said, "I am going to die." It is believed, though, that he kept an inviolable silence. Heart's desire was near. . . .

The camel drivers did not undo the cords which were attached to his hands, but knowing that Christians put their dead in a coffin, they covered the body with stones and pieces of paper and fragments from the wooden cases.

On December 17th, the commanding officer of the Hoggar started off in pursuit of the Fellagas; he caught up with them and killed several. But it was only on December 21st that Capitaine de la Roche was able to get to Tamanrasset. He took a sergeant and a soldier with him. The first thing he did was to put more earth over the bodies; over Charles's tomb he placed a wooden cross. Then he gave them military honours.

After that, Capitaine de la Roche went into the fort. A devastating sight met his eyes; everything had been pillaged, anything of any value. But all the papers and books had been scattered and torn and left behind in the chapel and in the room. However, by taking great care, they were able to piece together the leaves of the dictionary which had been his life work, and the two volumes of poetry. They found the letters that he had written earlier on the day of his murder.

Amongst the things left behind as of no value were Charles's rosary and the Way of the Cross that he had drawn on pieces of wood, and a very beautiful picture of the Crucified on a wooden cross. And then, buried in the sand, they suddenly found a very small monstrance. "Look, it seems as if the Host is still inside."

Capitaine de la Roche picked up the monstrance with great respect, dusted it and then wrapped it up in a piece of clean linen. He felt very worried. He thought to himself, "It is not I who should be carrying God in this way."

The time came for him to leave Tamanrasset. He took the little monstrance and put it in front of him on the saddle of his camel and rode thus, very carefully, the fifty kilometres from Tamanrasset to Fort Motylinski. As René Bazin has said so admirably, "It was, in the Sahara, the first procession of the Blessed Sacrament."

This humble, devout young French officer was able to do what Charles had never been able to accomplish: to carry the Body of the Lord through those desert wastes which He had created and which had never before received His bodily presence in so strange a procession.

To the Catholic brought up in awe of the Real Presence this is such a stupendous thing that one must ponder on its mystical implications for a moment. The theological genius, St Thomas Aquinas, spent himself in composing sequences and hymns in honour of this great Sacrament. And Charles who had loved the *Lauda Sion salvatorem* would have sung it inwardly, had he been there in the flesh: *Ecce panis angelorum*, silently, and not in his croaking old voice which he used to joke about, quietly, for the law of the desert is a law of silence. Seven hundred years after Aquinas, another Dominican mystical theologian, Père Garrigou-Lagrange, referring to Charles in his book on Divine Providence, emphasized that the greatest of his works was to bring the Blessed Sacrament to vast and arid regions where It had never been brought before.

Throughout the world, during the Catholic centuries of Christendom, artists such as embroiderers, goldsmiths and jewellers, have spent, have lavished their art on beautiful vestments and canopies, censers, candelabra and monstrances gleaming with rare jewels, to honour the Blessed Sacrament carried in procession during the feast of Corpus Christi, or on Maundy Thursday. Even in the present day, when men are aware of world poverty, you cannot prevent them from creating beautiful things for God. These processions of the Host, in whatever part of the world, have inspired their art, whether it be in the Basilicas of Rome, such as St Peter's, or in Holy Week, the cloister garth of

the monks of Solesmes, where the brothers robed in darkest sym-
bolical crimson, walk and chant against the dark green yew
hedges, singing their Gregorian plain-song; or in the streets of
some ancient Spanish city, strewn with millions of scented rose
petals, or in a humble French village or park, where faces which
one does not usually notice much during the year, suddenly, on
that day, in some strange way, seem transformed in adoration of
the Host. At Genzano, near Rome, on a hill near Lake Nemi, the
main street on Corpus Christi day is completely hidden by the
scattered masses of flower petals. And Christ's bodily presence, in
that procession, heals, as at Lourdes. Every free moment that he
could spare, Charles had spent at the foot of the altar adoring
the Blessed Sacrament. His gift of himself, afterwards, in welcoming the poorest of Christ's flock, his gift of hospitality, was the
fruit of this Eucharistic contemplation, for he was given, almost
consumed by others, as Christ is, in the form of Bread. . . .

One thing which gave Charles patience in the apparent
sublime failure of his life, in which he made pretty well no converts and attracted no companions, was that he was persuaded
that the Blessed Host would Itself act directly on the people It
approached. In the old days, when Jesus was passing by in the
crowd, the mere touch of His garments wrought miracles of heal-
ing. And now, for the first time for twenty centuries, since that
night in the Upper Room when He first instituted the Eucharist,
He came, carried on camel-back by an obscure French officer; in
all the beauty of His Sacred Humanity, He came to these hostile,
splendid and arid immensities. No marble floors, no rose-strewn
streets, but the sand dunes, sometimes gold, sometimes apricot, or
turning from rose red to russet. And the architect of these sand
dunes was the wind, shaping them into strange patterns, hollow
dips, rills and waves—that sand which had burned the feet of
his poor servant Charles, as he trudged many a weary mile behind
his camel.

Before he died, when he wrote the Rule for the Brethren of
the Sacred Heart of Jesus, he outlined a landscape quite exquisite in its evangelical appeal. And this Rule is the fruit of
his incessant Eucharistic adoration, of a life hidden and lost
with Jesus in silence and solitude, in nightly vigils before the
Host.

As he rode on in silence, Capitaine de la Roche had long, long thoughts. Suddenly he recalled a conversation he had had with Charles a long time ago. The captain had said to him, "You have permission to keep the Blessed Sacrament; but if some misfortune should befall you, what should one do?" He now remembered that Charles had answered, "There are two solutions: make an act of perfect contrition and then give yourself Holy Communion, or else send the consecrated Host through the post to the White Fathers."

"No, I can't send the Host through the post," he thought to himself. "I can't do that." At last he reached Fort Motylinski and dismounted. He went to his tent and summoned a subaltern of the post who had once trained for the priesthood and had remained a very ardent Christian. Capitaine de la Roche explained the whole situation, and they had a quiet discussion together. The subaltern said, "I think it would be best if either you or I should give ourselves Holy Communion."

The officer went out, and came back in a few moments holding a pair of white gloves. "I've never worn them before." And then he opened the little door of the monstrance to make quite sure that he was not mistaken and that the Host really was there. It was.

"Who will receive Holy Communion? I cannot. I'm unworthy," he said.

"We are all unworthy."

Then the subaltern knelt down and gave himself Holy Communion.

The last Host consecrated by Charles's hands, and adored by him in the fort where he was murdered, was consumed by an obscure French soldier whose name has not even gone down to posterity.

And now, the uttermost corners of the world, even as far as frozen Alaska, are filled with Charles's Little Brothers and Sisters of Jesus. They earn their living among the forsaken ones they wish to serve—in prisons, factories, farms. And yet, it is a contemplative Brotherhood, whose Rule ordains at least one hour of adoration daily before the Blessed Sacrament Exposed. They are also vowed to the strictest poverty. Their service to men is rooted and nourished in their deep love for Jesus, dwelling in His Sacrament. Pope Paul VI said that Père de Foucauld's charity won him the title of "Universal Brother". It was this Eucharistic food which had filled him with such burning love for men.

He was a child of the Desert, and a child of that Eucharist which he brought to the Desert, thereafter aiding the suffering human beings who were drawn to him, because he had become Love.

Father Martin D'Arcy, S.J., has said: "*Sileant creaturae, silentium est Christus.* Let creatures hush; the silence is Christ. . . . It is in this silence that the marriage hymn begins, between Christ and the soul."

APPENDIX

THE CAUSE of the beatification of Père Charles de Foucauld is not at the time of writing formally or officially opened; that is, a petition has not yet been made to the Pope. No doubt this is because there are so many letters and documents (photocopies of relevant papers must be made) and witnesses to be examined. The Cause is progressing normally and has had the interest and sympathy of Pope Paul VI.

The Fraternity of the Little Brothers and Sisters of Jesus was conceived by the Père de Foucauld, but not founded by him as he attracted no followers in his lifetime. It was founded by Rev. Père Voilliume of Marseilles in 1933 in the Sahara, seventeen years after the assassination. In 1968, it was approved by the Holy See as a congregation under papal jurisdiction.

The Brothers have fraternities in many different countries throughout the world. The communities of fraternities are set up in ordinary rented lodgings in towns and cities, among nomadic tribes, slum dwellers, in prisons, in the desert, or on the roads. They live among those without name or influence, sharing the hardships and instability which are an inseparable part of the human condition. The Brothers are dedicated to the contemplative life of worship, prayer, and meditation. They wear no distinctive habit, because they share their everyday life with those who ignore Jesus or have forgotten Him. Their life is marked by its simplicity and friendship. They rise early, say the Lord's Prayer together, meditate briefly on the Gospel and hear Mass. After breakfast, they go to work on a building site, in a factory, or workshop. They, like their fellow workers, suffer the boredom and fatigue of manual labour, the difficulties of finding employment, social injustice, racial and religious tension, and other everyday toil. In the evening, after work, the Blessed Sacrament is exposed (one room is arranged as a chapel), and the Brothers spend one hour in silent adoration.

The heart of the Brothers' lives is prayer. They imitate the example of the life of Jesus and seek intimacy with Him through constant prayer. They must learn from Him to regard every man with gentleness and to love their fellow men like brothers and friends. They especially love those who bear more particularly the consequences of the world's weight. And, of course, there is a deep brotherly charity among the Brothers themselves. First and foremost they strive to imitate the poverty, simplicity, and humility of Jesus; and with this, love's aim, they take vows of chastity, poverty and obedience: "The first effect of my love is imitation." From time to time they spend a month or forty days in the desert, alone, desiring to contemplate His face and to pray intensely for men. They work as they do and where they do because Jesus so worked. A Brother should have an aptitude for contemplation, equanimity, a sense of purpose, and a strong will. They must be capable of adjusting themselves to a life in a community which demands a close and frank life together. They must have a certain degree of maturity, both human and spiritual.

The Little Sisters were founded in 1939 and have now spread over five continents. The Sisters work in factories, prisons, hospitals, and for the poor and those unable to help themselves. They, like the Brothers, are dedicated to a loving intimacy with Jesus, His life, and His works. Unlike the Brothers, they have a habit: they wear a blue cotton dress, brown leather belt, dark blue head veil, blue cape and a brown cross with a heart on it, sandals and no stockings, even in winter. They say the Lord's prayer and Vespers—recited because Brother Charles wanted very simply to put them all at their ease.

In a desire to be universal the Regimes are established both in the Latin Church and the Eastern Churches. St Thomas Aquinas is their guide and hence the presence of the great French philosopher, Jacques Maritain, among the Little Brothers. There is a fraternity of theological studies under the direction of the Dominican Fathers: in France at Toulouse, in Great Britain in London, in Spain at Avila. They spend the last period of their novitiate at Rome, to draw from the Church the sense of unity, of Catholicism and of filial attachment to the Church and the Holy Father. Pope Paul VII addressed them at Castel Gandolpho in October 1955, "We cherish the great hope that the world will recognize the presence of God in you."